CRITICAL THEORY OF RELIGION

MARSHA AILEEN HEWITT

CRITICAL THEORY OF RELIGION
A Feminist Analysis

FORTRESS PRESS   MINNEAPOLIS

CRITICAL THEORY OF RELIGION
A Feminist Analysis

Cover design: Judy Swanson

Library of Congress Cataloging-in-Publication Data
Hewitt, Marsha, 1948–
    Critical theory of religion : a feminist analysis / Marsha Aileen
Hewitt.
        p.   cm.
    Includes bibliographical references and index.
    ISBN 0-8006-2612-5 (alk. paper) :
    1. Religion.   2. Critical theory.   3. Feminist theory.   I. Title.
BL48.H445   1995
200'.82—dc20   94-32897
                                                                         CIP

The paper used in this publication meets the minimum requirements of American National Standard for Information Sciences—Permanence of Paper for Printed Library Materials, ANSI Z329.48-1984.   ∞™

Manufactured in the U.S.A.   AF 1-2612

99   98   97   96   95   1   2   3   4   5   6   7   8   9   10

Preface   ix

1. To Change the World   1
Theory as praxis, praxis as theory 5
Critical theory and feminist theory: a shared interest 15
The dialectics of domination 17
Beyond "dialectic of enlightenment" 27
Feminist directions 34

**2. Woman, History and the Family:
The Dialectics of Non-Being**   37
The "unreal, insubstantial shadow": Hegel's "woman" 42
Karl Marx and Friedrich Engels: woman and class
   society 49
Sigmund Freud: woman as innate insufficiency 62
Women: civilization's discontents 68

**3. Shrew, She-Man, Slave:
Images of "Woman" in Critical Theory**   77
Negative dialectics 80
Ironies of negative dialectics 86
Self-perpetuating victims of patriarchy 89
Loss of the family 93

Toward resolving the sexist problematic 100
Eclipse of the individual 105

4. **Unreason and Revolution:
   Herbert Marcuse, Mary Daly,
   and Gynocentric Feminism**   113
   Resistance and transformation 114
   Mary Daly's elemental females 127
   Spinning new reifications 133

5. **Memory, Revolution, and Redemption:
   Walter Benjamin and
   Elisabeth Schüssler Fiorenza**   147
   Walter Benjamin and the puppet of history 151
   Emancipation and absolving soteriology 155
   The mother and the whore 159
   The prophetic power of redemptive memory 162

6. **The Radical Vision:
   Utopia, Socialism, and Humanist Feminism
   in Rosemary Radford Ruether**   171
   Christianity's latent emancipatory power 173
   The Goddess revealed 184
   Patriarchal invaders revisited 187
   Women of Stature: Minoan and Etruscan cultures 190
   Patriarchy triumphant: J. J. Bachofen 192
   Working women: an alternative view
       of feminist prehistory 196
   The human face of feminism 198

7. **Toward a Feminist Critical Theory
   of Religion**   207
   Beyond theology 207
   Negating oppression 213
   Intimations of utopia 221

Index   230

For Jessica, Nathan, and Justin,
who patiently waited for me to finish writing

The right consciousness in the wrong world is impossible.
—*Theodor W. Adorno*

*Religion is on sale, as it were. It is cheaply marketed in order
to provide one more so-called irrational stimulus among many
others by which the members of a calculating society are cal-
culatingly made to forget the calculation under which they
suffer.*
—*Theodor W. Adorno*

RATHER THAN REJECT RELIGION ALTOGETHER, THIS BOOK
arises out of the conviction that religion, with the aid of critical social
theory, may once again emerge as an emancipatory force within history. Recent developments in certain areas of Christian thought clearly
show strong affinities between religion and critical theory that remain
largely unarticulated. Although dialogue has taken place for some years
between North American and Western European theologians and the
heavily revised version of critical theory of Jürgen Habermas, the far
more interesting dialogue, yet to take place, will juxtapose the "early"
Frankfurt theorists and feminist liberation theology. The Frankfurt
theorists I have in mind are Max Horkheimer, Theodor W. Adorno,
Herbert Marcuse, and Walter Benjamin. The feminist liberation theologians and theorists whose work most closely resonates (at times in

contradictory ways) with the central preoccupations of critical theory are Mary Daly, Rosemary Radford Ruether, and Elisabeth Schüssler Fiorenza.

Despite the significant differences among these thinkers, they share a utopian commitment to the realization, within history and society, of a more humane world—one that clearly is not yet but nonetheless might one day be. Residing within the work of all these thinkers is the hope, however tentative and fragile, that present conditions may harbor the seeds of a transformed world. A striking characteristic of this group is that they hold in common the courage to think against current reality no matter what the consequences to themselves or the status quo. In this way they encourage hope in the genuine possibility of a future transformed human condition wherein people may finally encounter justice, freedom, and happiness as the most ordinary and taken-for-granted experience in all aspects of their daily lives. This is a hope that is all the stronger and more courageous in that it does not require belief in the inevitability of its own realization to be sustained.

This hope in the real possibility of a better world that might never come into being sustains both critical theory and feminist liberation theology and philosophy. It is also the point at which they intersect. Despite the antitheological character of most critical theory, it nonetheless preserves a kind of nontheistic religious longing for what can and should be, through a sustained negative confrontation with the world as it is. This is an attempt on the part of critical theory to articulate the inexpressible, while at the same time refusing to construct detailed portraits of what ought to be. It does not indulge in romantic, programmatic speculations of what an alternative society will look like. However disappointing this refusal might be to those committed to changing the world, it nonetheless constitutes one of critical theory's greatest strengths. In a critical attitude sometimes described as "immanent critique," "determinate negation," or "negative dialectics," critical theory commits itself to articulating the suffering of others while trying to account for the conditions that produce that suffering. As such, critical theory harbors an ethical vision that is clearly partisan; it takes sides with the vanquished, voiceless victims of history and the marginalized, oppressed others who have long been relegated to the refuse heap of civilization by their conquerors.

As a comprehensive (rather than "totalizing") negative critique of the human condition as it has been historically, culturally, and socially produced and maintained—and which critical theory unequivocally condemns—it not only shares much with contemporary forms of feminist liberation theology, it clearly anticipates it. This anticipation is, however, thoroughly nontheological, although not necessarily *non-religious*. Its effectiveness and power lie in its unwavering commitment to a sociological, philosophical, and psychoanalytic critique that identifies and accounts for domination in many of its material forms. The preoccupation with changing the world in concrete ways is central to feminist liberation theology as well. It is one of the major reasons why the latter must seriously consider critical theory in order to enhance, sharpen, and clarify its own theoretical and practical work.

Feminist liberation theology needs critical theory, in part at least, to understand the limitations that theology places on critical thought. These limitations are twofold insofar as they derive from a rudimentary social analysis that cannot fully theorize the complex interstructures of domination because of an inability—or unwillingness—to move beyond a theological mode of thought and linguistic expression. While many of the main themes of feminist liberation theology are at times unconscious, warmed-over revisitations of different aspects of critical theory, feminism shows a tendency to foreshorten the directions of its own thought by falling back into a distinctive theological discursive mode that is precritical and therefore inadequate to address the increasingly complex problems of humanity under contemporary conditions. From the perspective of critical theory, theological discourse and its corresponding institutions are so intertwined and embedded within the status quo that they have lost their prophetic, negative power to resist a world that is fundamentally antihuman. The implication for feminist liberation theology is that if it aspires to be a seriously emancipatory practical theory, it must break with most dimensions of the theological traditions out of which it comes. Otherwise it risks promoting, however unintentionally, a deeper accommodation with the status quo by removing itself further from concrete reality.

One of the major but unfinished achievements of critical theory in general lies in its capacity to remain loyal to the possibility of a transformed future while resisting the temptation to spell out what that future must be. In its continuing effort to articulate what ultimately cannot—and should not—be spoken, critical theory is able to intimate that which ought to be, but is not yet. Its steadfast refusal to articulate the contours of the new society suggests that it aspires to be in itself— in terms of the very process of its own thinking—a self-critical, emancipatory praxis. Part of the tragedy of the human condition, however, is that intention and its realization tend to fall short of one another. No matter how vigilant critical theory may be in guarding against the tendencies of thought toward the exercise of power and domination by exposing them via an ongoing act of sustained negative critique, critical theory harbors its own impulses to domination and irrationality. This becomes apparent when feminist analysis examines the treatment of women and conceptualizations of "the feminine" in critical theory. A feminist critique of critical theory reveals two seemingly paradoxical truths: (1) critical theory reproduces and sustains sexism while seeking to expose it; (2) critical theory provides a rich resource for feminist theorizing that is indispensable to a feminist critical theory of religion and society.

Finally, it will become apparent throughout this book that while critical theory rejected theology as woefully incapable of sustaining (not to mention realizing) the utopian hopes of suffering humanity, it nonetheless, *despite itself,* indicates that the religious longings articulated in Christianity are not necessarily exhausted by the political accommodations of theology and the churches with the status quo of past historical epochs. That is to say, what some feminist liberation theologians insist on as the liberating impulse of the Christian message—that which offers hope to the victims of the brutality and oppression of history—might still motivate human beings to participate in active struggles to transform the world in the light of concrete, contemporary human needs. The question is, how might this process of political mobilization come about in such a way as to avoid reproducing forms of domination and oppression within the illusory guise of transformative praxis? Beyond this lies the deeper and more troubling question of how this emancipatory impulse within Christianity might be retrieved from centuries of embeddedness in authoritarian theological traditions and oppressive ecclesial institutions that have mediated and hermeneutically transmitted the gospel message. Is such a retrieval even possible?

While this book does not attempt to answer these and other related questions directly, it does seek to intimate directions as to *how to think about how* to answer such questions. To this end I bring the critical theorists and selected feminist liberation thinkers together, but not with the intention of synthesizing or integrating their thought. Besides being impossible, it would be of no purpose to try to integrate these thinkers in some systematic grand theory that solves the problems that arise when theology enters into a consciously innovative dialogue with progressive social theory. Rather, I arrange the critical theorists with respect to the feminist theorists in a way that allows reciprocal illumination of certain aspects of their work. In situating Horkheimer, Adorno, Marcuse, Benjamin, Schüssler Fiorenza, Daly, and Ruether in "conversation" with one another I can only hope that sparks will fly that will light up, however momentarily, possible future paths toward a viable feminist critical theory of religion.

The main difficulty with acknowledgments is that it is impossible to make them all-inclusive. It is impossible to name everyone who has made some helpful contribution toward writing a book. Some of the most important influences on one's thinking happen by chance, in conversation or in reading things with no apparent relation to the subject with which the author struggles. Such chance occurrences may not only lend a certain shape and direction to a book—they may even be instrumental in bringing a book into being.

One such chance occurrence took place in Los Angeles in 1991 at the annual meeting of the Society of Christian Ethics, where I presented the plenary address that eventually became this book. Beverly Harrison kindly agreed to respond to my paper; her response was followed by a lively discussion between Beverly, the audience, and me. I remember the entire event with great fondness, and I recall the challenging questions posed to me by Beverly, members in the audience, and the referees who recommended publication of the address in the Society's *Annual*. Their critical responses not only helped me to strengthen the article, they also contributed toward my refining the thinking that resulted in the eventual book.

The person who was most crucial at that time to making this book become a reality is Michael West, the senior acquisitions editor at Fortress Press. He approached me shortly after my presentation with the simple question, "Do you have any plans to write a book out of this paper?" With this question, not to mention his faith in the project and steady encouragement while I was writing it, Michael has done more toward contributing to the realization of this book than he will ever know.

I also thank my colleagues and friends who read the manuscript during various stages of the writing and who took the time to give me helpful critical commentary. In particular I thank Donald Wiebe, who rarely agrees with anything I write but who read the manuscript thoroughly and provided, as usual, insightful critical responses. Thanks also to Graeme Nicholson and Eva Neumaier-Dargyay for their comments on portions of the text. My grateful appreciation to Béla Szabados, who not only read parts of the manuscript, but also provided me with the space necessary to complete the work. To the graduate students at the Toronto School of Theology and the Centre for the Study of Religion at the University of Toronto who have taken my course in critical theory and feminist religious thought over the last few years, and to those who have chosen to write theses on the subject, my gratitude for their keen and lively interest. I have learned much from them, and continue to do so.

My deepest gratitude, however, is reserved for Alexander Rueger, who without hesitation gave me far more help with his patient and careful, critical reading of the entire manuscript than I had any right to ask. There are no words to express my thanks for what was so obviously, in retrospect, a sustained labor of love.

CHAPTER 1

To Change the World

In her book on feminist literary theory, Toril Moi notes that few feminist critics have given serious attention to the work of Marxist theorists such as Theodor Adorno or Walter Benjamin "in order to see whether their insights into the problems of representing the tradition of the oppressed can be appropriated for feminism."[1] Moi's observation is equally applicable to the field of feminist studies in religion, particularly Christianity, and might well be expanded to include other Frankfurt theorists such as Max Horkheimer and Herbert Marcuse. I propose to take up the implicit challenge to feminist theorists posed by Moi. From the point of view of feminist critical liberation theology, or religious thought, I propose to examine critically the Hegelian Marxian tradition of critical social theory as developed by all these Frankfurt theorists. I do so in an effort to identify and appropriate their analysis of domination for the future formulation of a feminist critical theory of the Christian religion.

Contemporary feminist critical liberation theology on the whole ignores this intellectual tradition. Yet a remarkable degree of political and theoretical affinity exists between them and needs to be brought out. Some of the major thinkers in the area of feminist theology are heir to some of the most important themes developed in the tradition

---

[1] Toril Moi, *Sexual/Textual Politics: Feminist Literary Theory* (London and New York: Methuen, 1985), 95.

of Frankfurt critical social theory—sometimes known as "critical Marxism" or "Western Marxism." More deeply, they share a concern with forging a practical theory and immanent critique of oppression and injustice that aspires at the same time to abolish the conditions that produce them. Many feminists have abandoned Marxism as another patriarchal "grand theory" of modernity, incapable of adequately addressing the specific nature of women's subjugated condition. Yet I contend that we should take another look, with a view to sharpening and deepening feminism's own critical power, at Marxian social philosophy as it was critically reexamined and appropriated by the Frankfurt theorists.

This is an especially important task for feminist liberation theology. As a critique of the Christian theological, biblical, and ecclesial traditions, feminism has largely succeeded in exposing the specific ways in which those traditions have marginalized, silenced, and oppressed women. Feminist critiques of Christianity continue effectively to expose the deep contradiction of a religious tradition that purports to embrace all of humanity while actively excluding half of it through a variety of discriminatory, subjugative practices. As Valerie Saiving observed many years ago, the universalism of Christian theology actually champions an androcentric, pseudo-universalist perspective that presumes maleness as the measure and norm of humanness.[2]

Yet such an "ideology critique" of Christianity from a feminist perspective is in itself insufficient for the ultimate goal of the liberation of women. Feminist theology itself attests to this insufficiency, at least implicitly, insofar as it is compelled to branch out and incorporate the analytical insights of other disciplines, such as philosophy, literary criticism, and ecology, in an attempt to account for the ways in which Christian patriarchal traditions intersect with other cultural forces. This feminist approach reveals a highly complex collusion between theology and a variety of cultural forces that produce and sustain interlocking structures and relations of domination of women. If feminist liberation theology is to continue in this direction of increasingly comprehensive

---

[2] Valerie Saiving, "The Human Situation: A Feminine View," in Carol Christ and Judith Plaskow, eds., *Womanspirit Rising: A Feminist Reader in Religion* (San Francisco: Harper and Row, 1979), 25.

social and political critique, it will need to recognize that the specifically *theological* resources of the Christian tradition are by now exhausted in terms of whatever potential they may have held for the full emancipation of women. Once this has been fully grasped, feminist theology will become conscious of the necessity of transforming itself from within, pushing beyond the parameters of theological discipline and further into a comprehensive critical theory of culture, society, and religion. This entire feminist enterprise is driven by an explicit emancipatory interest. As it overcomes and moves beyond theology, feminist religious thought will be better able to articulate its utopian hopes for a more humane world in ways that may become more relevant to the actual, concrete condition of women.

As part of this self-transformative process, a feminist critical theory of religion must look to those nontheological intellectual traditions with which it has the strongest affinities, probing and appropriating their emancipatory potential by developing and reconstructing them in the light of feminist theoretical and practical goals. It must further identify the emancipatory potential of religion, in this case specifically Christianity, as it pertains to the full social, political, economic, cultural, and individual liberation of women and all humanity. Such a feminist critical theory of religion must transcend theology in its relentless exposé of theology as it interlocks with other systems of thought, belief, authority, and political power structures that are reflective of, and deeply implicated in, the prevailing forms of domination that pattern the entire social fabric. In its critique of theology, a feminist critical theory of religion breaks through the established boundaries of theology and its oppressive internal and external apparatuses to release whatever emancipatory elements remain, having survived in subterranean, repressed form in the various theological traditions. To realize this task, a feminist critical theory of religion at the same time requires assistance from those intellectual and practical traditions that harbor a conscious solidarity with the downtrodden and oppressed and that include an explicit political motivation to realize whatever concrete emancipation might be possible under current conditions.

The social theory elaborated by the Frankfurt thinkers offers a feminist theory of religion one such important resource through which it may not only hone and refine its own critical, transformative potential but also bring to fuller consciousness many of feminist theory's implicit roots as a practical theory of liberation. In the necessary transition from a feminist *theology of liberation* to a feminist *critical theory of religion,* feminism must carefully examine the themes and insights of critical theory to see what may be appropriated, built upon, and transformed for a feminist approach adequate to the multiple forms of domination that are becoming more sophisticated, remote, invisible, but no less oppressive in the capitalist world of late modernity.

In the dialectical interaction or dialogue that follows, I will situate feminist liberation theology and critical theory in relation to each other as mutually illuminating constellations[3] rather than as potentially integrated or synthetic theories. My intention is not to collapse critical theory and feminist religious thought into a grand, polished whole. To attempt to do so would be to undermine the integrity of each and destroy their mutually clarifying potential. Another important reason for constellating rather than integrating these theories has to do with the sexist moments within critical theory that surface in its idealizations and reifications of women. They would be obscured by a wholistic approach. A further point in favor of positioning feminism and critical

---

[3] The term *constellation* comes from Walter Benjamin. For him, ideas, concepts, images, or fragments from the past reveal meaning when arranged in the form of "critical constellations" or "dialectical images," in which the past meets the present in ways that explode with insight. For Benjamin, ideas relate to each other more authentically when they are arranged like stars in a constellation, rather than as concepts in a tightly closed system. His approach to the dialectical critique of history, for example, does not take the form of a "calm, contemplative attitude," but rather strives to "become aware of the critical constellation in which precisely this fragment of the past is found with precisely this present." See his "Eduard Fuchs, Collector and Historian," in *One-Way Street and Other Writings,* trans. Edmund Jephcott and Kingsley Shorter (London: New Left Books, 1979), 351. Benjamin's notion of constellations influenced the thought of Theodor W. Adorno, who also used the term. Thinking in constellations rather than in conceptual systems that impose identity between subject and object is highly relevant to contemporary feminist concerns with otherness and difference. The relationship between non-identity thinking as it was understood by the Frankfurt theorists (particularly Adorno) and contemporary feminist theory is discussed in chapter 3.

theory together in the form of reciprocally illuminating constellations is that only in this way can a creative tension be generated and sustained between them. Constellating remains faithful to the contradictoriness of human experience, which is characterized by nonhomogeneity, multiplicity, difference, and infinite particularity. This refusal to seek identity and integration between feminist and Frankfurt critical theory is requisite to the formation of a distinctly feminist critical theory of religion, as well as to the possibility of realizing a genuine democratic political praxis.

To begin pursuing these avenues of inquiry, it is necessary to consider some key themes in the social philosophy of Karl Marx. This is, after all, where the roots of critical theory lie.

Theory as Praxis, Praxis as Theory

THE FAMOUS CONCLUDING LINE OF KARL MARX'S *THESES ON Feuerbach*—"Philosophers have only *interpreted* the world, in various ways; the point, however, is to *change* it"—encapsulates the substantive nucleus not only of Marx's thought but also of a wide range of twentieth-century theories of liberation. They, too, are oriented, among other things, to healing the perceived breach between theory and practice. The critical relationship between theory and practice is a central preoccupation of a feminist theory that is committed to concrete changes in the situation of women that will contribute to their emancipation on all levels of experience. Debates about the theory-praxis relationship, however, can be misleading insofar as theory and practice are formulated as if they are separate entities. Some liberation theologians in the Latin American context have attempted to resolve the theory-praxis dilemma with the concept of *orthopraxis,* an unsatisfactory term because of its inescapable latent dogmatism that implies the existence of "correct praxis," which is no more helpful than assertions of "correct theory" or "orthodoxy."[4] A more nuanced and promising

---

[4] Gustavo Gutiérrez explains that the term *orthopraxis* does not intend "to deny the meaning of *orthodoxy,* understood as a proclamation of and reflection on statements considered to be true. Rather, the goal is to balance and even to reject the primacy and almost exclusiveness which doctrine has enjoyed in

approach to resolving the theory-praxis question has been put forward by other liberation theologians. It speaks of a "progressive theology" that is itself "liberative," as distinct from one that contents itself with merely "talking about liberation."[5]

The notion that theory is more than about or oriented toward particular ends, such as emancipation, but that theory may be in itself liberative, implies that thinking is also a practical activity. The notion of the practical character of thought must be consciously considered by contemporary theories of liberation, including feminism in its efforts to formulate a theory-praxis relation adequate to the complex realities of women's oppression in highly advanced capitalist societies. To do so, feminism must sift through the emancipatory discourses and theories of Western modernity and reclaim and adapt what is most helpful to a contemporary feminist theory and practice of liberation.

One of the most powerful emancipatory discourses of modernity is found in the work of Marx. The practical nature of thought is central to his entire social theory. It is clearly stated in his second thesis on Ludwig Feuerbach:

> The question whether objective truth can be attributed to human thinking is not a question of theory but is a *practical* question. Man must prove the truth, i.e., the reality and power, the this-worldliness

---

Christian life and above all to modify the emphasis, often obsessive, upon the attainment of an orthodoxy which is often nothing more than fidelity to an obsolete tradition or a debatable interpretation. In a more positive vein, the intention is to recognize the work and importance of concrete behavior, of deeds, of action, of praxis in the Christian life." *A Theology of Liberation: History, Politics and Salvation*, trans. and ed. Sister Caridad Inda and John Eagleson (Maryknoll, N.Y.: Orbis Books, 1973), 10. The term *orthopraxis,* however, implies more than a balance between doctrine and action; it implies the concept of a *correct* form of action that in itself harbors an authoritarian element. Who decides what action is correct or right? What criteria are involved? In this sense the term *orthopraxis* contains a contradiction since, in seeking to counter an "obsessive" reliance on doctrinal truth, it does so by establishing its own form of "truth" and "correctness" with respect to action.
[5] Juan Luis Segundo, *Liberation of Theology*, trans. John Drury (Maryknoll, N.Y.: Orbis Books, 1976), 9. For Segundo, the practical interest of the theology lies in the beginning of the theology itself, transforming it throughout.

of his thinking in practice. The dispute over the reality or non-reality of thinking which is isolated from practice is a purely *scholastic* question.[6]

Understood in this way, the practical nature of theory means that theory holds a political dimension as well. The argument concerning the practical nature of thought does not mean, however, that theory and practice are (or should be) perfectly integrated, or that they are identical. A tension always exists between them that is a necessary part of their highly mediated, dialectical relationship.[7] It allows for the flexibility necessary for theory and practice to alter and change one another. Such an approach empowers human beings with the insight that history is not apart from or immune to their actions. Such a relationship has other implications as well.

An understanding of the connection between theory and praxis in terms of a mediated and dialectical relationship further reveals that there is no such thing as "value neutrality," nor "pure," "disinterested" knowledge as such. The concept of knowledge as neutrally corresponding to the order of facts in nature, with its "calculated mathematization," classification, and categorization of "factual reality," is a fairly recent historical development. It surfaces in modernity in what Timothy Reiss calls the "analytical-referential"[8] discourses of scientific and philosophical thought represented in the works of Galileo, René

[6] Karl Marx, "Theses on Feuerbach," in Karl Marx and Frederick Engels, *Collected Works*, vol. 5 (New York: International Publishers, 1976), 3.

[7] Marx understands the theory-praxis relationship as both mediated and dialectical when he writes, "It is not enough for thought to strive for realization: reality must itself strive towards thought." "Contribution to the Critique of Hegel's *Philosophy of Right:* Introduction," in *Collected Works*, vol. 3 (1975), 183. Perspectives on the theory-praxis relationship that attempt to formulate it as a harmonious unity reassert the primacy of theory as an abstract category that exercises a coercive, regulative force on praxis, whereby it subsumes human action in its attempt to bring it into conformity within its own dictates. This is the kind of approach that is illustrated in former Soviet-style theories of "scientific socialism," where political activity must conform to preestablished "laws of history."

[8] Timothy J. Reiss, *The Discourse of Modernism* (Ithaca, N.Y., and London: Cornell Univ. Press, 1982), 352, 52.

Descartes, and Francis Bacon. According to Reiss, the rise of "analytical-referential" discourse at the beginning of modernity corresponds to an increased usage of the discursive "I" of mastering subjectivity. The "I" imposes itself upon the world through its imperialistic, conceptualizing practices, in which objective, material reality is coerced to fit given concepts.

For Reiss, analytical-referential modes of thought are represented in the discourses of experimental science that were appropriated and adapted to the political discourses of the geographic expansion of Europe in its military and ideological conquests of the Americas and other parts of the world. A conscious, fundamental premise of early scientific thought was that in science, knowledge and power converge, with the result that analytico-referential discourse became established as a powerful instrument of scientific knowledge and technical skill, while at the same time absorbing all other discourses pertaining to nonscientific human actions and experience.[9] This "discursive development toward dominance"[10] that Reiss locates at the beginning of modernity brought with it a new concept of subjectivity in the form of the self-creating, dominating, and commanding "I," for whom nonhuman nature and those "others" associated with it were considered as little more than objects of its (his) potentially limitless powers of manipulation and control. The consequences of the analytical-referential concept of knowledge remain with us still. They are profoundly political, especially in their implications for all those not included within the concept's self-interested categories and constructs of what constitutes authentic humanity.

This understanding of theory as a conceptual apparatus of power for the classification, analysis, and domination of human and nonhuman nature was already criticized by Max Horkheimer in his classic 1937 essay, "Traditional and Critical Theory."[11] Horkheimer's description and critique of "traditional theory" anticipate Reiss's account of the rise of analytical-referential scientific and intellectual discourses of

---

[9] Ibid., 319–20.
[10] Ibid., 52.
[11] Max Horkheimer, *Critical Theory: Selected Essays*, trans. Matthew J. O'Connell et al. (New York: Continuum, 1972).

modernity and their consequences, but Horkheimer probes this phenomenon on a more philosophical plane. Horkheimer charts the colonizing expansionist tendencies of the scientific, technical-instrumental
rationality of the natural sciences, with its logic of "purely mathe-
matical system[s] of symbols,"[12] to include "all the disciplines dealing
with social life," which he associates with "the Anglo-Saxon universities."[13]

In the traditional theories of modernity, reason becomes technique
rather than praxis[14] and is thereby divested of its substantive content,
including notions of justice, freedom, and human happiness. Horkheimer's critique of instrumental reason includes the way in which
knowledge conceals its ideological substrate, thereby masquerading
its impulse to domination, utility, and profitability for the benefit of
the various ruling elites of capitalist societies. Epistemological practices
are presented as "natural" or "neutral," with the result that their latent
power interest remains obscure and mystified. In this way the social,
historical, and political nature of thought becomes invisible in an
uncritical sacralization of "real" knowledge as above and untouched
by the human condition. This is what Horkheimer means when he
writes, "The conception of theory was absolutized, as though it were
grounded in the inner nature of knowledge as such or justified in some

---

[12] Ibid., 190.

[13] Ibid., 191.

[14] Here I follow Charles Davis's interpretation of the Aristotelian distinction
between *praxis* and *techne;* that is, the distinction between practical philosophy,
which attends to ethical and political activity, and technical mastery, achieved
through instrumental modes of production. Like Horkheimer, Davis also
recognizes what he calls the "new habit of conceiving all human action on
the model of a making or producing and the application of the techniques of
empirical science to the knowledge and control of social processes," which
leads to a corresponding notion of politics as the "administration of society
through the exercise of technical control." *Theology and Political Society* (Cambridge, England: Cambridge Univ. Press, 1980), 21. Behind the idea of politics
as administration stands Theodor Adorno's concept of an "administered
world," where phenomena such as mass culture and commodity exchange act
as regulating, leveling principles that undermine the possibility for critical
subjectivity.

other ahistorical way, and thus it became a reified, ideological category."[15]

To expose the hidden admixture of power, domination, and knowledge that resides at the very core of "traditional theory," what is required, according to Horkheimer, is no less than a "radical reconsideration, not of the scientist alone, but of the knowing individual as such."[16] The act of knowing does not occur in the isolated mind of the contemplative subject who disinterestedly exercises his or her innate power for rational reflection and penetration of the secrets of a static, external world. Rather, knowing activity is thoroughly social, to the extent that even the way human beings "see and hear is inseparable from the social life-process as it has evolved over the millennia."[17] Not only is human perception forged in long historical experience, but the objects we confront in the external world are themselves products of socialized and historical processes. Each generation confronts history as the accumulated sedimentation of the cultural, social, and cultural products and achievements of previous generations. This accumulated sedimentation of previous historical epochs that becomes congealed in each successive period is the result of human activity, a fact not always visible to human consciousness when knowledge is understood as separate from or somewhere above history.

Horkheimer's view of history in this essay echoes Marx's words in *The Eighteenth Brumaire:*

> Men make their own history, but they do not make it just as they please; they do not make it under circumstances chosen by themselves, but under circumstances directly encountered, given and transmitted from the past. The tradition of all the dead generations weighs like a nightmare on the brain of the living.[18]

Part of Horkheimer's task in his critique of traditional theory is to expose the thoroughly historical, interested character of knowledge

---

[15] Horkheimer, "Traditional and Critical Theory," 194.
[16] Ibid., 199.
[17] Ibid., 200.
[18] Karl Marx, *The Eighteenth Brumaire of Louis Bonaparte*, in *Collected Works*, vol. 11 (1979), 103.

and the social character of history, thereby enabling human beings to break through the illusion that history is an objective or blind force over which they have no control and are therefore helpless to change. Behind Horkheimer's argument stands the Marxian distinction between ideology and theory,[19] formulated by Horkheimer in terms of the contrast between traditional theory and critical theory, whose aim is to restore agency and historical subjectivity to human consciousness. Critical theory "considers the overall framework which is conditioned by the blind interaction of individual activities . . . to be a function which originates in human action and therefore is a possible object of planful decision and rational determination of goals."[20]

Horkheimer's understanding of human beings as historical agents responsible for the general condition of a given society is not to be confused with concepts of subjectivity in terms of a commanding ego described above. Although I will argue later that Horkheimer's thought is profoundly humanist, it is not the humanism so often identified

---

[19] The distinction between ideology and theory derives from Marx's notion of the relationship between ideas and material interests, or forces. In "The German Ideology," Marx writes that the "ideas of the ruling class are in every epoch the ruling ideas: i.e., the class which is the ruling *material* force of society, is at the same time its ruling *intellectual* force." He goes on to illustrate how the ideas of the ruling elites become detached from their material base, with the result that hegemonic or prevailing ideals and values appear to have an independence and life of their own, finding their "legitimation" from within, as opposed to being determined by external conditions of class society. What Marx sets out to do is to pierce the illusion that "history is always under the sway of ideas" by exposing their roots in class interest. Severing ideas from their material basis supports the status quo; for Marx, this is ideology. "The ruling ideas are nothing more than the ideal expression of the dominant material relations, the dominant material relationships grasped as ideas." When oppressed humanity is able to see that its condition is not somehow "natural" or "unavoidable," but rather the result of humanly produced class division, it will become motivated to struggle against those material conditions of injustice. In this sense, Marx's entire work is directed to exposing what he would call the "real" nature of the human condition under capitalist society; this may be understood as the opposition between ideology and theory. See "The German Ideology," in *Collected Works*, vol. 5, 59. In fashion analogous to Marx, Horkheimer opposes critical theory against traditional theory.
[20] Horkheimer, "Traditional and Critical Theory," in *Critical Theory*, 207.

with the Enlightenment view of man as the creator-subject.[21] Neither Horkheimer nor his colleagues espoused an anthropomorphic, species imperialism that legitimates "man's" self-professed right to dominate and manipulate human and nonhuman nature to his own self-serving, self-profiting ends. The humanism that surfaces in Horkheimer's 1937 essay is one that rather seeks to empower real human beings in their struggle for a better life. In his view (a belief he held throughout his life), humanity is drifting deeper into irrationality, dehumanization, and barbarism. In outlining the main features of a critical theory of society, Horkheimer hoped as well to provide a theory of the irrational inhumanity of contemporary life in capitalist societies that would, in its very negativity, reveal possibilities for a transformed human and humane future infused with reason, justice, and happiness. For him, the role of theory is indispensable to this practical task.

The inseparability of social and individual freedom and enlightened thought[22] informs most of Horkheimer's writing, including this earlier piece. The task of theory is to expose the inhumanity and irrationality of the social relations of exploitative class society as a necessary part of the practical activity of social transformation. The theoretician does not work apart from or beyond the situation she or he analyzes, but rather is implicated in it in a consciously partisan way, "forming a dynamic unity with the oppressed class, so that his presentation of societal contradictions is not merely an expression of the concrete historical situation but also a force within it to stimulate change." In this way, "his real function emerges."[23] The critical theorist's "own thinking is a part and not something self-sufficient and separable from the struggle"[24] against the inhumanity of class society. Critical theory harbors a conscious emancipatory interest in its commitment to the "reasonable conditions of life." In the light of this interest, critical theory is "the unfolding of a single existential judgement": that the

---

[21] For a fuller discussion of the concept of humanism in critical theory, see Martin Jay, "The Frankfurt School's Critique of Marxist Humanism," *Social Research* 39 (1972): 285–305.

[22] Max Horkheimer and Theodor W. Adorno, *Dialectic of Enlightenment*, trans. John Cumming (New York: Continuum, Seabury Press, 1972), xiii.

[23] Horkheimer, "Traditional and Critical Theory," 215.

[24] Ibid., 216.

commodity economy of class societies in modern capitalism, despite its technological advances and temporary emancipations of some human beings, is driving humanity "into a new barbarism."[25]

Critical theory, as formulated by Horkheimer here in one of his most important writings, is both the theory and practice of emancipation. What this means is that thinking is a practical activity that is integrally associated with transformative action in ways that are deeply political. Although Horkheimer's analysis and explication of the main contours of critical theory are closely linked to a Marxian critique of political economy, his insights into the dynamics of domination are not limited strictly to the field of political economy. For that matter, neither were Marx's. Where Horkheimer differs from Marx, and significantly so, is in his refusal to identify a collective revolutionary subject or group, such as the proletariat, upon whom the hopes of a liberated humanity rest. For Horkheimer, the possibility of a revolutionary subject is limited to scattered, "small groups of men" who, in spite of their small numbers, "may at the decisive moment become . . . leaders"[26] in the struggle for social change. Even this possibility is extremely tentative and slight.

Horkheimer is well aware that theories and conscious struggles for emancipation do not of any inherent necessity bring about a transformed, liberated society and unalienated humanity. Rather, a sense of fragility belongs to the very project of critical theory. In part this is because to be adequate to history, critical theory requires a certain flexibility that will allow it to respond to the particular forms of injustice located in specific social situations. As well, Horkheimer is fully aware of the prevalent "hostility to theory" that resists "the transformative activity associated with critical thinking." Horkheimer accounts for this hostility as the result of a perceived threat to "the vast majority of the ruled," a threat that confronts them with the reality that their "painfully won adaptation to reality" was both "perverse and unnecessary."[27]

---

[25] Ibid., 199, 227.
[26] Ibid., 241.
[27] Ibid., 232.

Critical theory, as articulated here by Horkheimer, represents a form of praxis philosophy,[28] primarily because of its conscious commitment to theory as a practical, transformative, and political activity. As critical theory pursues this path, it intensifies its own self-understanding as comprehensive critique, in Marx's sense of "ruthless critique" that he announced as the purpose of his own life's work:

> Hitherto philosophers have had the solution of all riddles lying in their writing-desks, and the stupid exoteric world had only to open its mouth for the roast pigeons of absolute knowledge to fly into it. Now philosophy has become mundane, and the most striking proof of this is that the philosophical consciousness itself has been drawn into the torment of the struggle, not only externally but also internally. But, if constructing the future and settling everywhere for all time are not our affair, it is all the more clear what we have to accomplish at present: I am referring to *ruthless criticism of all that exists,* ruthless both in the sense of not being afraid of the results it arrives at and in the sense of being just as little afraid of conflict with the powers that be.[29]

What Marx defines as his social philosophical task requires the actualization of philosophical ideals in material reality, such as justice and

---

[28] The term *praxis philosophy* formally refers to a specific group of Marxist intellectuals living and working in the former Yugoslavia. Formerly concentrated in the main universities and research institutes of Yugoslavia, these thinkers and activists represented and developed the humanist tradition of Marxism that was sharply opposed to the official state Marxism of Tito's Communist regime. Many of these intellectuals lost their jobs and suffered various forms of harassment and even persecution, and their official journal, *Praxis,* was banned by the state in 1975. Philosophically, they belong to the Hegelian Marxian tradition of the Frankfurt School, which is sometimes referred to as Western Marxism. What these variants of Hegelian Marxism share is a view of human beings as historical agents who possess the capacity to transform social and individual reality by overcoming the pervasive alienation that divides humanity antagonistically from nature, from other human beings, and from itself. It is a philosophical approach committed to actual transformation, with a utopian dimension that strives for the inbreaking of future possibilities into present conditions. For an informative discussion of praxis philosophy and its representatives, see Gerson S. Sher, *Praxis and Marxist Criticism and Dissent in Socialist Yugoslavia* (Bloomington: Indiana Univ. Press, 1977).

[29] Karl Marx, "Letter to Arnold Ruge," in *Collected Works,* vol. 3, 142.

freedom. In the course of their realization, these ideals emerge as the "ruthless criticism" of everything existing, because the existent is the alienated negative embodiment of those ideals. With the social theory of the Frankfurt School, philosophy becomes practical critique: for the Frankfurt theorists, a comprehensive critique of society, using the conceptual and analytical tools of philosophy, sociology, and psychoanalysis, takes precedence over prescriptive, programmatic action. In the tradition of Marx, but different, critical theory not only does not offer solutions, it refuses to speculate on ready-made solutions for all time. As Herbert Marcuse was to remark much later, critical theory, as a wholly negative critique, offers no bridge between the present and its future,[30] no historical blueprint for social transformation.

Critical Theory and Feminist Theory: A Shared Interest

CONTEMPORARY FEMINIST THEORY SHARES A COMMON INterest with the notion of critical theory as formulated by Horkheimer insofar as it too participates in the deconstruction of Western intellectual traditions and their imperialist humanist theories that privilege Man as the self-creating, commanding, and regulating subject over other human beings and nature. At the same time, feminist critical theory must recognize that this concept of subjectivity is not an uncontested, singular concept structuring all of Western thought. The "master narratives" of modernity that have come under the scrutiny of contemporary postmodernist critiques[31] do not constitute a seamless garment of Western discourses, as a close reading of most works produced by the Frankfurt theorists will readily demonstrate. Prior to hasty adoptions of any of the variety of "post-isms" that proliferate throughout the contemporary disciplines, be they of a postmodernist, posthumanist, or even post-Christian type, feminist theory must commit

---

[30] Herbert Marcuse, *One-Dimensional Man: Studies in the Ideology of Advanced Industrial Society* (Boston: Beacon Press, 1968), 257.
[31] The term *master narrative* is used by Jean-François Lyotard, *The Postmodern Condition: A Report on Knowledge*, trans. Geoff Bennington and Brian Massumi (Minneapolis: Univ. of Minnesota Press, 1984).

itself to a reexamination of the emancipatory counterdiscourses of modernity with their corresponding democratic and socialist political expressions that continue to exist, stubbornly preserving notions of justice, freedom, and happiness for all humanity. As feminist theorist Andrea Nye recognizes, "If culture is sexist culture, feminist theory may have to be generated out of whatever lifelines that culture concedes."[32]

A feminist critical theory conceived in this way may refuse to repudiate such concepts as autonomy and subjectivity. Rather it reclaims and reconstructs them as vital to empowering women in their struggles to change the conditions that oppress and subjugate them. Building on the work of the Frankfurt theorists, feminists may retain the notion of subjectivity for women while renegotiating and revising it, shifting its location from the abstract subjectivity of the commanding self to an intersubjective, relational understanding of subjectivity and agency. In this way, the practical nature of the theory becomes evident in the theorist's act of solidarity with suffering women, who will together work to overcome their subjugated condition. This is the feminist elaboration of Horkheimer's view of the "dynamic unity" between the theoretician and the "oppressed class," where feminist critical theory consciously aspires to become a force within history to stimulate change. A feminist critical theory in the tradition of Horkheimer's 1937 essay is able to envision human liberation at the very least as "a *minimal utopia* of social life characterized by nurturant, caring, expressive and nonrepressive relations between self and other, self and nature."[33]

Such a feminist critical theory focuses not only on the actual social, economic, political, and institutional structures and power relations of oppression. It must also include cultural and psychoanalytical analyses in its effort to account for the manifold interlocking dynamics of

---

[32] Andrea Nye, *Feminist Theory and the Philosophies of Man* (London: Croom Helm, 1988), 4.

[33] Seyla Benhabib and Drucilla Cornell, "Introduction: Beyond the Politics of Gender," in S. Benhabib and D. Cornell, eds. *Feminism as Critique: On the Politics of Gender* (Minneapolis: Univ. of Minnesota Press, 1987), 4.

domination that reverberate throughout Western civilization.[34] A feminist critical theory that "begins from the recognition that individuals are feminine and masculine, [and] that individuality is not a unitary abstraction but an embodied and sexually differentiated expression of the unity of humankind,"[35] must expose the false universalism of Western intellectual traditions with its hidden political agenda that establishes power and privilege of a particular sex-specific group. In this vein feminist critical theory deconstructs the abstract humanism of Western intellectual and political discourses in order to reconstruct and restore a concrete humanism that affirms and promotes human beings in all their difference and diversity as not only ends in themselves, but as ends in relation to other selves and to nature. To recover the critical, concrete humanism that lies buried within Western civilization and cultures, feminist critical theory must further deconstruct the mechanisms through which women have been subject to sustained historical, intellectual, religious, and political processes of dehumanization. Such processes identify women with nonhuman nature, coercing them in their "bodies and . . . minds to correspond, feature by feature, with the *idea* of nature that has been established for us."[36]

The Dialectics of Domination

A MAJOR SOURCE OF WOMEN'S OPPRESSION RESIDES IN THIS enforced identity between woman and nature, with the result that women, by virtue of the association with nature historically thrust on them, represent the antithesis of civilization and potential negation of its achievements. They therefore must be contained as a dangerous

---

[34] Iris Marion Young, *Throwing Like a Girl and Other Essays in Feminist Philosophy and Social Theory* (Bloomington and Indianapolis: Indiana Univ. Press, 1990), 4.

[35] Carole Pateman, "Introduction: The Theoretical Subversiveness of Feminism," in Carole Pateman and Elizabeth Gross, eds., *Feminist Challenges: Social and Political Theory* (Boston: Northeastern Univ. Press, 1986), 9.

[36] Monique Wittig, "One Is Not Born a Woman," *Feminist Issues* 1 (Summer 1980): 47.

threat to that which Man has struggled to create in intellectual and physical labor. Many feminists agree that socially constructed categories of gender, where maleness corresponds to the products of history while femaleness corresponds to nature, have no basis in "natural" sexual difference. Rather, the social repression and marginalization of women are rooted in the domination of nature, and, by association, the repression of the feminine in the male self. The suppression of the feminine in the male, however, is not the suppression of what is alien or different from the male, although it is perceived as such. Rather, "exclusive gender identity is the suppression of natural similarities"[37]— that is, *human* similarities. The suppression of the feminine as connected with the suppression of nature in the self leads to the much more disturbing insight that what is renounced and feared by patriarchal culture is the very humanity that men and women share.

As time passed, critical theorists shifted their emphasis from the injustices directly associated with class society and political economy to focus their analysis on the noneconomic forms of domination.[38] They concentrated in particular on the domination of nature and its consequences for Western civilization. At the same time, their account of the dynamics of domination and its reverberations throughout society and culture delved into its specific, concrete forms in modern, capitalist societies. With Horkheimer and especially Theodor Adorno, critical theory moved away from the notion of the explicitly practical, transformative power of the theory itself, as it was formulated by Horkheimer in his 1937 essay. Rather, critical theory understood its task as an attempt to confront and expose the "consummate negativity" that pervades human existence, inspired by the hope that in doing so,

---

[37] Gayle Rubin, "The Traffic in Women: Notes on the 'Political Economy' of Sex," Rayna Reiter, ed., *Toward an Anthropology of Women* (New York and London: Monthly Review Press, 1975), 180.

[38] I do not want to suggest that either Horkheimer, Adorno, or Marcuse abandoned Marxian social theory. Rather, they expanded its field of analysis beyond direct issues of class in an effort to understand and account for domination as integral to the development of Western civilization, in terms of its intellectual traditions, social institutions, and the internal psychic structures of human beings.

the "mirror-image" of its opposite might be revealed.[39] For Adorno in particular, critical theory "is a theory of human relations only to the extent that it is also a theory of the inhumanity of those relations."[40]

Horkheimer and Adorno's effort to account for the inhumanity of human relations reached its fullest statement in their jointly authored *Dialectic of Enlightenment*. Their analysis of the etiology of domination in Western civilization remains one of the most penetrating, perhaps prophetic insights into enlightenment's self-betrayal. Some commentators, such as Martin Jay, describe *Dialectic of Enlightenment* as a "radical and sweeping . . . critique of Western society and thought" that replaces critical theory's earlier interest in political economy and class conflict with the discovery of "a new motor of history . . . the conflict between man and nature both without and within."[41] In Jay's view, Horkheimer and Adorno came to recognize that domination assumes "increasingly direct, uneconomic forms," and that the domination specific to capitalist societies could only be understood within an expanded analysis of the progress of domination throughout the development of Western civilization. At the center of that development lies the human striving to control and manipulate nature, with the result that human reason inevitably evolves into the calculating, instrumental rationality of Western science and technology criticized by Horkheimer in "Traditional and Critical Theory." In the struggle against nature for the self-preservation of the species, humanity becomes locked in a struggle against nature within the self. This struggle results paradoxically in the purchase of self-preservation with the currency of ruthless repression and denial of the very self it seeks to preserve. Capitalism represents a specific historical form of the dynamics of domination that is all the more insidious than what existed in previous epochs by virtue of its power to generate the illusion that the struggle against nature has been largely won through unprecedented technological capacity.

---

[39] Theodor Adorno, *Minima Moralia: Reflections from Damaged Life*, trans. E. F. N. Jephcott (London: Verso, 1985), 247.

[40] Theodor W. Adorno, *Prisms*, trans. Samuel Weber and Shierry Weber (Cambridge, Mass.: MIT Press, 1990), 41.

[41] Martin Jay, *The Dialectical Imagination: History of the Frankfort School and the Institute of Social Research, 1923–1950* (Boston: Beacon Press, 1973), 256.

The question that lies at the heart of Horkheimer and Adorno's negative vision is this: Given the "great discoveries of applied science" in the twentieth century, with their dual promise of emancipation of humanity from the drudgery of labor and the possibility of a happier, freer, more humane future, "why mankind, instead of entering into a truly human condition, is sinking into a new kind of barbarism."[42] In an effort to account for the human condition in advanced capitalist societies that could adequately address the profound contradiction of a society that is as highly developed on the level of technology as it is regressive on the level of humane ethics and values, Horkheimer and Adorno attempted to provide a kind of genealogy of the paradoxical nature of reason. For the Enlightenment and modernity, reason represents the human potential for realizing justice, freedom, and happiness within history. For Horkheimer and Adorno, as well as for Marx, a society is irrational as long as injustice, exploitation, and suffering constitute the given condition of certain social groups whose oppressed condition is the prerequisite of the perceived freedom and well-being of other groups, in whose service the exploited work and live. A rational world, according to Enlightenment and modernist ideals, is a just, humane world that is able to overcome alienation both socially and on the level of individual consciousness and interpersonal relations.

Reason is in itself an ambiguous phenomenon, however, in that it is both instrumental and technical as well as substantive and emphatic. Instrumental reason occupies its proper field in science and technology, while emphatic, substantive notions of reason as grounding justice, freedom, and happiness belong to the world of social praxis and ethics. The latter concept of reason has become submerged by the hegemonic pervasiveness of an instrumental, calculating reason that has increasingly colonized what Jürgen Habermas calls "the lifeworld,"[43] thereby intensifying dehumanization and alienation both within human beings and between them. For Horkheimer and Adorno,

---

[42] Horkheimer and Adorno, *Dialectic of Enlightenment*, xi.
[43] Jürgen Habermas, *The Theory of Communicative Action*, vol. 2, trans. Thomas McCarthy (Boston: Beacon Press, 1987).

the roots of this displacement and discrediting of substantive reason lie in the domination of nature.

As part of their genealogy of hegemonic, instrumental reason, Horkheimer and Adorno look to the epic of Homer's *Odyssey* as an originating narrative of the emergence of Western civilization that takes place within the struggle of the Enlightenment to free itself from myth and the unpredictable power of nature. The hero of the story, Ulysses, represents for Horkheimer and Adorno the prototype of the modern, bourgeois subject whose unfolding self-consciousness is forged in his battle for self-preservation and liberation from mythic forces, through the exercise of a progressively ego-centered, cunning rationality. His encounters with mythological figures such as the Cyclops, Circe, and the Sirens represent a contest with nature that is won largely through the deceptive, calculating practices of an instrumental reason that fears nature as the embodiment of the negative principle of its very existence. Ulysses' self-discovery as a mastering ego with the power to subject nature and other human beings to his commanding will must be atoned for in a repetition of self-sacrifice, in the form of intensified domination and control of the nature in him that is the result of each encounter with mythic forces. This dialectic of self-preservation and self-sacrifice both prefigures and encapsulates the structure of Western civilization from its earliest beginnings to its apex in capitalist societies. It also anticipates the struggle of reason against itself that is part of the subterranean history of Western cultures.

According to Horkheimer and Adorno, the story of Ulysses charts the "prehistory of subjectivity,"[44] in which the hero's struggle against myth and nature signals the rising "sun of calculating reason," the basis of the possibility of science in the modern era. For Horkheimer and Adorno, the key episode of *The Odyssey* is found in Ulysses' encounter with the Sirens. In this "presentient allegory of the dialectic of enlightenment,"[45] Ulysses successfully resists succumbing to the Sirens' "promise of pleasure," thereby preserving patriarchal order.[46] In order to navigate his way through the dangerous passage where

---

[44] Horkheimer and Adorno, *Dialectic of Enlightenment,* 54.
[45] Ibid., 34.
[46] Ibid., 33.

the Sirens sing their enchanting song, Ulysses has himself bound to the mast so as to be physically incapable of responding to them; meanwhile his laborers row, impervious to the Sirens' song because their ears have been plugged. This division of labor that Ulysses imposes between himself and his sailors establishes an irrevocable split between work and enjoyment, as well as between mental and physical labor, thus instantiating and prefiguring the contradictory antagonisms inherent in the alienated nature of work that characterizes capitalist societies.

This split between manual and mental labor, which lies at the "root of the dialectic of enlightenment,"[47] interlocks with the "mistaken" premise of prevailing modern philosophies that reproduce and preserve the mental/manual division of labor in the alienation of thought, the inevitable outcome of their insistence on the rigid separation between theory and praxis.[48] For Horkheimer and Adorno, the episode of Ulysses' escape from the Sirens seals the fate of Western man, who will be condemned to suffer the consequences of renewed and intensified self-denial throughout the course of history:

> This very denial, the nucleus of all civilizing rationality, is the germ cell of a proliferating mythic irrationality: with the denial of nature in man not merely the telos of the outward control of nature but the telos of man's own life is distorted and befogged. . . . Man's domination over himself, which grounds his selfhood, is almost always the destruction of the subject in whose service it is undertaken; for the substance which is dominated, suppressed, and dissolved by virtue of self-preservation is none other than that very life as functions of which the achievements of self-preservation find their sole definition and determination: it is, in fact, what is to be preserved. . . . The history of civilization is the history of the introversion of sacrifice . . . the history of renunciation."[49]

Domination, which structures Western civilization and rationality from within, arises at the point where Man attempts to control not

---

[47] Martin Jay, *Adorno* (Cambridge, Mass.: Harvard Univ. Press, 1984), 114.
[48] Gillian Rose, *The Melancholy Science: An Introduction to the Thought of Theodor W. Adorno* (London: Macmillan Press, 1978), 68.
[49] Horkheimer and Adorno, *Dialectic of Enlightenment,* 54–55.

only nature, but nature *in him*. More alarmingly, what the Sirens episode tells us is that this struggle to control nature necessarily involves the renunciation of the feminine, not merely as representative of nature without, but as part of nature within man's own being. In doing this, Man repudiates his own humanity, for it is nature, or naturalized humanity, that men and women share. Horkheimer and Adorno recognize that the domination of women is embedded in the very foundations of Western civilization, a conviction that becomes further reinforced with their reading of the story of Ulysses' manipulation of the courtesan Circe.

In Horkheimer's and Adorno's interpretation, Circe represents and affirms "an older form of life" that is prior to the patriarchal order represented by Ulysses. In Circe, the ambiguity of nature remains undivided and undifferentiated, so that she is associated with the realm of promiscuous, unordered sexuality. She represents as well the promise of the liberation of repressed instinct, the psychic bedrock of the self-reflective, individual, mastering ego, without whom it would be impossible to forge a decisive separation between the human and the animal world of nature. Circe's ability to transform men into animals represents her capacity to effect a reconciliation between human and nonhuman nature, assuring "happiness and [destroying] the autonomy of the one she makes happy." The capacity of her erotic and magical power to effect the reversion of the willful, autonomous ego to archaic consciousness results not in physical annihilation, but in nature realized and reconciled in peace and harmony with itself:

> The enchanted men behave like the wild animals who hear Orpheus playing. The mythic commandment to which they succumb liberates at the same time the repressed nature in them. What is recalled in their reversion to myth is itself myth. The repression of instinct that makes them individuals—selves—and separates them from animals, was the introversion of repression in the hopelessly closed cycle of nature, to which—as an older theory has it—the name Circe alludes. The forceful magic, on the other hand, which recalls them to an idealized prehistory, not only makes them animals, but . . . brings about, however delusive it may be, the illusion of redemption.[50]

---

[50] Ibid., 70.

By the time of *The Odyssey*, the promise of a reconciliation with inner nature, as well as reconciliation with the feminine, is already discredited as a sign of degradation of the properly human being, who is male. This leads Horkheimer and Adorno to dwell further on the humiliation and subjugation that mark the condition of women in Western civilization. Horkheimer and Adorno treat the relationship between Ulysses and Circe as anticipatory and paradigmatic of the relationship between men and women in Western bourgeois societies. The identification of women with nonhuman natural forces inscribes them as "other," as Woman, who can never be considered as human in the same way Man considers himself to be human. If nature is perceived as the antithesis of the human, then for Man to understand himself as fully human, Woman must remain outside the realm of full humanity. There she performs the function of representing to Man the ambivalent power of nature that both repels and fascinates him, with which he dares allow himself only limited contact under circumstances he controls and defines. In this way Man allows himself the illusion of gratifying the nature within himself, while preserving his humanity intact.

As part of nature, Man cannot totally escape its demands. In acts of repeated and more intense self-repression that are the precondition of his deluded sense of overpowering subjectivity, however, Man projects his internal nature onto domesticated, benign external objects—women—whom he has stripped of their independence and power. What he does not see is that in the mutilation of others, he loses himself. Horkheimer and Adorno well understood that male domination is the result of "a permanent deprivation of instinct" and "self-mutilation on the part of the man."[51] Ulysses only allows himself intimate contact with Circe after she has capitulated to his will, thereby satisfying the needs of nature in him, but in an illusory, self-stultifying way. In subjecting herself to Ulysses' will, Circe prefigures what woman is destined to become in bourgeois society, "the enigmatic image of irresistibility and powerlessness. In this way she reflects for domination the pure lie that posits the subjection instead of the redemption of nature."[52]

---

[51] Ibid.
[52] Ibid., 72.

The resumption of patriarchal order with Ulysses' return home is predicated on his reassertion over his own household, and especially on the reestablishment of ordered sexuality framed within the rights acquired in the possession of property. When Penelope meets Ulysses after his long years of absence, she assures herself of his identity by posing deliberately misleading questions about the construction of their marriage bed. Ulysses built the bed long before from an olive tree growing in the center of the room, but Penelope speaks of it as if it were movable. By Horkheimer's and Adorno's wry account, Ulysses, "furious . . . answers her with a detailed account of his longlasting piece of woodwork."[53] The reunion of husband and wife after years of separation succeeds on account of a piece of furniture. For Horkheimer and Adorno, Ulysses and Penelope are the prototypical bourgeois couple for whom desire and recognition are mediated—and alienated—by property and the propertied sexual relations of monogamous marriage. Husband and wife become reunited in resolving the controversy over the bed, the symbol of their mediated relationship as a bond "between sex and property."[54]

Penelope, who has remained faithful to her husband during his absence, is implicitly contrasted with the courtesan Circe, so that both women are interpreted as prefiguring the erotic division of labor characterized by the different roles of wife and prostitute in bourgeois society. By virtue of a coercive marriage tie, Penelope was compelled to repress nature in herself by maintaining her chastity during her husband's absence, as a precondition of protecting her status, her wealth, and her very life. Circe, in contrast, is not restricted by these particular limitations, although the sexual "labor" in which she engages with Ulysses occurs under conditions of domination and alienation established by him. She is not able to sleep with Ulysses on her terms, or even on terms of equal reciprocity, but strictly on his terms. As a result she loses her female, magical power.

As the embodiment of promiscuous sexuality, Circe must submit to the domination and control of the male, thereby sealing not only

[53] Ibid., 74.
[54] Patricia Jagentowicz Mills, *Woman, Nature, and Psyche* (New Haven and London: Yale Univ. Press, 1987), 189.

her fate, but that of woman in subsequent Western cultures. Circe symbolizes the degraded nature of female sexuality that elicits male fascination, revulsion, and fear that will mark the humiliated, subjugated condition of women throughout the course of Western civilization. Yet Penelope is able to maintain for herself a very different kind of power in terms of property, status, and wealth, although completely derived from her husband and enforced by the fear of death. The stories of Circe and Penelope are the metaphorical pillars that structure and limit female possibility, and in the shadow of which most women live out their lives: "Prostitute and wife are the complements of female self-alienation in the patriarchal world: the wife denotes pleasure in the fixed order of life and property, whereas the prostitute takes what the wife's right of possession leaves free, and— as the wife's secret collaborator—subjects it again to the order of possession: she sells pleasure."[55]

The transformation of erotic pleasure into a commodity item of market exchange reduces women to interchangeable objects whose use value supersedes their human value. This is further demonstration of the degree to which the effort to master and control nature is inescapably linked to the repudiation of the human. The dichotomization of female sexuality in terms of illegitimate pleasure associated with prostitutes on the one hand, along with the respectable sexuality of monogamous legal marriage and its mediated relations of contract and property on the other, has its roots then in the domination of nature. As we have seen in Horkheimer's and Adorno's reading of Ulysses' encounters with various female characters, the domination and repudiation of nature are interlinked with the domination of woman and female sexuality. The domination of women thus is part of the innermost structure of Western cultures.

The struggle for domination and repression of nature within the self becomes ultimately aporetic in the sense that its logical outcome implies self-annihilation. Thus humanity is locked in a perpetual struggle against itself, because nature within must find gratification and satisfaction. Alienated and distorting social structures evolve in the course of this struggle against nature and abet it, resulting in a deformed

---

[55] Horkheimer and Adorno, *Dialectic of Enlightenment,* 73–74.

and disabling satisfaction of needs that drives human beings and nature into deeper forms of abasement. As civilization progresses with its new developments in technology and science that appear to offer seemingly limitless possibilities for happiness and satisfaction, new forms of repression and domination, both internal and external, must be devised in order that Man not lose control and succumb to nature's demands.

The struggle against nature that Horkheimer and Adorno locate at the very root of Western civilization can never be won but only perpetually renewed and reenacted. With each historical epoch, domination reformulates and reinforces itself on higher levels established by the prevailing social conditions. The progress of history is therefore illusory; advances in science and technology that are capable of realizing emancipation and human happiness are transformed into their negation, so that the domination of nature, women, and those "others" associated with nature (that is, nonwhites) is simply repeated and reinforced. Man becomes a myth to himself, an abstract, reified category of a self-creating, commanding self, made in an equally alienated image of God. The very cosmos has become for him an "immense hunting ground" where he exercises "sovereignty over existence, in the countenance of the lord and master, and in command. Myth turns into enlightenment, and nature into mere objectivity."[56] Thus enlightenment becomes myth in the perpetual and inescapable cycle of intensified domination; "the awakening of the self is paid for by the acknowledgement of power as the principle of all relations."[57]

Beyond "Dialectic of Enlightenment"

IF WE ACCEPT THE MASSIVE INDICTMENT OF NOT ONLY THE Enlightenment, but also of the very possibility of enlightenment's self-actualization as against its apparent total self-betrayal, then we are forced to ask if there is any possibility for emancipation in modernity

---

[56] Ibid., 9.
[57] Ibid.

on any level, let alone for the emancipation of women. This question is especially acute for feminism, if it is indeed the case that the very structure of civilization is tainted at the source with domination of women as its own precondition. An increasing number of feminist theorists maintain that modernity and its intellectual traditions hold no possibility for the emancipation of women. In postmodernist fashion, they argue for the death of the commanding subject, Western metaphysics, and the "master narratives" with their totalizing accounts of reality. One postmodernist feminist theorist goes so far as to assert that "belief in something called the modern has itself been a mistake."[58]

Ironically, many feminist theoretical perspectives most closely associated with postmodernism would in several respects agree with Horkheimer's and Adorno's account of the prehistory of enlightenment and its devastating consequences for all those considered beyond the pale of Eurocentric, androcentric concepts of what is human. The decisive difference is that while critical of modernity, Horkheimer and Adorno do not take the step to a complete rejection of it,[59] despite the depth and range of their critique. For many feminist theorists, especially those who embrace a Foucauldian-style critique of the intertwinement of knowledge and power as constitutive of the "grand narratives" of enlightenment and its modernist traditions,[60] the Enlightenment (and modernity) has not only failed to realize its ideals

---

[58] Donna Haraway, "The Promises of Monsters: A Regenerative Politics for Inappropriate/d Others," in L. Grossberg, C. Nelson, and P. Treechler, eds., *Cultural Studies* (New York: Routledge, 1991), 304. Haraway, a biologist and historian of science, has written a number of articles and books that are distinctly postmodern in their critique of science as a cultural phenomenon. See her collection of essays, *Simians, Cyborgs, and Women: The Reinvention of Nature* (New York: Routledge, 1991), especially the essays "A Cyborg Manifesto" and "Situated Knowledges." These essays are fairly representative of feminist postmodernist approaches to epistemology, identity formation, and relations between human and nonhuman nature. For a critique of her thinking from a critical theory perspective, see Marsha Hewitt, "Cyborgs, Drag Queens and Goddesses: Emancipatory-Regressive Themes in Feminist Theory," *Method and Theory in the Study of Religion* 5, no. 2 (1993): 135–54.
[59] Jürgen Habermas, *Autonomy and Solidarity: Interviews with Jürgen Habermas*, rev. ed., ed. Peter Dews (London: Verso, 1992), 152.
[60] See, for example, the work of Judith Butler, as in her *Gender Trouble: Feminism and the Subversion of Identity* (New York and London: Routledge, 1990).

for human emancipation, it directly works against them, devising new forms of domination and enslavement. The task of feminist theory is therefore understood as a thoroughgoing critique and repudiation of modernity with its social, political, and intellectual practices in favor of more differentiated, partial, decentered theoretical perspectives, "situated knowledges" and provisional alliances that allow for a democratic politics of inclusion of the traditionally marginalized.

For commentators who do not hold a postmodernist perspective, Horkheimer's and Adorno's critique of domination as the ascendancy and hegemony of instrumental reason is problematic because it appears to terminate in an impossible contradiction that destroys the very basis of critique, thereby foreclosing on the possibility of social and individual transformation. Jürgen Habermas accuses Horkheimer and Adorno of producing an "astoundingly" oversimplified image of modernity,[61] insofar as they fail to differentiate the logical structures pertaining to the different spheres of society. Habermas's critique proceeds from his understanding of modern capitalist societies in terms of the categorial framework of "system" and "lifeworld." The former is structured along the lines of a systems-theoretic or functionalist mode of rationality, and the latter according to socially integrated action contexts in which different actors coordinate their activities discursively and with reference to agreed-upon norms and values.

The existence of these distinct spheres of rationality constitutes one of the paradoxes of modernity, in that the mode of rationality most appropriate to the lifeworld involves conscious agents engaged in discursive practices whereby they are able to agree on the legitimacy (or nonlegitimacy) of given norms, values, and worldviews, as well as to reach agreement and mutual understanding as to courses of action. Against Adorno in particular, Habermas proposes the "structure of a rationality which is immanent in everyday communicative practice," where an alternative to instrumental reason is preserved in the "resistant structure"[62] of communicative rationality. The systems realm is structured in terms of a different mode of rationality, what Max

---

[61] Jürgen Habermas, *The Philosophical Discourse of Modernity*, trans. Frederick Lawrence (Cambridge, Mass.: MIT Press, 1990), 112.
[62] Habermas, *Autonomy and Solidarity*, 153.

Weber referred to as "purposive-rational," or calculating, instrumental reason driven by the nonreflexive steering mechanisms of power and money. This mode forms the logical structures of technology, organization, and administration. Habermas's theory of society identifies the possibilities for emancipation from, withdrawal from, and resistance to the encroaching colonizing expansionism of the systems-integrated field as located along the "seams between system and lifeworld,"[63] in the places where communicative practices may occur.

Habermas takes issue with Horkheimer's and Adorno's failure sufficiently to recognize the "differentiation of value spheres" characteristic of modern societies and their attendant logics. This differentiation provides opportunities for the exercise of the discriminating capacity of critique. For Habermas,

> It is true that with the capitalist economy and the modern state the tendency to incorporate all questions of validity into the limited horizon of purposive rationality proper to subjects interested in self-preservation and to self-maintaining systems is also strengthened. But the far from contemptible compulsion toward the progressive differentiation of a reason that, moreover, assumes a procedural form—a compulsion induced by the rationalization of world views and lifeworlds—competes with this inclination toward a social regression of reason. The formation of expert cultures, within which carefully articulated spheres of validity help the claims to propositional truth, normative rightness, and authenticity, attain *their own logic* . . . and this development competes with the naturalistic assimilation of validity claims to power claims and the destruction of our critical capacities.[64]

From this perspective, not only do Horkheimer and Adorno fail to "do justice to the rational content of cultural modernity" that informs bourgeois ideals, the uncompromising negativity of their indictment of the Enlightenment results in "a critique that attacks the presuppositions of its own validity." It ends in an aporetic, "performative contradiction inherent in an ideology critique that outstrips itself."[65]

---

[63] Habermas, *Theory of Communicative Action*, vol. 1, "Translator's Introduction," xxxv.
[64] Habermas, *Philosophical Discourse of Modernity*, 113.
[65] Ibid., 127.

Other commentators refer to Horkheimer's and Adorno's "relentless pessimism" and "totalizing critique"[66] of enlightenment, which in the end leaves no possibility for the "recuperation of reason,"[67] thereby offering no space for the restoration of substantive reason. Some critics are troubled by the scope of Horkheimer's and Adorno's critique, charging that it engages in a "destructive, negative hermeneutics . . . of all civilization" that in the end leaves "no locus of liberation [that is] available in either past, present or future culture."[68] Others argue that the "self-destructive intellectual hyper-radicalism" of *Dialectic of Enlightenment* is part of an "over-politicization of theory [that] leads logically to the substitution of theory as a surrogate for politics—an *Ersatzpolitik*."[69]

If *Dialectic of Enlightenment* is read in the light of Marx's self-professed commitment to the "ruthless criticism" of the current social reality, however, as well as in the context of its authors' other writings, it may be interpreted as a much more hopeful diagnosis of Western civilization than some critics are prepared to allow. For Horkheimer and Adorno especially, but for Herbert Marcuse as well, the only hope

---

[66] Seyla Benhabib, *Critique, Norm and Utopia: A Study of the Foundations of Critical Theory* (New York: Columbia Univ. Press, 1986), 166, 167. Albrecht Wellmer's discussion of *Dialectic of Enlightenment* is similar in tone to that of Habermas and Benhabib. In his view, the expression of critical theory put forward in the *Dialectic*, which occupies "a key position in regard to the later development of the critical theory of the Frankfurt school," "establishes . . . that the fateful process of 'rationalization' of all processes of social life does not find its preordained end in an emancipated society, but—in accordance with its inward logic—is compelled instead to end in the opposite of emancipation: in the subjection of men, too, to the domination over nature that they themselves have achieved." *Critical Theory of Society*, trans. John Cumming (New York: Seabury Press, 1974), 135, 132.

[67] Robert Hullot-Kentor, "Back to Adorno," *Telos* 81 (Fall 1989): 13. Kentor criticizes Habermas's reading of *Dialectic of Enlightenment* along lines that I find persuasive.

[68] Andrew Arato, "Introduction" to Part One, *The Essential Frankfurt School Reader*, ed. Andrew Arato and Eike Gebhardt (New York: Continuum, 1982), 24.

[69] Göran Therborn, "The Frankfurt School," *New Left Review* 63 (September–October 1970), 88, 73.

for a transformed future lay in a sustained, unflinching, and negative critique of the existent. In the famous concluding lines of the "Finale" of *Minima Moralia*, Adorno defines "the task of thought" as directed toward fashioning perspectives that "displace and estrange the world, reveal it to be, with its rifts and crevices, as indigent and distorted as it will appear one day in the messianic light."[70] This is the expression of a negative utopianism that does not settle for premature or cheap reconciliations and false harmonies by offering "constructive," clearly laid out solutions to contemporary problems. For Horkheimer and Adorno, the "insanity systematized"[71] of late capitalist societies in the West reflects the internalized inhumanity and irrationality of humankind. The only possibility for transcendence of the current situation in which humanity finds itself, and in the creation of which it is profoundly implicated, lies in an understanding and critical insight that is commensurate with reality. For them, constructive solutions that precede the required analysis can only result in an accommodation to the status quo that reinforces and legitimates it.

Critics of *Dialectic of Enlightenment* have not given serious enough attention to Horkheimer's and Adorno's stated purpose in the work: to enable enlightenment's own self-critique, whereby it may "consider itself, if men are not to be wholly betrayed. The task to be accomplished is not the conservation of the past, but the redemption of the hopes of the past."[72] This articulated hope in the recuperation and regeneration of enlightenment is the animating force of the work, and as well accounts for the scope and depth of a critique that counterpoints enlightenment against itself.

What Habermas describes as a performative contradiction at the heart of Horkheimer's and Adorno's critique, which "radicalize[s] the critique of reason to the point of self-referentiality,"[73] might also be read as a performative enactment of self-disclosure that reveals the self-redemptive and self-rehabilitative potential of reason that renders the depth of its self-criticism even possible. The utopian hope that

---

[70] Adorno, *Minima Moralia*, 247.
[71] Wellmer, *Critical Theory of Society*, 134.
[72] Horkheimer and Adorno, *Dialectic of Enlightenment*, xv.
[73] Habermas, *Autonomy and Solidarity*, 152.

sustains Horkheimer's and Adorno's analysis is one that is painfully conscious of its own fragility yet marshals the courage to take seriously the very real possibility of its ultimate impossibility. This is apparent at various stages in the book, particularly in the fragments toward the end, which reaffirm the absolute necessity of a negative consciousness that does not shrink before the "horror of destruction"[74] that humanity has bequeathed to itself. The courageous and tenacious hope that stubbornly persists throughout Horkheimer's and Adorno's sustained "existential judgment" of enlightenment becomes all the stronger precisely because of their uncompromising negativity:

> It is not the portrayal of reality as hell on earth but the slick challenge to break out of it that is suspect. If there is anyone today to whom we can pass the responsibilities for the message, we bequeath it not to the "masses," and not to the individual (who is powerless), but to an imaginary witness—lest it perish with us.[75]

The insistence on dwelling on the "negative side" of the historical process, on "the gruesomeness and injustice of it all," along with the resolute refusal to "describe how people are to escape from the charmed circle of the status quo,"[76] constitutes the motivational core or animating impulse of the critical theory of Horkheimer and Adorno that is sustained throughout their entire work. Although critical theory refuses to speculate on the detailed nature of the transformed future society it clearly anticipates, and despite the expansive, uncompromising nature of its critique of enlightenment, it nonetheless insists on the "utopian potential of modern society," an insistence and political commitment that is grounded in a consistent hope for a better world.[77] This sustained hope in the face of profound despair, which pervades critical theory, constitutes one of its most important potential intersections with religion, despite the fact that none of the Frankfurt theorists adhered to any religious beliefs, at least in any conventional sense.

---

[74] Horkheimer and Adorno, *Dialectic of Enlightenment,* 215.
[75] Ibid., 256.
[76] Max Horkheimer, "The Concept of Man," in *Critique of Instrumental Reason* (New York: Seabury Press, 1974), 32.
[77] Jay, *Adorno,* 179, note 52.

Perhaps the strong sense of hope that surfaces repeatedly in the writings of the Frankfurt theorists is what, in my reading of their work, prevents their negative critique of enlightenment and modernity from ending in the aporetic impasse attributed to it by other commentators. The emancipatory, politically committed, and practical nature of theory elaborated by Horkheimer in the 1937 essay has not been abandoned or swallowed up in a pessimistic, destructive hermeneutic of Western civilization that leads straight to political paralysis and sterility. What Horkheimer wrote about as theory that forms "a dynamic unity" with its object, namely oppressed and exploited humanity, *becomes itself* that dynamic unity in the *Dialectic of Enlightenment,* by virtue of the depth of its condemnation of enlightenment's self-betrayal. In this way, Horkheimer's and Adorno's loyalty to modernity's as yet unfulfilled promise becomes apparent. "Only the conscious horror of destruction," they write, "creates the correct relationship with the dead: unity with them because we, like them, are victims of the same condition and the same disappointed hope."[78] Thus they offer the testimony, as it were, of those disappointed hopes to an "imaginary witness," so that at the very least, critical consciousness of the contradiction between what could be and what is may not be extinguished. *Dialectic of Enlightenment,* as negative critique and analysis of the multiple forces of domination that inform the civilizing processes of the West, is also a powerful counterdiscourse of modernity whose range and comprehensiveness provide a critical resource for other counter-discourses of modernity.

Feminist Directions

THE QUESTION THAT MUST NOW BE CONSIDERED IS: WHAT does the critique of domination put forward in the *Dialectic of Enlightenment* have to offer feminism? How can the insights of Horkheimer and Adorno be appropriated by a feminism that consciously positions itself as the "imaginary witness" of critical theory? The assumption of this book is that contemporary feminist theory, and feminist

---

[78] Horkheimer and Adorno, *Dialectic of Enlightenment,* 215.

religious thought in particular, needs to fashion itself as a conscious counterdiscourse of modernity that seeks to restore enlightenment ideals by reconstructing them in the light of feminist goals.

The analysis of domination that situates the mastery of nature and of women as integral to the history of Western civilization and its intellectual traditions has much to offer contemporary feminist theory. At the same time, the critical theory of the Frankfurt School, for all its recognition of the inextricable linkages between the domination of nature and the domination of women, nonetheless fashions this critique in ways that undermine the agency and full humanity of women. Despite the fact that the critical social theory of the Frankfurt School is the most emancipatory and perhaps most highly "developed philosophical thought of our times,"[79] it nonetheless harbors serious blind spots concerning women that not only indicate its inability to see women as concrete historical agents in spite of their oppressed condition, but further indicate its own irrational, nonemancipatory moments. In this way critical theory forecloses on its emancipatory potential. To overcome this condition, critical theory requires a feminist critique of its inherent and potentially disabling contradictions. Such a critique will necessarily take the form of a feminist critical theory that interrogates and reexamines cultural modernity in order to discover what possibilities for emancipation exist there, in however distorted, repressed, or elusive form.

Of particular interest to this study is the identification and location of those emancipatory possibilities within contemporary feminist approaches to Christianity with a view to constructing the contours of a feminist critical theory of religion that is part of a more comprehensive feminist critical theory of society. In pursuing this task, and as part of its critical appropriative work, feminism must look more closely at the irrational moments harbored by critical theory that surface in its treatment of women and that are carried over from the main intellectual traditions out of which it is formed (represented mainly in the work of G. W. F. Hegel, Karl Marx, Friedrich Engels, and Sigmund Freud). The pejorative images of woman as less-than-human

---

[79] Mills, *Woman, Nature, and Psyche*, xi.

portrayed by these writers bear striking similarity to those unfortunate naturalized attributions imposed on women by Christian theology.

Western intellectual and theological traditions share a great deal in common when it comes to theorizing about women. One of the tasks for a feminist critical theory of religion must be to expose those similarities, showing how a feminist critique of theology is useful to a more expanded critique of Western conceptions of women. In demonstrating the relevance and power of feminist theology's capacity to reveal the interlocking and mutually reinforcing structures of sexism of philosophical and theological thought, it will become increasingly apparent that feminist liberation theology strongly intimates a feminist critical theory of religion. Before moving into this discussion, however, it is necessary to examine some of the intellectual roots of critical theory's unsettling accounts of women.

Woman, History, and the Family

The Dialectics of Non-Being

ONE OF CRITICAL THEORY'S MOST PUZZLING IRONIES IN-volves its treatment of women, or more accurately, woman,[1] since women, conceived as concrete, historical agents, do not on the whole exist in Frankfurt School theory. For all its attention and often moving sensitivity to the subjugated plight of women, including its insightful account of patriarchal domination as an integral part of Western civilization, critical theory does not consider women's experience of domination as it is lived from their point of view in history, society, and the family.

Max Horkheimer's, Theodor Adorno's, and Herbert Marcuse's critiques of contemporary society take serious account of the family, including its role in the education and socialization of human beings, as part of their more comprehensive analysis of the dynamics of domination and its accompanying tendencies toward intensified dehumanization within contemporary capitalism. Their analyses of the family, however, do not focus on women's subjective experience, whether as mothers, wives, or daughters. Their attempt to understand

---

[1] I will use the term *woman* when referring to concepts of abstract female essence, category, or principle, as found in the writers under study here. I refer to *women* as *woman's* direct opposite: as concrete, real, sensuous, individual, living, suffering, historical human beings. While Hegel usually understands women as *woman*, Marx and Engels tend to swing between *women* and *woman,* a contradiction that will be addressed in this chapter.

the differentiated logic of the contemporary family both as a discrete unit and as a socializing interface with respect to the larger community utilizes insights and concepts appropriated and reconstructed from philosophy, sociology, and psychoanalysis. The family is not only discussed in terms of its internal psychodynamics, but also in terms of its complex relationship to the demands of the prevailing socio-cultural reality within which it exists and which it serves.

For all this, *woman* in the end fails to appear as anything other than an abstract principle or category; when her role and situation in the family are commented on, they are in static, wooden terms. In the Frankfurt thinkers's theorizing of the family, *woman* never comes to life, because she is not allowed to achieve full humanity; she is usually portrayed as the object of masculine fantasy. What critical theory provides with respect to women is an insight into woman-as-object within masculine consciousness, an insight that reveals little of how women perceive themselves or understand their own experiences. It may be further stated that critical theory shows no interest in un-derstanding or articulating women's subjective experience.

This inability to see women as fully human in the sense of active, self-conscious, historical, and moral agents and to consider domination and suffering from their particular point of view presents feminism with a serious dilemma, as was indicated in the previous chapter. If critical theory is to be considered as one of the most significant eman-cipatory discourses of modernity, as I am arguing here, and as pro-viding one of the richest resources for a feminist theory and practice, how do we deal with its problematic treatment of women?

It is not news to feminists that most of the intellectual traditions of the West, no matter how rich with revolutionary potential, are inadequate with respect to their treatment of women. At the same time, feminist critique, consciously understood as a situated, historical, and comprehensive metacritical discourse,[2] itself arises out of a variety

---

[2] By *metacritique* I mean that feminism is not only a critique of the conditions that contribute to and maintain women's subordination and suffering. It is also a *critique of those critiques of the existent situation,* such as found in Marx or critical theory, as well as being an ongoing critique of itself, constantly revising its own insights.

of discourses that critically interrogate prevailing concepts and ideological legitimations of reality. Feminist critique does not originate from a point beyond history and society, but is deeply embedded and implicated in them, so that it is compelled to forge its practical vision within the conditions it already confronts. For these reasons, feminism must examine and appropriate those theories whose emancipatory potential lends itself to specifically feminist goals. The process of a feminist examination of critical theory promises to result in a feminist critical theory that is capable of restoring and reconstructing the former's emancipatory integrity through an uncompromising confrontation with its inherent sexist (and therefore irrational) moments.

To account adequately for the irrational, contradictory elements of critical theory that are primarily situated in its treatment of women, feminist analysis must further examine critical theory's intellectual roots in a Hegelian-Marxian discourse of modernity, whose treatment of women is equally inadequate. What this reveals is the extent to which critical theory on the whole maintains an unreflective attitude to women as less-than-human other, an attitude largely sustained in the work of those theorists associated with the Hegelian-Marxian tradition who exerted the most powerful influences on the development of critical theory. An examination of the work of G. W. F. Hegel, Karl Marx, Friedrich Engels, and Sigmund Freud shows that with respect to women, critical theory does not advance beyond their work. In fact, critical theory at times falls below the level of Marx and Engels with its resuscitation of abstract, static Hegelian concepts of woman. The image of woman that appears in critical theory recalls Hegel's treatment of women without moving significantly beyond it. This is also true in many respects with Freud, although the same claim does not apply in quite the same fashion to Marx and Engels, whose treatment of women is often—but not consistently—more differentiated and complex, and thus more compatible with feminist insights than any of the others. Some Hegelian echoes remain, however, in their theory and in a fairly unmodified form when it concerns the question of *woman*.

What is striking about the work of these theorists is that they are inheritors of the Enlightenment tradition and its critique of traditional worldviews and concern with the realization of freedom and justice through the activity of reason. The philosophical, social, and cultural theories advanced by Hegel, Marx, Engels, Freud,[3] and later on by the Frankfurt School, constitute some of the most significant critical discourses of modernity on the question of human freedom. They contain an important but latent, as yet unrealized potential for a feminist critical theory and praxis. Why latent and unrealized? Why is it that these discourses of modernity with their often progressive, emancipatory insights into the human condition, remain not only conservative and ineffective with respect to the question of woman, but actually serve to reinforce the reproduction and maintenance of women's oppression? How does it happen that when it comes to women, these thinkers appear to abandon their own emancipatory logic? Why do their discussions of freedom and their insights into and concerns with injustice and human suffering not extend with the same rigor and clarity to include women?

A typical answer to such questions is that, especially with respect to Hegel, Marx, Engels, and Freud, they were "men of their time" and cannot be expected to reflect attitudes to women any different from those of the prevailing society and culture. It is neither reasonable nor fair to expect, so this line of argument continues, that they could have possibly diverged from the dominant views of women of their day. These views held, among other things, that women were naturally suited to marriage and domestic activity and thereby had no need, for example, of access to forms of education beyond their inherent feminine capacities. For these and other reasons, one could hardly expect these nineteenth- and early twentieth-century products of a Victorian outlook to champion the emancipation of women.

---

[3] My treatment of Freud in this chapter will consider his work from the perspective of sociocultural theory rather than clinical practice. In approaching Freud in this way, I follow interpreters of his work such as Herbert Marcuse, Russell Jacoby, and Juliet Mitchell, although without necessarily agreeing with them on all points. What interests me about Freud is his analysis of culture and civilization, the relationship between ontogenetic and phylogenetic psychic formation, the individual and society, sexuality, and the possibilities of rethinking his insights from a feminist perspective.

This apologetic fails on a number of grounds, not least of which pertains to the critical, revolutionary nature of the theories advanced by these thinkers. Nor does the argument suffice that appeals to the limitations imposed by the worldviews belonging to particular historical epochs. Women's liberation had already been placed on the political agenda of the day by intellectuals such as Mary Wollstonecraft, John Stuart Mill, and Harriet Taylor Mill. Moreover, the eighteenth and nineteenth centuries were times of revolutionary ferment in many parts of Europe, and notions of the inalienable, natural rights of man had already been articulated on both sides of the Atlantic, in the American Declaration of Independence (1776) and in the French Declaration of the Rights of Man (1789).[4]

In the case of Hegel, who died in 1831, his conservative, regressive attitude to women cannot be excused simply with platitudes about an inconvenient *Zeitgeist* as yet unfamiliar with concepts of women's emancipation. According to one of his feminist commentators, Hegel's " 'time' was a revolutionary one, and in the circles closest to [him], that of his Romantic friends, he encountered brilliant, accomplished and nonconformist women who certainly intimated to him what true gender equality might mean in the future. Hegel saw the future, and he did not like it."[5]

As for Karl Marx, his scathing criticisms of Hegel and the German philosophical Idealism he epitomized do not apply themselves with equal force and insight to Hegel's treatment of women. In some respects, Marx even preserves Hegel's views. While on the whole Engels follows Marx, in this respect he too has a more highly developed materialist and political approach to women's exploitation in their

---

[4] Eighteenth-century feminists such as Mary Wollstonecraft embraced Enlightenment concepts of human dignity and rights and sought to extend them to women. According to Josephine Donovan, Wollstonecraft dedicated her *A Vindication of the Rights of Woman* (1792) to French minister Talleyrand in the hope of persuading him to include women in France's new constitution, thereby preventing France from remaining "a tyranny." See Donovan, *Feminist Theory: The Intellectual Traditions of American Feminism* (New York: Continuum, 1988), 1.

[5] Seyla Benhabib, *Situating the Self: Gender, Community and Postmodernism in Contemporary Ethics* (New York: Routledge, 1992), 254.

social roles as workers and as bourgeois wives. Freud implicitly incorporates many Hegelian prejudices into his discussions of women and female sexuality, while Horkheimer, Adorno, and even Marcuse tend to adopt uncritically Hegel's views on women in the family, which preserve to varying degrees both the idealized romanticism and occasional contempt of the Hegelian approach.

Yet Horkheimer and especially Adorno were critical of Hegelian philosophy, rejecting in particular what they saw as the logic of identity that structures his entire dialectic. Adorno's "negative dialectics" or theory of non-identity has become a powerful critical tool in contemporary feminism, despite the fact that many feminists who embrace non-identity theory do not acknowledge his work. As will be argued in the next chapter, Adorno's work provides feminist theory with a vital critical resource that he himself could not or would not develop with respect to women. Briefly stated, the treatment of woman in critical theory generates a contradictory impasse or aporia within the theory itself, one to which there can be no resolution unless it is subjected to a feminist interrogation of its philosophical prejudices regarding women. By examining the image of woman and its vicissitudes as carried over from Hegel, Marx, Engels, and Freud where they settle in critical theory—modified, but substantially untransformed—it becomes possible to dislodge the ideological and irrational elements of critical theory from within. Indispensable to this reconstructive task is a feminist critique that charts the evolution of images of women from Hegel to Freud. To that I now turn.

The "Unreal, Insubstantial Shadow": Hegel's "Woman"

HEGEL'S PHILOSOPHICAL EXPOSITION OF THE ETHICAL STRUCture and interrelationship between the family and the state[6] inscribes

---

[6] Hegel's distinction between the family and the state and the nature of their antagonistic or oppositional relation is found in the *Phenomenology of Spirit*. In his later work, the *Philosophy of Right,* Hegel introduces the triadic distinction between family, civil society, and state, and it is here that his treatment of woman and her role in the family is most fully stated. I begin with a brief

traditional gender-specific categories as representative of a "rational ontology" that is meant to "reflect the deep structure of *Geist*."[7] By Hegel's account, *Geist,* or Spirit, undergoes a restless process of "self-diremption" whereby it congeals in history, taking concrete form in manifold particularity that includes male and female as principles of *Geist's* own embodied reality. As *Geist* self-dirempts or differentiates into a multiplicity of forms within history, it manifests itself in modernity in the forms of family, civil society, and state,[8] all of which represent differing levels or degrees of its achieved universal essence and self-awareness.

While the family, civil society, and the state constitute different aspects of the "ethical order," the family as the least developed stands somewhat antagonistically in relation to the other spheres and is the domain of woman, the female principle. The family represents or manifests Geist in its ethical substance as Divine Law, which confronts the secular, human law or ethical power of the state, which is the law of universality, opposed to the law of individuality located in the family. For Hegel, "the ethical power of the state, being the movement of self-conscious action, finds its antithesis in the simple and immediate essence of the ethical sphere; as *actual* universality it is a force actively opposed to individual being-for-itself; and as actuality in general it finds in that *inner* essence something other than the ethical power of the state."[9]

The antagonism between family and state depicted in the *Phenomenology of Spirit* can only reflect a deeper antagonism between woman and man, since the family is the exclusive domain of woman, whereas man is destined to activity in the public realm of the larger society (although, unlike woman, he has the opportunity of moving

---

discussion of the *Phenomenology,* however, in order to illustrate that many of Hegel's views concerning women and their oppositional relation to civil society and the state are foreshadowed in the earlier work.

[7] Benhabib, *Situating the Self,* 245.

[8] Hegel introduces the concept of civil society into his later work, the *Philosophy of Right.* As Graeme Nicholson notes, in the *Phenomenology* Hegel refers to the family and the state as aspects of the community.

[9] *Hegel's Phenomenology of Spirit,* trans. A. V. Miller (Oxford, England: Oxford Univ. Press, 1977), 268.

between both realms). The family is a *"natural"* ethical community, representing the *"unconscious"* interior principle of the ethical order, and thus "stands opposed to its actual, self-conscious existence" in the nation: "as the *immediate* being of the ethical order, it stands over against that order which shapes and maintains itself by working for the universal; the Penates stand opposed to the universal Spirit."[10] The ethical existence of the family is characterized by immediacy, its ethical element the unrealized, intrinsic universal element.

For Hegel, the family acts as a training ground in preparing its sons for later active participation in the community, or life "in and for the universal."[11] An individual, particular human being remains so within the family, and it is only in leaving the family and taking up his destined role as citizen within the community that the son achieves "actuality" and "substantiality." As family member only, the individual male can be nothing more than "an unreal impotent shadow." Unlike the man, woman is by her nature a member of the family only; she has no option for becoming a citizen. She must remain at the level of unrealized, insubstantial shadow, not even capable of consciousness of herself as a particular person in relation to particular members of her own family. Hegel writes:

> In the ethical household, it is not a question of *this* particular husband, *this* particular child, but simply of husband and children generally; the relationships of the woman are based, not on feeling, but on the universal. The difference between the ethical life of the woman and that of the man consists just in this, that in her vocation as an individual and in her pleasure, her interest is centered on the universal and remains alien to the particularity of desire; whereas in the husband these two sides are separated; and since he possesses as a citizen the self-conscious power of universality, he thereby acquires the right of desire and, at the same time, preserves his freedom in regard to it. Since, then, in this relationship of the wife there is an admixture of particularity, her ethical life is not pure; but in so far as it *is* ethical, the particularity is a matter of indifference, and the wife is without the moment of knowing herself as *this* particular self in the other partner.[12]

---

[10] Ibid.
[11] Ibid., 269.
[12] Ibid., 274–75.

Hegel is clear that the women in the family, as either sisters or wives and mothers, must remain there, as "guardian of the divine law," whereas the male members of the household must leave, passing from "the divine law" to the "human law," where they find their "self-conscious being."[13] In the larger community, the male actualizes his conscious freedom as an active subject in the modern state. In the *Phenomenology,* Hegel appears somewhat contradictory in his account of the relationship between the family, as one element of the ethical realm, and the human community. At one point he describes the relationship in harmonious terms, explaining that the "antithesis" between them is "the authentication of one through the other." Where they come into "direct contact with each other as real opposites, their middle term and common element is their immediate interpenetration," the site of which is the union between man and woman.[14] A little later he tells us that the community achieves its existence by "interfering with the happiness of the family" by suppressing "womankind in general," its "internal enemy." Woman must remain in the domain proper to her nature, the family, otherwise she becomes a threat to the well-being of the community:

> Womankind—the everlasting irony [in the life] of the community—changes by intrigue the universal end of the government into a private end, transforms its universal activity into a work of some particular individual, and perverts the universal property of the state into a possession and ornament for the Family. Woman in this way turns to ridicule the earnest wisdom of mature age which, indifferent to purely private pleasures and enjoyments, as well as to playing an active part, only thinks of and cares for the universal.[15]

Hegel's views on woman and man and the relationship between the family and the state become clearer, more detailed, and more systematic in his later work, the *Philosophy of Right* (1821). Here Hegel elaborates his analysis of the physical, intellectual, and moral differences between woman and man, which he tells us have a "rational

---

[13] Ibid., 275, 276.
[14] Ibid., 278.
[15] Ibid., 288.

basis," thereby acquiring "intellectual and ethical significance." Man recapitulates Spirit's self-diremption toward complete self-consciousness in his public activity and exercise of "conceptual thought." Woman, in contrast, is "mind maintaining itself in unity as knowledge and volition of the substantive." He is "powerful and active," whereas she is "passive and subjective." For Hegel, it follows from all of this that

> man has his actual substantive life in the state, in learning, and so forth, as well as in labor and struggle with the external world and with himself so that it is only out of his diremption that he fights his way to self-subsistent unity with himself. . . . Woman, on the other hand, has her substantive destiny in the family, and to be imbued with family piety is her ethical frame of mind.[16]

The physical differences between man and woman[17] structure the opposition between them on all levels of existence, indicating an ontology of gender opposition that clearly privileges male over female in ways that essentialize both sexes. Hegel tells us that while women are capable of education, "they are not made for activities which demand a universal faculty such as the more advanced sciences, philosophy, and certain forms of artistic production." He goes on to compare men with "animals" and women with "plants, because their development is more placid and the principle that underlies it is the rather vague unity of feeling." Because of their capricious nature, women become a menace to the state if they get involved in government. He finally concludes in wonderment that, "Women are educated—who knows how?—as it were by breathing in ideas, by living

---

[16] *Hegel's Philosophy of Right*, trans. T. M. Knox (Oxford, England: Clarendon Press, 1949), 114.

[17] In Hegel's philosphical system, the differences between woman and man are rooted in their respective anatomies, which structure and account for all the other differences between them—ethical, intellectual, and ontological— and which further provide the rational grounding for their specific life activities. Toward the end of the *Philosophy of Nature,* Hegel provides a detailed and vivid description of the sexual dimorphism of male and female. He concludes that by virtue of their different genital formation, "the male is the active principle, and the female is the receptive, because she remains in her undeveloped unity . . . the truth is that the female contains the material element, but the male contains the subjectivity." *Hegel's Philosophy of Nature*, trans. A. V. Miller (Oxford, England: Clarendon Press, 1970), 413.

rather than by acquiring knowledge. The status of manhood, on the other hand, is attained only by the stress of thought and much technical exertion."[18] From all of this it seems clear that for Hegel, woman can never, by virtue of her female nature, achieve the same level of humanity as man.

What is even more interesting, given Hegel's comments on women, is the way in which he idealizes love in marriage and defends women's right to choose a husband on the basis of love, rather than to be forced into marriages arranged by parents. For Hegel, marriage ought not to occur as a "means to other ends"; indeed, forcing young people into arranged marriages indicates "scant respect" for the female sex among those cultures that encourage the practice.[19] As for the legal institution of marriage itself, although Hegel insists that it must be regarded as "in principle indissoluble, for the end of marriage is the ethical end," he also allows for the possibility of divorce in cases where the parties "are completely estranged," meaning by reason of adultery. To protect marriage from premature or frivolous dissolution on the basis of momentary "passion," however, Hegel charges that government and even the church must be prepared to permit divorce, while at the same time making marital "dissolution as difficult as possible . . . [by upholding] the right of the ethical order against caprice."[20]

Hegel's attitude to marriage posits love as its sole justification, its "subjective" and exclusive "originating factor."[21] Yet love also represents "the most tremendous contradiction" insofar as it negates self-consciousness, which one otherwise "ought to possess as affirmative."[22] In marriage, physical love finds its legitimation in being more than the satisfaction of "natural desire," which is secondary to the reciprocal affection between the man and wife. Sexuality outside marriage remains at the level of crude gratification, although the consequences for a woman engaging in sexual activity outside of marriage

---

[18] Ibid., 263–64, addition to par. 166.
[19] Ibid., 262, addition to par. 162.
[20] Ibid., 262, addition to par. 162; 263, addition to par. 163; 265, addition to par. 176; and addition to par. 163.
[21] Ibid., 262, addition to par. 162.
[22] Ibid., 261–62, addition to par. 158.

appear to be far graver than those for a man, since her proper realm of existence is within the family, while the man has open to him "a field for ethical activity outside the family." Woman has far more to lose than her male counterpart through illicit sexuality because of the fixed ontological and corresponding existential differences between them. Sexuality outside marriage violates both the woman's own essence and that of the marriage bond for which she is destined, as it is "demanded of her that her love shall take the form of marriage."[23] For Hegel, one can only conclude that woman is a being of a different kind than man.

A feminist analysis of Hegel's treatment of woman in the *Phenomenology* and the *Philosophy of Right* reveals the presence not only of sexist prejudice, but also of a significant contradiction that undermines Hegel's own claims to a universal system wherein all opposition, dualism, and antagonism will be resolved in a higher unity of reason fully conscious of and identical with itself. The dialectical movement of *Geist* through the self-diremptive process of issuing into its Other, or seeming opposite, where it finds self-recognition, and from there continuing its movement of negation, preservation, and finally transcendence[24] that sustains difference in an ever-widening, higher unity, is betrayed by the static position of woman. The development of the male from his membership in the family to his self-conscious, active participation in the life of the community and state is a necessary part of his coming into full humanity, and is necessitated by *Geist's* own restless movement. This possibility of self-actualization is not open to the woman, since her "law" is that of "substantiality" and "inwardness." Unlike the male, she can never achieve or participate in universality.[25] Not only this, she remains incapable of concrete particularity as a fully self-conscious person, even in relation to the

---

[23] Ibid., 263, addition to par. 164.

[24] The term used by Hegel to describe the ceaseless movement of *Geist* through history is *aufheben*, which means literally "to pick up, or lift up." The noun *Aufhebung* means cancellation, abrogation, or dissolution. Hegel uses the word to indicate a process of negation, preservation, and supersession that occurs as a single movement.

[25] Patricia Jagentowicz Mills, *Woman, Nature, and Psyche* (New Haven and London: Yale Univ. Press, 1987), 48.

members of her own family. There is no place for *Geist's* coming into self-awareness in the interiority of her mind.

Hegel's treatment of women can, finally, be accounted for only by a prejudice that belongs to him personally and to his time, rather than by reason. At the same time, the inner logic of his philosophy is neither necessarily nor inevitably sexist, although that is its result. Hegel's account of men and women and their respective positions in the unfolding of *Geist* indicates a lack of critical awareness that might well have extended many of his own insights into the dialectic of freedom to include women.

This is not to pass judgment on Hegel but to draw a conclusion that applies not only to his philosophy, but to the social theories of those who follow him, whose work often resonates in various ways with similar Hegelian prejudice concerning women. Many of those theorists who criticize Hegel's philosophy do not extend their criticisms to his discussions of women, but rather reproduce and sustain many of his views. In some respects, the influence of Hegel on his critics shows clearly in their discussions of woman and her role in the family. I will restrict my examination of the authors under discussion here to their presentations of women, attending especially to the ways in which Hegelian images resurface without substantial transformations. My purpose here is to demonstrate the ways in which women become inscribed and reinscribed in Western thought as less-than-human-Other, as the passive, somewhat deficient object of analysis rather than being taken account of as subjects in possession of active, historical agency. What is both remarkable and disturbing is that these traditions are among the most highly developed theories of human emancipation in the West—except with respect to the subject of women.

Karl Marx and Friedrich Engels: Woman and Class Society[26]

IN KARL MARX'S WORK, WOMEN ARE TREATED ABSTRACTLY in their function of humanizing principle, and also as concrete human

---

[26] In this section I discuss Marx's and Engels's views on women together. Marx

beings who are victimized and exploited within bourgeois marriage and as laboring proletarians. The same is true with respect to Friedrich Engels. Although, like Hegel, Marx and Engels present women from a transsubjective[27] rather than intersubjective perspective, their materialist approach to history prevents them from lapsing into the same type of idealization and even reification[28] that occurs in Hegel's discussions of woman. That Marx and Engels are able to apprehend the

---

and Engels were close collaborators until Marx's death, and their treatment of women is quite similar. Even in his own text, *The Origin of the Family, Private Property and the State,* published after Marx's death, Engels describes his work as based on Marx's researches, and as a "meagre substitute for that which my departed friend was not destined to accomplish." Preface to the

[27] I use the term *transsubjective* in similar fashion to Seyla Benhabib, who defines it with respect to Hegel as the perspective of the third person who presumes that he is in possession of privileged insight into the nature or essence of others. It does not, nor cannot, stand as the point of view of social actors themselves. *Critique, Norm and Utopia: A Study of the Foundations of Critical Theory* (New York: Columbia Univ. Press, 1986), 103.

[28] I use the term *reification* in relation to Hegel's view of woman in a modified version of Georg Lukács's definition of the concept. In his discussion of the "essence of commodity-structure," Lukács describes its basis as that of "a relation between people [which] takes on the character of a thing and thus acquires a 'phantom objectivity,' an autonomy that seems so strictly rational and all-embracing as to conceal every trace of its fundamental nature," which is its human nature. *History and Class Consciousness,* trans. Rodney Livingstone (London: Merlin Press, 1971), 83. Although Hegel does not treat women as commodities, he does objectify them in a way that obscures and reduces their humanity, rendering them as inferior or less adequate instruments of *Geist's* self-becoming. Thus reification is objectification of an alienated kind, in that it undermines and suppresses the humanity of people and their relationships. It is more accurate to describe Hegel's treatment of woman as a form of reification rather than objectification, insofar as his is indeed a "phantom objectivity" in relation to woman.

The distinction I have in mind between objectification and reification relies on Herbert Marcuse's interpretation of Marx's concept of alienated and unalienated labor. For Marx, according to this reading, objectification is a social activity that occurs within labor as a free activity and the universal self-realization of human beings. Objectification is not, then, necessarily tied to domination. Within the alienated conditions of this laboring activity produced

concrete (what Marx would call "real") sufferings and exploitation of women is to be accounted for by a conscious materialist approach that shifts the rational movement of history from *Geist,* or Spirit, to human activity. For Marx, laboring human beings, not *Geist,* create history. Whereas Hegel theorizes human freedom in terms of the self-unfolding of *Geist* into absolute self-consciousness, Marx insists that human liberation is a historical rather than a mental act, requiring specific material conditions for its actualization. "People cannot be liberated," he wrote, "as long as they are unable to obtain food and drink, housing and clothing in adequate quality and quantity."[29] Contrasting his materialist conception of history, which, in self-conscious contrast to Hegel ascends from "earth to heaven," Marx reiterates that "life determines consciousness," and consciousness belongs to "real living individuals."[30]

The decisive factor that differentiates Marx from Hegel, despite the strong influence of the latter on his thought, is the insight that human survival is the precondition of history. The medium through which human beings sustain themselves is labor, which for Marx is a social activity in which individuals realize themselves and affirm their being. Following Hegel's concept of labor as an ontological category, Marx describes labor as both the creation and appropriation of the

---

by capitalism, objectifying action becomes reifying action, in that the products of human labor, along with their corresponding social relationships, have little to do with humanity's real needs and creative capacities *qua* human. This results in a situation where human beings experience the world as hostile and themselves as helpless objects of blind forces. According to Marcuse, "There are . . . two conditions for breaking through reification . . . the objective relations must become human—i.e. social—relations and they must be recognized and consciously preserved as such." *Studies in Critical Philosophy*, trans. Joris De Bres (London: NLB, 1972), 34. It is important that the distinction between objectification and reification be maintained; in many critiques of Marx, including those from a feminist perspective, "objectification" is often used when the sense of the text implies "reification." This distinction becomes especially important with regard to nature and human activity in relation to nature, as will be seen in chapter 6 on Rosemary Radford Ruether.

[29] "The German Ideology," in Karl Marx and Friedrich Engels, *Collected Works,* vol. 5 (New York: International Publishers, 1975–92), 38.

[30] Ibid., 37.

objective world that manifests human reality and is the expression of genuine freedom. As a social activity, labor allows for the establishment of intersubjective relations that promote reciprocal recognition between the agents as reflecting, confirming, and celebrating each other's distinct humanity. Marx's description of unalienated, nonexploitative labor brings this out:

> Let us suppose that we had carried out production as human beings. Each of us would have *in two ways affirmed* himself and the other person. 1) In my *production* I would have objectified my *individuality, its specific character,* and therefore enjoyed not only an individual *manifestation of my life* during the activity, but also when looking at the object I would have the individual pleasure of knowing my personality to be *objective, visible to the senses* and hence a power *beyond all doubt.* 2) In your enjoyment or use of my product I would have the *direct* enjoyment both of being conscious of having satisfied a *human* need by my work, that is, of having objectified *man's* essential nature, and of having thus created an object corresponding to the need of another *man's* essential nature. 3) I would have been for you the *mediator* between you and the species, and therefore would become recognized and felt by you yourself as a completion of your own essential nature and as a necessary part of yourself, and consequently would know myself to be confirmed both in your thought and your love. 4) In the individual expression of my life I would have directly created your expression of your life, and therefore in my individual activity I would have directly *confirmed* and *realized* my true nature, my *human* nature, my *communal nature.*[31]

This long paragraph is worth quoting in full because it clearly indicates that for Marx, objectification is intrinsic to human interrelatedness and can take place in a nondominating, fully intersubjective fashion, promoting humane reciprocity at all levels of interaction. Marx's focus on the possibility for free, unalienated mutuality occurring between human beings through social labor must not be misread as a privileging of humanity over nature in ways that justify manipulation and exploitation of nature.[32] In the *Economic and Philosophical*

---

[31] Karl Marx, "Comments on James Mill, Eléments d'économie politique," in *Collected Works,* vol. 3 (1975), 227–28.

[32] Some feminist critics of Marx read his formulation of the concept of labor

Manuscripts of *1844,* Marx makes it clear that human and nonhuman nature do not exist in a state of true antagonism, since man lives on nature and "is a part of nature."[33] Human beings exist in an "abstract enmity" with nature under conditions of alienation produced by capitalism, where everything is transformed into commodities, generating profit for the owners of private property. When human beings realize their unalienated social essence, as described above, then they will be able to exist in a nonexploitative relation to nature. Since human beings are cut off from themselves in the form of the self-estrangement produced by class society, they are inevitably cut off not only from external

---

as privileging work and productivity as the overarching paradigm of human activity. They argue that such a narrow, restrictive understanding of labor is rooted in a subject–object logic, thereby excluding women's activities of child-bearing and childraising, which are intersubjective activities. See, for example, Seyla Benhabib and Drucilla Cornell, "Introduction: Beyond the Politics of Gender," in S. Benhabib and D. Cornell, eds., *Feminism as Critique: On the Politics of Gender* (Minneapolis: Univ. of Minnesota Press, 1987), 2. Linda Nicholson, "Feminism and Marx: Integrating Kinship with the Economic," 16–30 in the same volume, reads Marx's concept of labor predominantly in political economy terms, arguing that "Marx has eliminated from his theoretical focus all activities basic to human survival which fall outside of a capitalist 'economy' . . . [his] ability to do this was made possible by his moving from a broad to a narrow meaning of 'production.' " Ibid., 18.

A similar criticism is voiced by Donna Haraway, for whom Marxism is "polluted at the source" because of its "structuring theory about the domination of nature . . . and by its closely related impotence in relation to historicizing anything women did that didn't qualify for a wage." "Situated Knowledges: The Science Question in Feminism and the Privilege of Partial Perspective," *Feminist Studies* 14, no. 3 (Fall 1988): 578.

These critiques of Marx tend toward a serious simplification and reductionism of his philosophical anthropology, which structures much of his critical perspective on the political economic conditions that distort and alienate human capacities for intersubjective relationships. This includes all the ways in which human beings present themselves to themselves and to one another. Marx's thought is too often reduced to a critique of political economy—the result, I argue, of decades of Leninist-Stalinist varieties of interpretation that have effectively marginalized the critical, philosophical anthropological basis of his social theory.

[33] Karl Marx, *Economic and Philosophical Manuscripts of 1844* (Moscow: Progress Publishers, 1977), 72–73.

nature, but from their internal nature as well. Human beings in a condition of self-alienation are incapable of relating to nature or other human beings in ways that are anything but alienating. In Marx we can begin to see the preliminary interconnections between social and eco-justice that prefigure some contemporary feminist discussions. These connections will be addressed later. In a world where objectification devolves into reification, humanity becomes a "spiritual and physical monster."[34]

Marx's detailed, material analysis of labor within the conditions of alienation, along with his fragmentary vision of what a humanized world and its corresponding social relations might look like, allows him to focus on the concrete suffering experienced by both women and men in capitalist societies. Both he and Engels describe in detail the misery of women toiling in factories and the specific nature of women's exploitation in relation to men. In comparison to men, women are paid less, the "slaves of slaves."[35] Engels was fully aware of the existence of sexual harassment and intimidation of women in the workplace and their vulnerability to the predatory factory owner whose mill "is also his harem."[36]

Both Marx and Engels recount the devastating effects on proletarian families who are forced to send their children into the factories and mines for the economic survival of the family unit, although the employment of women and children often resulted in the outright dissolution of working-class families. Engels describes the brutal conditions of female labor, where women not only worked twelve- to thirteen-hour days even during the entire course of their pregnancy— "an infamous act of barbarism"[37]—but were compelled to return to their jobs three to four days after childbirth for fear of losing wages

---

[34] Marx, "Comments on James Mill," in *Collected Works* 3:220.

[35] Karl Marx, *Capital*, trans. Samuel Moore and Edward Aveling, ed. Friedrich Engels (Moscow: Progress Publishers, 1986), vol. 1, 469.

[36] Friedrich Engels, *The Condition of the Working Class in England* (London: Cox & Wyman, 1969), 177.

[37] Ibid., 188. Engels also describes the destructive effects on women's health of factory work, which often results in deformities of the pelvic area, making pregnancy and childbirth more difficult and dangerous.

or losing employment altogether.[38] Both he and Marx note the use of
narcotics as substitutes for nonexistent child care in the parents' absence, as well as other forms of abuse suffered by children in working-
class families. Marx does not, however, attribute the harsh treatment
of children among "the oppressed classes" to moral deficiency on the
part of the parents. Rather he lays the blame on "the capitalistic mode
of exploitation which, by sweeping away the economic basis of pa-
rental authority, made its exercise degenerate into a mischievous misuse
of power."[39]

Both Marx and Engels comment on the destructive effects on the
proletarian family that result from women leaving their husbands and
children to earn a wage. Engels betrays underlying assumptions about
male and female nature when he notes the role reversal between husbands and wives in many working-class families, where domestic
relations are "turned upside down" by the employment of the wife
in the absence of work for the husband. He speaks of men "condemned
to domestic occupations," citing the case of a man who felt humiliated
by the "bad work" of mending, caring for children, cooking, and
cleaning.[40] For Engels, such situations deprive both men and women
of dignity, emasculating the male and robbing the female of wom-
anliness. To dismiss Engels' observations as rooted in simple sexist
prejudice, however, misses his more profound critique of male-female
relations in general. The damaging emotional consequences of domestic role reversal, especially for men, leads Engels to question the
very structures that privilege male power in the first place:

> If the reign of the wife over the husband, as inevitably brought about
> by the factory system, is inhuman, the pristine rule of the husband
> over the wife must have been inhuman too. If the wife can now base
> her supremacy upon the fact that she supplies the greater part, nay,
> the whole of the common possession, the necessary inference is that
> this community of possession is no true and rational one, since one
> member of the family boasts offensively of contributing the greater
> share. If the family of our present society is being thus dissolved,

[38] Ibid., 171–72.
[39] *Capital*, 1:459–60.
[40] Engels, *Condition of the Working Class,* 173–74.

> this dissolution merely shows that, at bottom, the binding tie of this family was not family affection, but private interest lurking under the cloak of a pretended community of possessions.[41]

The role of private interest or property in marriage is taken up by Marx, for whom the "first form" of property "lies in the family, where wife and children are slaves of the husband."[42] Marx rejects the ideological "clap-trap" that mystifies the real basis of family relations within bourgeois society; for him, capital and private property are the material force that binds the family members together. The bourgeois family with its corresponding sentimental ideological veil generates its own negative complement in the form of the proletarian family, on which it preys in order to exist. Marx protests the havoc and ruin inflicted on proletarian families who are forced to turn their children into mere "articles of commerce and instruments of labor"; with the transcendence of capitalism, both the bourgeois and proletarian family forms will come to an end.[43] In the bourgeois family, women are exploited as "instruments of production," and their economic dependence in marriage is a form of private prostitution. Under communism, the prostitution of women, both private and public, including the more "general" prostitution of the laborer who is forced to sell himself as well as his wife and children for a wage, will be abolished.[44]

Marx also recognized the concrete possibilities for women's emancipation, however, along with the formation of new or "higher" forms of the family and interpersonal relationships that would result from women's entry into the workplace.[45] The option for women to leave the domestic sphere in order to participate in public life, however alienated it might be, would have been unacceptable for Hegel; for Marx, it provided a precondition for women's eventual liberation and the transformation of the family.

---

[41] Ibid., 174–75.

[42] Marx, "The German Ideology," in *Collected Works* 5:46.

[43] "Manifesto of the Communist Party," in Marx and Engels, *Collected Works*, 6:501–2.

[44] Marx, *Economic and Philosophical Manuscripts*, 94.

[45] Marx, *Capital*, 1:460.

Marx's treatment of women is not, however, without contradictions. His materialist analysis of women in the bourgeois and proletarian family, along with his uncompromising account of their brutal exploitation as workers, brings women to life as concrete human beings in their specific social, familial, and economic circumstances. One can derive from Marx's writing something of what it must have been like to be a working woman in the nineteenth century. At the same time, these women also fade away into the highly abstract, ontological, and anthropological category of *woman*,[46] the humanizing principle of family life, particularly in relation to the male. Through woman, man finds his capacity for transcending his self-alienation in a relation of reciprocity and recognition with her:

> The direct, natural and necessary relation of person to person is the *relation of man to woman*. . . .From this relationship one can therefore judge man's whole level of development . . . the relation of man to woman is the *most natural* relation of human being to human being. It therefore reveals the extent to which man's *natural* behavior has become *human,* or the extent to which the human essence in him has become a *natural* essence—the extent to which his *human nature* has come to be *natural* to him. This relationship also reveals the extent to which man's *need* has become a *human* need; the extent to which, therefore, the *other* person as a person has become a need— the extent to which he in his individual existence is at the same time a social being.[47]

This paradigm of genuine human relationships is explicitly one-sided in its focus on the male who realizes his naturalized humanity through the woman, who mediates his relation with himself. Through her, the male becomes conscious of his social being, so that the natural and human elements become fully integrated in him, thereby allowing for his full self-awareness as potentially unalienated humanity. What is absent from Marx's account of the male-female relation is the woman's experience in it. Marx gives no indication if woman experiences the man in the way he experiences her, nor if she has an active self-awareness at all. The dialectic of the humanization of nature and the

---

[46] Juliet Mitchell, *Woman's Estate* (New York: Vintage Books, 1973), 78.
[47] Marx, *Economic and Philosophical Manuscripts*, 95–96.

naturalization of the human is presented exclusively from the male perspective, focusing on his potential for unalienated subjectivity alone. Marx's portrait of the male-female relation preserves the Hegelian gender division in similarly ontological terms, contrasting male activity with female passivity. Marx's abstract treatment of women as outlined here turns into reification when he categorizes their condition in capitalist society as an "index of general social advance."[48]

The abstract, idealized approach that dissolves living women into a functional category is taken by Engels as well. Both Marx and Engels absolutize the oppression of women by men as the originating act of domination and class exploitation. For Engels, the antagonism inherent in monogamous marriage, the foundation of patriarchal domination, represents the "first class oppression."[49] Monogamy is a benefit only to males by ensuring the transmission of property through the male line; it brings misery and repression to women as the "subjection of one sex by the other."[50] Civilization is marked by patriarchal power, generating the "absolute domination of the male over the female sex as the fundamental law of society."[51] The monogamous bourgeois family is a microencapsulation of class society with all its exploitative antagonisms and contradictions that destroy woman's dignity and respect. Women's humiliated condition in civilization proceeds from the "world-historic defeat of the female sex" by male force, resulting in the enslavement and degradation of women into "mere instrument[s] for breeding children."[52] In Engels's view (with which Marx apparently

---

[48] Mitchell, *Woman's Estate*, 78. Marx takes the idea of woman as an indicator of the general condition of society from Charles Fourier, whom he quotes: "The degree of emancipation of woman is the natural measure of general emancipation." Cited in "The Holy Family," in Marx and Engels, *Collected Works*, vol. 4, 196. Marx fully recognized and maintained that the position of women in modern society is "inhuman."

[49] Engels, *Origin of the Family*, 66.

[50] Ibid., 65.

[51] Ibid., 67.

[52] Ibid., 57. Several contemporary feminist authors have taken up the view that women suffered a decisive overthrow by patriarchy, with the result that the peaceful, egalitarian, partnership modes of social organization became superseded by societies based on violence, domination, and competition. See,

agreed) patriarchy is fundamental to civilization, while female power in the form of mother-right is prehistoric. The one exception to the universal domination of women is found among the working classes, who by virtue of their dispossessed condition have no motive to "assert male domination."[53]

Here Engels betrays a remarkable incapacity to follow through on his earlier, acute insights into the destruction of working-class families and the breakdown of relations between family members generated by capitalist exploitation. His romantic idealization of the egalitarian, loving relations between men and women of the oppressed classes indicates a kind of momentary self-amnesia that undermines his own materialist analysis and betrays the women whose emancipation he advocates. Women are vulnerable to and often experience all kinds of abuse in their domestic environments, irrespective of their class position. Domestic violence, as is true of violence against women in general, crosses class lines; it is a fundamental problem between the sexes rather than a specific form of behavior of certain classes. Engels's idealization of sexual relations among oppressed people cloaks the reality and pervasiveness of domination and violence against women. In agreement with Marx, however, Engels too understands that women's entry into the paid workforce is a step toward the abolition of male domination; moreover, it is the precondition of their emancipation.[54]

The treatment of women in the work of Marx and Engels contains an ambivalence in terms of its abstract idealizations on the one hand, and its specific, concrete analysis that focuses on women as suffering,

---

for example, the work of Elizabeth Gould Davis, Merlin Stone, and Riane Eisler. Authors such as Gerda Lerner are far more careful in their claims, arguing that although there is no proof for the existence of matriarchal societies on a universal scale in the prehistoric world, there is evidence to suggest that alternate models to patriarchy did exist. See Gerda Lerner, *The Creation of Patriarchy* (Oxford, England: Oxford Univ. Press, 1986), 35. She also maintains that enslavement of women by men is prior to enslavement of men by other men (p. 87), and generally she appears to agree with Engels's postulation of the domination of women as the root of domination within history.

[53] Engels, *Origin of the Family*, 71.

[54] Ibid., 72, 74.

living human beings on the other. Marx's entire social theory is in many respects an extended critical response to Hegelian idealism, which it seeks to overcome and refute by shifting the motor of history from *Geist* to human activity; Marx nonetheless preserves Hegelian moments within his own thought on the question of women. This becomes especially clear in Marx's comments on marriage and divorce, which carry over Hegel's views virtually intact.

In an early, brief text on divorce (1842), Marx recapitulates the Hegelian view of marriage as possessing its own "essence," having its "moral substance" in the family, and therefore in need of protection from whimsical, arbitrary destruction. If marriage were not the basis of the family, there would be no need for legislation ensuring the rights of the parties. Like Hegel, Marx acknowledged the necessity of divorce in cases where the essence of marriage was already destroyed.[55] As well, it is the duty of the state to ensure that divorce is permitted only in cases where the essence of marriage is irrefutably dissolved. The perspective of the wife, for whom the marital experience may have become intolerable, is not considered here. This omission is curious given Marx's not too much later views of the depth of women's exploitation within marriage, his references to "private prostitution," and his location of private property as constituting the real bond between husband and wife in bourgeois marriage.

The tendency to idealize women by transforming them into abstract categories or ontological, anthropological principles that is evident in Hegel and carries through to Marx and Engels is doubleedged. With Hegel, woman's emotional and domestic sensibilities are celebrated and accounted for by her unsuitability for life beyond the family. In Marx and Engels, the domination of women is the first cause of all oppression within history, so that their condition functions as a measurement of social progress. Despite their subjugated position, which Marx fully recognizes, he can still expect women to be ultimately responsible for the humanization of men, by virtue of their natural attributes.[56] Engels, however, understood that the "natural"

---

[55] "The Divorce Bill," in Marx and Engels, *Collected Works*, 1:307–10.

[56] Marx cites the explanation given by one manufacturer concerning his preference for employing women, especially those who are the sole breadwinner

characteristics traditionally associated with women depend on social and cultural conditions, so that the experience of women in the harsh environment of the nineteenth-century factories stunted and shattered their domestic and maternal potentialities, rendering them unfit for family life.[57]

For Hegel women possess a distinct female nature or essence to which all women must conform, otherwise they endanger both the state and family security. Although Marx and Engels do not share this view, they nonetheless presume the existence of an ideal feminine nature or anthropology that is capable of transforming male alienation. In marriage woman is subordinated to the higher demands of the moral substantiality of the family. She is bound to its abstract essence at the expense of her specific experience, thereby severely restricting the possibility for her of divorce, which might well be in her best, individual interest. It is up to the state, not to a wife, to decide if her wish to end her marriage is justified or capricious. Yet both Marx and Engels are fully aware of the structural nature of oppression and exploitation in proletarian and bourgeois marriages under capitalism, and its particular effects on women.

---

for their families: their "attentiveness" and "docility" and "all that is most dutiful and tender in [their] nature is made a means of [their] bondage and suffering." Marx's comment is that the "excessive addition of women and children" to the workforce seriously undermines the resistance put up by male workers against "the despotism of capital." *Capital*, 1:379–80, note 2.

[57] "It is self-evident," Engels writes, "that a girl who has worked in a mill from her ninth year is in no position to understand domestic work, whence it follows that female operatives prove wholly inexperienced and unfit as housekeepers." Hard work and long hours away from home as well destroy women's capacity for maternal feeling, since a woman who spends twelve to fourteen hours a day at work "can be no real mother to the child," to whom she inevitably grows "indifferent" and "unloving." *Condition of the Working Class*, 175–76, 172. The conclusion that working women cannot be feeling mothers is not only related to the particular type of work women may be involved in, such as in the mills and mines, but seems in itself to be the result of women leaving the family to work outside the home. The somewhat contradictory view expressed by Engels—who, as we have seen, acknowledged as well the possibility for women's emancipation through employment—is maintained to the point of prejudice in the work of the Frankfurt theorists, especially Theodor Adorno and Max Horkheimer, as will be argued in the next chapter.

The diverse but contradictory elements in the treatment of women found in Hegel, Marx, and Engels are repeated in critical theory, which bears even stronger traces of Hegelian influence concerning the location of women in the family. In contrast with Marx and Engels, Horkheimer, Adorno, and even Marcuse express negative reservations about women going out to work because of the harmful psychological effects that would inevitably result to the sons. The conclusion that the maternal bond is threatened by the mother working outside the home follows from maintaining the abstraction of woman that carries over from Hegel, with some mediations through Marx but especially Engels, and lodges within critical theory as a counter-emancipatory moment.

Before proceeding to an examination of the theme of woman in critical theory, it is necessary to consider Freud's discussion of femininity and female sexuality and the way in which his work provides a kind of bridge between Hegel, Marx, and Engels on the one hand and critical theory on the other. Given that psychoanalysis is an important component of critical theory, it is all the more necessary to consider the impact of Freud's theories of female sexuality and his treatment of women in general on critical theory. This is important because many of Freud's views of women are appropriated by critical theory with little revision or modification.

Sigmund Freud: Woman as Innate Insufficiency

WHILE THE IMAGE OF WOMEN IN MARX AND ENGELS IS MORE historical, concrete, and differentiated than in Hegel, this is not exactly the case with respect to Sigmund Freud. Freud's more general conclusions concerning female sexuality and the nature of "femininity" and his observations of the quality of the female character itself indicate an attitude to the question of *woman* that resonates with Hegelian prejudice. His comments on the relationship between women's psychosexual development and their capacities for ethical reasoning proceed from the transsubjective perspective of the observing, normative male point of view that reserves for itself the right of uncontestable interpretation and conclusion.[58] The value of a feminist examination of Freud's views on women and femininity is not to pass judgment on Freud's misogynistic tendencies, but rather to use his theories for a greater understanding of the condition of women in Western culture that he describes.

Here I follow Juliet Mitchell's approach, which treats Freud and psychoanalysis "not [as] a recommendation *for* a patriarchal society, but [as] an analysis *of* one."[59] The claim that Hegelian views of women surface in psychoanalysis is not advanced to prove that Freud consciously appropriated Hegel (or even read him, for that matter), but to illustrate the persistent resilience and strength of those social, cultural, and individual attitudes to women that uncritically preserve assumptions of their less-than-human status. These premises structure and inform social relations throughout Western culture, operating in an unreflective, taken-for-granted fashion that reverberates throughout this culture's most developed intellectual discourses. In psychoanalytic discourse, the assumption of women's "natural" or "innate" inferiority ossifies into "science," thus becoming even more unshakably embedded in the social psyche.

Freud's accounts of women, which are by no means without self-expressed doubts on his part, reveal the ways in which women's oppression "courses through the mental and emotional bloodstream"[60] of our culture, posing further questions about the integral importance of patriarchy within Western civilization. Even those psychoanalytic interpretations of female psychosexual development that many feminist critics find so repugnant, such as the Oedipal drama[61] and penis

---

[58] It must also be pointed out, however, that Freud did not assume an inflexible approach regarding many of his psychoanalytic insights, including those he derived from his long experience with women clients. Freud revised and rethought many of his own theories, and he was capable of admitting his bafflement with respect to female sexuality. According to Juliet Mitchell, Freud was aware, somewhat self-critically, that his models for understanding female sexuality were exclusively masculine. See Juliet Mitchell, *Psychoanalysis and Feminism: Freud, Reich, Laing and Women* (New York: Vintage Books, 1975), 308.

[59] Ibid., xiii.

[60] Ibid., 362–63.

[61] Andrea Nye asks, with a great deal of justification, "Who is this Oedipus,

envy, offer invaluable insight into the psychic bedrock of sexism produced and sustained in Western culture, irrefutably demonstrating that the "longevity of the oppression of women" is rooted in far more than "biological handicap" or "economic exploitation."[62] In this sense Freud has contributed to advancing our thinking about the nature of the domination of women.

Freud's most significant statement on female sexuality appears in the essay "Femininity," written late in his life (1931) and incorporating a number of ideas on women outlined in previous texts.[63] Feminist critics such as Luce Irigaray (to whom I return later) claim that this text provides a clear example of ideological bias operating under the guise of science. In this text, Freud utilizes an exclusively masculine model as the normative framework for interpreting the development of human sexuality and, in particular, of female sexuality. Here Freud is unequivocal in his understanding of the relation between anatomy and character; in a fashion similar to Hegel, Freud also postulates a gender dualism whose underlying structure originates with anatomical difference.

His disclaimers notwithstanding (namely, that anatomy cannot adequately account for definitions of masculinity and femininity, and that concepts associating maleness with activity and femaleness with passivity are socially mediated), Freud nonetheless applies a rigorously masculine model when drawing conclusions about female sexuality and character development. The inevitable result of his logic inscribes women's less-than-human status into an unassailable scientific "fact." Women are, as it were, prisoners of their biological destiny. Freud assures his audience, however, that in spite of the overwhelming impact of women's peculiar sexuality on all aspects of their emotional

---

whose love for his mother and murder of his father are supposed to be the primary structure of the psyche? Does the feminine need to be theorized in terms of a prologue or supplement to this primal scene?" *Feminist Theory and the Philosophies of Man* (London: Croom Helm, 1988), 155. That the feminine *is* theorized in such terms, however, illustrates that sexism is a part of the earliest intrapsychic formation of human beings, where it becomes lodged in the unconscious.

[62] Mitchell, *Psychoanalysis and Feminism*, 362.
[63] Sigmund Freud, "Femininity," in *New Introductory Lectures on Psychoanalysis*, trans. James Strachey (New York: W. W. Norton, 1931), 112, note 1.

and moral development, "we do not overlook the fact that an individual woman may be a human being in other respects as well."[64]

Freud begins his discussion of "the riddle of the nature of femininity" by establishing male psychosexual development as the measure of that of females.[65] From this comparison, Freud discovers that women's sexuality proceeds in a more troubled and overburdened fashion than that of men, subject to more complex pressures that men never experience. The root difficulty a little girl encounters in her psychosexual life arises out of the shock she suffers from the realization that she has no penis. With this realization, the little girl angrily turns against her mother, whom she concludes is the person responsible for her "castrated" condition.

Prior to the awareness of her humiliating situation, the little girl experiences a "phallic phase" of development, in which she manifests an active aggressivity not dissimilar to that of boys, rendering her "a little man."[66] This phase of life corresponds to her experience of pleasure achieved in masturbation, "carried out on [her] penis–equivalent," the clitoris, which substitutes for the truly feminine pleasure of the yet-to-be-discovered vagina.[67] At this stage her clitoris functions as the "leading erotogenic zone"; it will be abandoned as she enters a stage of repression that is requisite for her to develop into a mature woman—that is, becoming transformed from a "little man" to a truly feminine woman. For this to happen, the girl must shift the location of her erotic experience from the clitoris to the vagina. This is a difficult task for her and takes its toll on her long-term psychic life. In Freud's view, the establishment of the primacy of the vagina over against the more infantile, masculine clitoris is the inevitable precondition of the successful entry of a female into mature womanhood. He further recognized that this psychosexual transfer did not occur without intense emotional stress, representing the first "burdensome task" of a woman's emotional and sexual life.

---

[64] Ibid., 135.
[65] Ibid., 117.
[66] Ibid., 118.
[67] Ibid.

A related "burdensome task" for the girl involves the corresponding shift of affection from her mother, to whom she was powerfully
attached in the pre-Oedipal stage, to her father. According to Freud,
a girl's entry into the Oedipal situation offers her a "haven of refuge"[68]
from the frustration and pain associated with the mother's betrayal
and deception of her. The girl's transition from the masculine phase
associated with pre-Oedipality to the feminine-directed Oedipal stage
is precipitated by her discovery that she has no penis. She interprets
this as being castrated (she must have had a penis, since boys do), a
situation caused by her mother. Her pre-Oedipal love for her mother
is revealed as an illusion, since the object of her love was the "*phallic
mother.*"[69]

Betrayed by her mother, who she discovers is also castrated, and
humiliated by her deficient condition, the girl rejects her equally deficient mother with anger and hostility, gives up masturbation (if she
can), and turns to her father. Her father represents for her the future
masculine promise of symbolic wholeness, wherein she may obtain a
substitute penis in giving birth to a child. As her wish for a penis is
replaced with a wish for a baby, the "feminine situation" becomes
established; however, she will wait a long time to be at peace with
herself (if in fact she ever attains such peace). Her initial rebellion
against her mother may be replaced with a protracted, mimetic struggle
against her husband, for which divorce and remarriage may be the
only solution (but not resolution). A woman's only possibility for
"unlimited satisfaction" can be realized in the birth of a son, which
provides her with "the most perfect . . . of all human relationships."[70]

The difficult process of female psychosexual development results
in long-lasting effects to a woman's character formation. It leaves her
something of an emotional, moral cripple in comparison to men. The
man is privileged by biology, so that he is not forced to transfer the
site of his sexual pleasure from one location on the body to another,
nor must he repudiate his mother in the decisive way required for the
feminization of the girl. Because he is compelled to work through his

---

[68] Ibid., 129.
[69] Ibid., 126.
[70] Ibid., 133.

Oedipal phase and overcome his fear of castration by giving up his desire for the mother, he is able to clear away the Oedipal conflict for the establishment of the superego, "heir" to the Oedipal complex.[71] Girls, however, having no penis, no castration anxiety, and therefore no motive for resolving their Oedipus complex,

> remain in it for an indeterminate length of time; they demolish it late and, even so, incompletely. In these circumstances the formation of the superego must suffer; it cannot attain the strength and independence which give it its cultural significance, and feminists are not pleased when we point out to them the effects of this factor upon the average feminine character.[72]

Having internalized the prevailing cultural view of women as debased creatures, girls soon begin to harbor intense feelings of penis envy that will mark their character throughout life. The lingering disabling effects of penis envy dispose women to jealousy and envy that divest them of the capacity for justice and leave them with little interest in social affairs.[73] Because they are deprived of the "superior equipment" of masculinity,[74] women are especially vulnerable to feelings of shame, which Freud identifies as the motive force behind their single contribution to "the discoveries and inventions in the history of civilization": weaving. According to Freud, women's proclivity for weaving is a symbolic activity of concealment, in which the absence of a penis is repeatedly covered up. Women's achievements in the field of textile production are thus reduced to the level of an unconscious compulsion rooted in the shame of castrated being.

Freud irrevocably closes the iron gate of biology on women, reducing their historical accomplishments, emotional and moral character, and capacity for social relationships to the *absence* of the male bodily organ. Freud's account of the psychic structure of women fuses myth with ontology, where the original loss of a sacred object transforms the inner being of half of humanity. An analysis of the concept

---

[71] Ibid., 129.
[72] Ibid.
[73] Ibid., 134.
[74] Ibid., 126.

of *woman* reveals an ontology of gender division at the heart of psychoanalysis that paradoxically condemns the theory itself to failure. As far as women are concerned, psychoanalysis can do little to release them from their intrapsychic conflicts. It can only attest to their flawed being.

Women: Civilization's Discontents

FROM THIS PORTRAIT OF WOMEN WE CAN ONLY CONCLUDE that for Freud, women's less-than-human status renders them fit for little more than family life. In the family at least, women may satisfy their drive toward maternity, resolve some of their frustration with their condition of biological insufficiency, and generally turn their attention to matters more compatible with their nature. Vain, narcissistic, desirous of being loved rather than loving, devoid of strong ethical sensibility, and oblivious to the demands of justice,[75] woman stands in enmity against the interests of civilization.

In *Civilization and Its Discontents* (1930), Freud refers to the "retarding and restraining influence"[76] of women with respect to civilization. The reasons behind this statement are to be found in Freud's concept of love and its relation to civilization. Civilization is founded upon love,[77] the origins of which are found in the genital love between man and woman; this love issues in the formation of the family. The

---

[75] Freud's belief in women's incapacity for a sense of justice has much in common with philosophers other than Hegel. For example, Arthur Schopenhauer (1788–1860), whom Freud read, refers to women as "mental myopic[s]" whose "fundamental defect" is a "lack of a sense of justice" the origins of which are to be found in their "want of rationality." For Schopenhauer, what women lack in "power of reasoning" they make up for through "cunning" and "dissimulation." Women are the "*sexus sequior*," "the inferior second sex in *every* respect . . . the man . . . is the actual human being." For Schopenhauer, women's intellectual defects correspond to their "unaesthetic" anatomy. "On Women," in *Essays and Aphorisms*, trans. R. J. Hollingdale (Harmondsworth, England: Penguin Books, 1985), 80–88.

[76] Sigmund Freud, *Civilization and Its Discontents*, trans. Joan Riviere, revised and newly edited by James Strachey (London: Hogarth Press, 1973), 40.

[77] Ibid., 38.

love that founds the family branches out to bind people together in increasingly larger units, so that groups of people become capable of cooperating in the interests of civilization. As these social cultural groupings become larger and more complex, differentiating love into genital and various "aim-inhibited" forms, "the relation of love to civilization loses its unambiguity. On the one hand love comes into opposition with the interests of civilization; on the other, civilization threatens love with substantial restrictions."[78]

Women, who "represent the interests of the family and . . . sexual life," turn hostile to that very civilization whose foundations they established by virtue of the "claims of their love." In a condensed recapitulation of Hegel's view of the relation between the family and state, Freud presents a cultural psychoanalytic description of the deepening antagonism between family and civilization in terms of the development of the individual family member, who realizes his conscious individuality by moving away from the family to participate in the public realm. "Detaching himself from his family becomes a task that faces every young person, and society often helps him in the solution of it by means of puberty and initiation rites. We get the impression that these are difficulties which are inherent in all psychical . . . and . . . organic development."

As civilization becomes more complex, its demands and tasks become correspondingly difficult, which is why "the work of civilization" becomes "the business of men," who are far more capable of "carry[ing] out instinctual sublimations"[79] than are women. As civilization progresses, it demands a greater share of masculine activity, diverting the man's attention and psychic energy away from his family and sexual life. Freud concludes that man's "constant association with men, and his dependence on his relations with them . . . estrange him from his duties as a husband and father. Thus the woman finds herself forced into the background by the claims of civilization and she adopts a hostile attitude towards it."[80] The Hegelian notion of woman as guardian of the family, unfit by virtue of her nature for the higher

---

[78] Ibid., 40.
[79] Ibid.
[80] Ibid., 41.

forms of education on which a complex society depends, resurfaces in the Freudian psychoanalytic depiction of the male-female, family-civilization dialectic. Traces of Engels also appear in Freud's conclusion that civilization as such is patriarchal.[81] Freud accounts for this in terms of the innate inferiority of woman; if history had been left to her, humanity would not have advanced beyond cave life, beautiful tapestries notwithstanding.

A feminist examination of the notion of *woman* in Hegel, Marx, Engels, and Freud reveals the depth and extent of women's oppression in Western culture. From the perspective of feminist critical theory, the different accounts of the human condition in these thinkers offer insight into the structures of domination that exist in history and are reproduced in their own work. What they all share is an interpretation of woman as a reified category, wherein the particular humanity of women dissolves into elements or principles of ontology and anthropology whose aim is a greater understanding of masculine development. The process of reification as it applies to women in their work reflects the manifold ways in which women's humanity is undermined in the social realm, where it lies concealed within pervasive sexism. Hegel, Marx, Engels, and Freud further illustrate the incapacity of even the most progressive thinkers of a given epoch to see women as fully human. The domination of women, an integral part of the development of Western civilization, is enacted on all levels of human experience, legitimated and reproduced in its most highly advanced intellectual traditions.

However dispiriting this realization may be, much can be gained here in the struggle for women's liberation. Feminist critical theory looks to Freudian psychoanalysis as exposing the underlying juncture where history and psyche meet. In this way Freudian psychoanalysis provides feminist critical theory with a rich resource in its identification of the inevitable connections between culture and psyche, which point toward possibilities for the emancipatory transformations of both.

Following Russell Jacoby's[82] Marcusian interpretation of Freud, we may agree that Freud's biologically rooted concepts of sexuality,

---

[81] Mitchell, *Psychoanalysis and Feminism*, 366.
[82] Russell Jacoby, *Social Amnesia: A Critique of Contemporary Psychology from Adler to Laing* (Boston: Beacon Press, 1975).

repression, and instinctual life demonstrate the massive impact of society's norms and values on the formation of the individual psyche. Following this approach with respect to women, it becomes apparent that the pressure inflicted on little girls to abandon their active, "masculine" phase of sexuality through externally and internally induced acts of psychic repression attests to "the power of society in and over the individual."[83] The ideal of "true femininity" to which all women must ultimately conform is generated by an androcentric, patriarchal society. This ideal introjects itself in the unconscious, with the further result that women and men internalize gender opposition and the value hierarchy that accrues to it. The perilous journey of female development—with its complex, disfiguring transformations from an infantile, clitoral-dominant stage of sexuality to the mature, vaginal-dominant sexuality of adult womanhood—recapitulates a historical cultural process that becomes hardened in intrapsychic nature. What Freud represents as the internal psychosexual development of women is mediated by an internalized accumulation and sedimentation of historical processes, "so long monstrously oppressive . . . that it congeals." What appears in Freud's account as "female nature" or "feminine essence" is "frozen history that surfaces as nature."[84]

Freud was aware of the historical dimension of sexuality and the effects of "external inhibitions" on the modification of the sexual instinct.[85] At the same time, he appears incapable of understanding female sexuality in any other terms than those of masculine development, which he repeatedly privileges as normative. His assertion of the primacy of the vagina over the clitoris as the authentic location of mature female sexual satisfaction is a significant illustration of ideological prejudice that conceals male interest within scientific discourse. Freud dismisses the diversity of female sexuality with the unfortunate term "polymorphous perversity"; if persisting beyond childhood, this becomes an attribute of the "uncultivated woman."[86]

---

[83] Ibid., 79.
[84] Ibid., 31.
[85] Sigmund Freud, *Three Essays on the Theory of Sexuality*, trans. James Strachey (London: Hogarth Press, 1970), 28, note 2.
[86] Ibid., 57.

His accounts of penis envy, women's inevitable hatred of their mothers, the desire for giving birth to sons, and so on, reflect the values of a culture that postulates masculinity as normative humanity.

From a feminist critical theoretical perspective, Freud indeed is an expositor of the psychosexual development of women under the conditions of ubiquitous patriarchy. Freud does more than reveal the social and individual psychodynamics of the domination of women, however; he reproduces them by validating them, thereby participating in them.

Freud's conclusions about femininity and the nature of female sexuality are connected with an important insufficiency on his part—namely an inability to accept women as independent agents whose insights into their own behavior might at times be more accurate than his own. When his female colleagues objected that male bias in psychoanalysis results in incomplete research, his unserious, somewhat flip response was that women intellectuals are obviously more masculine than feminine.[87]

Freud's overall resistance to accepting the validity of women's experiences of themselves and the meaning of their relationships is poignantly apparent in his treatment of Dora, whose story (insofar as we have it) concludes this chapter. With Freud's attitude to Dora, we gain insight into the uneasy role of woman in psychoanalysis, a role that moves between the contradictory polarities of (active) "agent" and (passive) "patient."[88] Dora occupies both roles at once, being situated in a painful dialectic of competing interests in which her doctor, Freud, insists on the truth of his transsubjective interpretation of her life experience, which she understands differently. What is wrong in Freud's approach is not only his stubborn contestation of her perspective, but his refusal to consider the truthfulness of her point of view. Freud insists on what he refers to as the abnormality of Dora's rejection of a married man who attempted to seduce her. This insistence begins to appear as if motivated by an interest, however unintended,

---

[87] Freud, "Femininity," 116–17.

[88] Jane Gallop, *The Daughter's Seduction: Feminism and Psychoanalysis* (Ithaca, N.Y.: Cornell Univ. Press, 1982), 136.

to soften the man's responsibility for the emotional torment Dora is forced to experience.

When Freud encounters Dora, a young woman still in her teens, she is literally being made ill by the actions of her father and his friend, Herr K., who attempt to exploit her for their own immediate interests. Dora's father, who is sexually involved with Frau K., consciously and tacitly colludes with Herr K.'s advances to his daughter so that his own affair may proceed undisturbed. According to Freud, Dora was "overcome by the idea that she had been handed over to Herr K. as the price of his tolerating the relations between her father and his wife; and her rage at her father's making such use of her was visible behind her affection for him."[89]

While Freud acknowledges the general validity of Dora's view, he goes on to say that it was "exaggerated" in that there was no "formal agreement" between the two men that she be "treated as an object for barter." Yet Freud is also aware of the extent to which both men were capable of avoiding insight into each other's behavior, "which would have been awkward for [their] own plans. It was possible for Herr K. to send Dora flowers every day for a whole year . . . to take every opportunity of giving her valuable presents, and to spend all his spare time in her company, without her *parents* noticing anything in his behavior that was characteristic of love-making."[90] What begins as identifying the father's responsibility in relation to Dora's plight thus suddenly expands to implicate her mother. This is curious inasmuch as the mother hardly appears as a significant figure in the whole corrupt situation.

Freud's acknowledgment of the unspoken collusion between Dora's father and Herr K. is as far as he will go in accepting his patient's version of her position. He refuses to believe that she was not attracted to Herr K. He goes so far as to suggest that her attachment to his children is a "cloak" disguising her real motivation—her love for their

---

[89] "Fragment of an Analysis of a Case of Hysteria," in *The Standard Edition of the Complete Psychological Works of Sigmund Freud*, vol. 7, trans. James Strachey (London: Hogarth Press, 1978), 34.

[90] Ibid., 35; emphasis added.

father.[91] Freud is incredulous at Dora's account of her feelings of revulsion and disgust at Herr K.'s forceful advances, since they ought
to have precipitated "a distinct feeling of sexual excitement in *a girl of
fourteen* who had never before been approached."[92] He does not consider that the girl's physical nausea is an understandable result of her
being terrified by Herr K., who she could easily have thought was
about to rape her.[93]

Freud chooses to take Dora's negative reaction as a sign of complete
hysteria: "I should without question consider a person hysterical in
whom an occasion for sexual excitement elicited feelings that were
preponderantly or exclusively unpleasurable." In addition, Herr K.
was an attractive man, "quite young and of prepossessing appearance."[94] At no point in the course of Freud's treatment of Dora does
he affirm the validity of her fear and revulsion concerning Herr K.;
he insists on her actual love for him, including a desire to bear his
child, in the face of such incidents as Herr K.'s univited intrusion into
her bedroom when she was alone in the house, or his repeatedly
following her in the street. Even Dora's slapping Herr K. is taken by
Freud as a further sign of her affection for him.[95] As there is nothing
Dora can do to convince Freud that her "no" to Herr K.'s advances
really means "no," she breaks off the analysis. Freud all too predictably
interprets this as "an unmistakable act of vengeance on her part."[96]

---

[91] Ibid., 37.

[92] Ibid., 28; emphasis added.

[93] That Dora, fourteen years old, could easily have been justified in having
such a fear of Herr K. is unwittingly confirmed in Freud's own description
of a scene recounted by Dora. Herr K. manages to have Dora meet him at
his office. Having "persuaded his wife . . . to stay at home, and sent away
his clerks . . . he was alone when the girl arrived. . . . [Herr K.] asked the
girl to wait for him at the door which opened on to the upper staircase leading
to the upper story, while he pulled down the outside shutters. He then . . .
suddenly clasped the girl to him and pressed a kiss upon her lips." Ibid., 28.
Note that Freud does not dispute the details of this incident nor question the
truthfulness of Dora's account; he rather questions the authenticity of her
response, which he describes as "reversal of affect."

[94] Ibid., 28, 29, note 3.

[95] Ibid., 109.

[96] Ibid.

The pathos of this case study involves both Dora and Freud. There are moments in the story when it is hard to determine who is the more victimized: Dora, subject to callous, manipulative treatment by her own father on the one hand, as well as the less callous but equally demoralizing lack of credulity of her doctor, on the other; or Freud as victim of himself, whose creative power of rational insight into the depth of human suffering caused by intrapsychic conflicts was finally incapable of transcending his own patriarchal prejudice to apprehend fully the appalling betrayal of a young girl. Freud's treatment of Dora indicates an inability to appreciate the full humanity of women that was to persist throughout his careful development and constant re-thinking of psychoanalysis and the nature of female sexuality. His fullest, most coherent theoretical statement on women, found in the essay on "Femininity," was already anticipated in his study of Dora.

In Freud's view of women, not only female sexuality but the entire female character is defined by "a series of lacks."[97] Not only does woman lack a penis, she lacks an adequate superego, which means she lacks the capacity for a fully developed ethical sensibility and interest in anything that transcends the immediate boundaries of her vain concerns. On each level of humanity, woman is defined as a deficient and atrophied creature in comparison with men who "alone hold a monopoly on value."[98] As heir to an " 'ideology' that he does not call into question, Freud asserts that the 'masculine' is the sexual model, that no representation of desire can fail to take it as the standard, can fail to submit to it."[99] Luce Irigaray's remarks on Freud apply with equal force to Hegel, as well as to Marx and Engels, insofar as their theoretical discourses situate women within the logic and economy of "the Same."[100]

Psychoanalytic thematizations of woman as "lack," "fault," or "flaw" carry over from philosophical discourses that equally position

---

[97] Janine Chasseguet-Smirgel, *Sexuality and Mind: The Role of the Father and the Mother in the Psyche* (New York: New York Univ. Press, 1986), 20.

[98] Luce Irigaray, *This Sex Which Is Not One*, trans. Catherine Porter with Carolyn Burke (Ithaca, N.Y.: Cornell Univ. Press, 1985), 69.

[99] Ibid., 72.

[100] Ibid., 74.

woman as deficient humanity. Western philosophical and psychoanalytic discourses are structured according to a "logic of identity" that
universalizes male particularity as the measure of what is human,
leaving no other option but to conceptualize woman as humanity's
damaged spot. The elevation of male partiality to the level of universality constitutes the ideological or irrational moment that is common to all these discourses, thereby undermining their claims to
relevant meaning for all humanity as well as compromising their emancipatory interest.

Although the dominating, violent effects of identity thinking became a central focus of Frankfurt School criticism, it too treats women
with a logic of abstraction and reification similar to that found in the
philosophical tradition deriving from Hegel. It will be the task of the
next chapter to show that from the perspective of critical theory, this
shared approach to the question of woman and the role attributed to
her in the development of Western civilization is not inevitably determined by the logic of the theory itself. Critical theory's restructuring
of the Hegelian–Marxian tradition and its emphasis on the social theoretical dimension of psychoanalysis allowed for the development of
analytical tools necessary to the formation of a comprehensive theory
adequate to challenge domination. What the critical theorists did not
do was extend their own insights in a way that could effectively negate
the ossified attitudes to women that they themselves identified as
thoroughly embedded at all levels of Western culture. This was a step
that Frankfurt theory could have taken, and indeed came close to
taking. Why it did not, or rather, *how* it did not take this step is our
next theme.

CHAPTER 3

Shrew, She-Man, Slave

Images of "Woman" in Critical Theory

THE MOST CURIOUS YET UNSETTLING CONTRADICTION within critical theory—at least for a feminist appropriation of its emancipatory power—is its treatment of women or, more accurately, what it refers to as the "woman question." In the work of Max Horkheimer and Theodor Adorno, women are situated within polarized images that evoke contempt and derision on the one hand and idealistic, romantic, and highly unreal sentimentalism on the other. The element of sentimental romanticism does not modify or soften critical theory's occasional contemptuous treatment of women, but rather serves to intensify the savagery of those directly pejorative attitudes that surface repeatedly throughout Horkheimer's and Adorno's writings.

While Herbert Marcuse shares their romantic idealism, he does not respond with the same cold ridicule that they express with respect to the struggles of women who attempt to change their life situation. Like his Frankfurt colleagues, Marcuse also tends to picture women in terms of abstract principles and concepts, but he does so within a different operational logic than Horkheimer and Adorno. For this reason Marcuse's treatment of women will be discussed in a separate chapter (chapter 4). Although the hostility to women that erupts repeatedly throughout Horkheimer's and Adorno's thought is largely absent in Marcuse, he nonetheless shares their underlying inability to confront women as concrete, fully human agents who reflect the individual diversity and distinct particularity that characterize the whole of humanity. In this sense Marcuse too participates in that deeper, more insidious violence inflicted on women that defines them utterly in terms of male-generated images and fantasies and reveals far more about the psychological prejudices of men than about the existential or ontological realities of women.

The conceptualizations of woman in Horkheimer, Marcuse, and Adorno imply a repressive effect or function that banishes living, suffering, oppressed women to a subterranean, marginal position that offers little possibility for them to become fully visible within the light of critical, compassionate reason. Adorno's statement, "No light falls on men and things without reflecting transcendence,"[1] does not apply to women at any point in his work, although it could have. In some respects, Horkheimer's and Adorno's incapacity or perhaps even refusal to confront the actual humanity of women is less excusable than Marcuse's in that their mode of theorizing lends itself more logically and effectively to feminist analysis. The difference between Horkheimer's and Adorno's conceptualizing practices and Marcuse's lies primarily in the commitment to non-identity thinking, which is not developed in the same way by Marcuse. Non-identity theory, so influential in contemporary feminism, is elaborated by Adorno in the form of negative dialectics whose purpose is directed toward unmasking the operation of domination and manipulation within the act of thinking itself. Although Adorno was unable to extend his negative dialectics to confront the condition of women, he nonetheless anticipated some of the most creative developments within contemporary feminist theory in his critique of identity thinking.

---

[1] Theodor W. Adorno, *Negative Dialectics*, trans. E. B. Ashton (New York: Continuum, 1983), 404. By "transcendence" Adorno means that everything is more than "nothing," that human and nonhuman nature possess their own specific vitality and distinctness, which is reflected in certain forms of art. For Adorno, the "light of transcendence" once cast by religion is replaced by the power of art to preserve nonsemblance in semblance, or the dissimilar in the similar. While a discussion of Adorno's aesthetics is well beyond the scope of this book, it must be pointed out that his understanding of the redemptive, reconciliatory potential of art can only be properly understood within his theory of negative dialectics. See James Harding, "Historical Dialectics and the Autonomy of Art in Adorno's Asthetische Theorie," *Journal of Aesthetics and Art Criticism* 50, no. 3 (Summer 1992): 183–95.

Horkheimer and Adorno were acutely aware of the intrinsic connection between domination, power, and theory. One commentator describes Frankfurt philosophy as "a permanent critique of the theory and practice of *'Identitätsphilosophie,'* [whose] aim is the rescue of the non-identical."[2] This statement most accurately describes the entire philosophical orientation of Adorno, whose interest in the particular and in sustaining and preserving difference marked his thinking throughout his intellectual career. Yet when it comes to the subject of women, Adorno's capacity to "see" let alone "rescue" that which is different and distinct collapses into what he would describe himself as a totalitarian theoretical mode bent on consuming the object.

Adorno and Horkheimer undercut the integrity of their own theorizing as they force women to conform to predetermined concepts of femininity that substantively possess no more relevance to women's humanity than any other irrational prejudices directed at a particular group. Their efforts at theorizing about women repeatedly dissolve into ideology as they revert to repeated usage of the conceptualizing imperialism of the masterful subject who, "tolerat[ing] nothing particular . . . reveal[s] [him]self as particularly dominant."[3] In this way women disappear within that all-too-familiar categorial abstraction *woman,* the inferior mirror image of the male, whose sole reason for existing is to guarantee and maintain his intrinsic superior value as the measure of full humanity. Horkheimer and Adorno sustain the image of woman as humanity's crippled moment that marks and mediates the main intellectual traditions of the West.

By their own standards, Horkheimer and Adorno may be seen to engage in acts of conceptual coercion that confine women within the prison-house of absolute identity. Preconceived assumptions of "woman" force living women to conform with those categories that are erected to define them. My purpose here is to demonstrate two main points. First, on the subject of women, the critical theory of Horkheimer and especially Adorno betrays its own integrity by sacrificing the particular—that is, the particularity of women—to the violent,

---

[2] Irving Wohlfarth, "Presentation of Adorno," *New Left Review*, no. 46 (November–December 1967): 65.
[3] Adorno, *Negative Dialectics*, 317.

coercive logic of identity. Second, paradoxically and simultaneously, Adorno's and Horkheimer's commitment to rescue the particular by letting it be, embracing it in all its difference and diversity by refusing the compulsory conformism latent within the relation between the conceptualizing subject and the object of its contemplation, reveals the rich potential of critical theory to burst the bonds of identity that have functioned to sustain and reproduce the subjugated condition of women throughout history. In my attempt to articulate this contradiction that lies at the heart of critical theory I intend, in the spirit of the theory, to think the theory *against itself*. I will do so by probing and deepening its internal negative dialectic in order to expose and overcome its turn toward noncritical positivity where the question of woman is concerned.

Negative Dialectics

FROM HIS INAUGURAL LECTURE TO THE PHILOSOPHICAL FACulty at the University of Frankfurt in 1931 until the publication of his most "mature" and sustained philosophical statement in *Negative Dialektik* in 1966, Adorno's "philosophical ambition" was to "redefine the subject and the object, and their relationship, without presupposing their identity, and to show that this can only be accomplished if the subject and the object are understood as social processes and not as the presuppositions of pure epistemology."[4] In his 1931 address, "The Actuality of Philosophy," Adorno rejected the traditional philosophical belief in the power of thought as somehow "sufficient to grasp the totality of the real." In Adorno's view, philosophy had failed in its efforts to construct a "grand and total" system. In the wake of this failure and the need to grasp it, Adorno posed the question of philosophy's possible "actuality." That is, he asked "whether . . . there exists an adequacy between the philosophic questions and the possibility of their being answered at all; whether the authentic results of the recent history of these problems is the essential unanswerability

---

[4] Gillian Rose, *The Melancholy Science: An Introduction to the Thought of Theodor W. Adorno* (London: Macmillan Press, 1978), 56.

of the cardinal philosophic questions."[5] In this respect Adorno orients himself toward the Marxian challenge that seeks to heal the breach between thought and reality.

For Adorno, the "cardinal philosophical questions" are not only unanswerable in themselves, but the very attempt to construct a final or totalizing interpretation of reality is expressive of those manipulating conceptualizing practices that drive toward control and mastery of the objects of philosophical thought. He also rejected philosophy's tendency to accommodate itself to current reality. This rejection led him to repudiate the idea that philosophy should engage in interpretations directed at discovering a fixed or immutable meaning of reality. As far as Adorno was concerned, interpretations of the meaning of the human condition amounted to the justification of the social forces that produce it.

Furthermore, grand interpretations of reality are based on the illusion of the existence of an ahistorical, underlying "whole," an unchanging truth or true Being to which the power of philosophical speculation has some privileged access. This view led Adorno to proclaim, "The whole is the false," a philosophical inversion of the famous Hegelian dictum. Adorno criticized Hegelian identifications of the rational with the real and the true with the whole, on the grounds that in Hegel's consistent sacrifice of particularity to the universal, his philosophy could only ultimately aid and abet the status quo. In Adorno's view, the pervasive injustice and suffering inflicted on humanity and nature demonstrated the profound irrationality of "the whole" and its untruth. Anticipating certain current postmodernist preoccupations, Adorno insisted that the "text" philosophy "reads" is "incomplete, contradictory and fragmentary." Given the fleeting, ever-changing, and unfinished quality of reality, the most philosophy can do is to "light up" philosophical questions "suddenly and momentarily,"[6] simultaneously consuming them, so that they may be reconsidered in accordance with specific historical contexts, rather than

---

[5] Theodor W. Adorno, "The Actuality of Philosophy," *Telos*, no. 31 (Spring 1977): 120, 124.
[6] Ibid., 127.

imposed on them. Adorno's philosophical "anti-system"[7] arranges ideas into "constellations," forming theoretical patterns of "changing trial combinations, until they fall into a figure which can be read as an answer, while at the same time the question disappears."[8]

Adorno approached philosophy as a tentative arrangement of conceptual elements within constellations, whereby the material integrity or concrete uniqueness of objects may be apprehended, however inadequately or incompletely. This approach reveals the strong influence of Walter Benjamin. For Benjamin,[9] who will be discussed at greater length in chapter 5, ideas most properly relate to phenomena as "juxtaposed rather than [as an] integrated cluster of changing elements that resist reduction to a common denominator, essential core, or generative first principle."[10] The most truthful interpretation possible can succeed only in arranging the smallest elements of reality within partial and contingent forms. In this way Adorno hoped to achieve a mode of thinking capable of realizing the desire for a noncoercive relation with an object. Adorno was not interested in fabricating a timeless epistemological structure in possession of a universal "validity isolated in itself."[11] Rather, he attempted to engage in a philosophical reversal that disavowed the primacy of the concept along with the thinking subject in favor of a tentative, partial, and constantly shifting approach that facilitated the "break-in of what is irreducible,"[12] that is, the object in all its unique, mysterious particularity.

Adorno's critique of totalizing philosophical systems contained the accusation of philosophical hubris, where philosophy's confidence in its own self-generated first principles led to its attempt to wield its power over the "totality of the real,"[13] thereby gaining access to and

---

[7] Rose, The Melancholy Science, 12.

[8] Adorno, "Actuality of Philosophy," 127.

[9] See chapter 1, note 3, above.

[10] Martin Jay, Adorno (Cambridge, Mass.: Harvard Univ. Press, 1984), 14–15. See chapter 1, note 3, above, for a fuller elaboration of Benjamin's use of constellations. See also Susan Buck-Morss, The Origin of Negative Dialectics: Theodor W. Adorno, Walter Benjamin, and the Frankfurt Institute (New York: Free Press, 1977), 91.

[11] Adorno, "Actuality of Philosophy," 132.

[12] Ibid.

[13] Ibid., 133.

control of it. His critique of the absolutizing thrust of philosophy allowed for the emergence of an alternative, historically mediated theory capable of "touching" reality and realizing its potential to participate in society and history, as well as contributing to their transformation. The compulsion to control and manipulate that motivates identity logic needs to be broken if philosophy is to abandon its collaboration with the social and historical forces of domination and begin to provide intimations of what a truly human and humane way of relating might look like.

Adorno's critique of philosophical idealism, especially of the Hegelian system whose ultimate effect he describes as the "liquidation of the particular"[14] in the final self-actualization of *Geist,* exposes the intrinsic violence of both identity thinking and the "specific historical mode of production" in which it operates. The force exerted by a masterful, knowing subject obsessed with the need to digest the object within its own conceptualizing activities results in the imposition of identity by the subject on the object. The subject's drive to consume objectivity within the validity-seeking bounds of its own epistemological structures "devours"—but incompletely—the object, disfiguring and distorting it beyond recognition. "The system is the belly turned mind," writes Adorno, "and rage is the mark of each and every idealism."[15] The driving impulse of identity thinking originates in the struggle for self-preservation, where the calculating ego seeks mastery and control of nature in its emergence from myth into enlightenment. The compulsion toward the enforced unity of subject and object, man and nature, provides the comfortable illusion that vanquished nature will not turn on man nor threaten his self-perceived mastery of the world.

Under conditions of capitalism, identity thinking finds expression in the process and principle of commodity exchange, where human labor becomes reduced to an "abstract universal concept of average working hours," thereby revealing its fundamental kinship with "the principle of identification." In the process of exchange, commodities

---

[14] Theodor Adorno, *Minima Moralia: Reflections from Damaged Life,* trans. E. F. N. Jephcott (London: Verso, 1985), 17.

[15] Adorno, *Negative Dialectics,* 23.

and people occupy the same category of value, reduced to inter-changeable and disposable items in the marketplace. According to Adorno, "it is through barter that non-identical individuals and per-formances become commensurable and identical. The spread of the principle imposes on the whole world an obligation to become iden-tical, to become total."[16] Identity thinking, expressed in capitalist econ-omies as modes of exchange, obliterates difference and diversity, making unlike into like, and finally transforming people and their relationships within the properties of things. The violence of the cap-italist economic principle of exchange mirrors the violence of the philosophical systematic method in its "ruthless disregard"[17] of par-ticularity and difference.

For Adorno, the ultimate result of "the *episteme* of pure identity"[18] in the twentieth century issued in the genocidal acts unleashed against the Jews, who were divested of all individuality and specificity to the extent that they became reduced to the absolute identity of a "speci-men" with all its accorded dehumanized attributes. This is the lesson of Auschwitz for Adorno: The victims became identical with the myth enclosed around them; whatever was left remaining or undigested was simply obliterated in their literal annihilation. Adorno's discussion of "pure identity" as mass death could easily be applied to deepen our understanding of the great witch-hunt of the late Middle Ages, where large numbers of women were reduced to specimens of the demonic, with which they became completely identified in much the same way as the Nazis ideologized the Jews.

For Adorno, "matters of true philosophical interest"— "noncon-ceptuality, individuality, and particularity"—have been dismissed and treated as unimportant by the main philosophical traditions since Plato.[19] Against this tradition, Adorno asserts

> the untruth of identity, the fact that the concept does not exhaust
> the thing conceived. . . . Aware that the conceptual totality is mere

---

[16] Ibid., 146.
[17] Ibid., 315.
[18] Ibid., 362.
[19] Ibid., 8.

appearance, I have no way but to break immanently, in its own measure, through the appearance of total identity. Since that totality is structured to accord with logic, however, whose core is the principle of the excluded middle, whatever will not fit this principle, whatever differs in quality, comes to be designated as a contradiction. Contradiction is nonidentity under the aspect of identity.[20]

Adorno's effort to undermine "explicit theoretical cohesion"[21] is motivated in part by an ethical materialism that insists on articulating the suffering of specific, concrete human beings who struggle for existence under conditions that foreclose on the possibilities for happiness and peace. Adorno's ethical materialism[22] forms part of a political demand that hunger, torture, murder, and brutality, along with the conditions that produce them, be abolished. The goal of an ethical and humane society "would be to negate the physical suffering of even the least of its members, and to negate the internal reflexive forms of that suffering."[23]

Adorno's political ethics envisages the need for transformation on the social and individual level, although he never attempted to articulate what that transformation would look like or how it would occur. He consistently rejected any engagement in constructivist, programmatic solutions since "the right consciousness in the wrong world is impossible."[24] Any formulation of an alternative society could only result in a premature, false reconciliation with the status quo that would be no more than the reconstruction of the existent. The best and only service the theoretician can offer humanity is to "scrutinize" life in its estranged immediacy, and to articulate "the objective powers that determine individual existence even in its most hidden recesses."[25]

A sustained negative consciousness provides the only hope for the objective to appear—if only momentarily—in all its contingency, specificity, and difference. Constructivist programs that attempt to outline

[20] Ibid., 5.

[21] Adorno, *Minima Moralia*, 18.

[22] Jay, *Adorno*, 88.

[23] Adorno, *Negative Dialectics*, 204.

[24] Theodor W. Adorno, *Introduction to the Sociology of Music*, trans. E. B. Ashton (New York: Seabury Press, 1976), 18.

[25] Adorno, *Minima Moralia*, 15.

solutions to human problems operate within identity logic, where reality is once again fitted to conceptual structures. Such efforts result in the production of ideologies, where difference vanishes. For Adorno, intimations of difference and of otherness can only reveal themselves in the crevices between "what things claim to be and what they are."[26] Justice and love require that the qualitative moments of the object are allowed to emerge, at least in thought. Utopia, for Adorno, is a "togetherness of diversity,"[27] and peace is the "state of distinctness without domination, with the distinct participating in each other."[28]

Love "is the power to see similarity in the dissimilar,"[29] and rescuing the particular is for Adorno an act of love. For Adorno, noncoercive ways of relating to the other that permit it to be itself in all its impenetrable difference are informed and mediated by an ethical love that has nothing to do with mere sentimentalism. Adorno's thought is stubbornly materialist in its unfailing concern for the actual, concrete conditions of life that produce real misery and suffering for living, laboring human beings. The precondition for truth, in his view, is the articulation of the suffering[30] that identity would prefer to silence and deny.

Ironies of Negative Dialectics

LOVE, FOR ADORNO, IS THE NEGATION OF FORCE, THE REfusal to annex otherness. It is the repudiation of all hierarchy and power as domination, where objects—be they human beings or nonhuman nature—are subjected to any form of mastery, even and especially on the level of thought. Conceptualizing practices that demand unity and integration of the subject and the object interlock with other forms of domination in the social, cultural, and political realms. A

---

[26] Adorno, *Negative Dialectics*, 150.

[27] Ibid.

[28] Theodor Adorno, "The Sociology of Knowledge and Its Consciousness," in Andrew Arato and Eike Gebhardt, eds., *The Essential Frankfurt School Reader* (New York: Continuum, 1982), 500.

[29] Adorno, *Minima Moralia*, 191.

[30] Adorno, *Negative Dialectics*, 17.

commitment to, solidarity with, and celebration of all that is different indicates for Adorno the measure of a genuinely humane condition where reconciliation among human beings and with nature becomes possible. According to Adorno, the capacity to embrace and appreciate difference is rooted in the capacity to apprehend the difference between men and women, which is requisite for a humanized consciousness: "That large sensitivity to difference which is the hallmark of the truly humane develops out of the most powerful experience of difference, that of the sexes."[31]

This statement, read within the theoretical context of Adorno's philosophy of negative dialectics and its sustained concern with rescuing particularity, easily could be indicative of a concomitantly "large sensitivity" to women and the specific nature of their subjugation in patriarchal society. Unfortunately, this is anything but the case when Adorno's treatment of "the woman question" is examined more closely.

Equally distressing is Adorno's belief that a humane sensibility understood in accordance with its capacity fully to experience the difference between the sexes necessarily leads to a repudiation of homosexuality. In Adorno's view, homosexuals lack the capacity for experiencing difference because of their "experiential color-blindness," which is related to their "incapacity to apprehend individuality [since] women are . . . 'all the same' to them."[32] The inability to experience difference that Adorno attributes to homosexual men (lesbians are not mentioned in this regard) relates to what he sees as the psychosexual dimension of fascism. He formulates this in the phrase, "Totalitarianism and homosexuality belong together."[33]

The homosexual's inability to perceive women in their diversity is evidence, for Adorno, of a constitutive deficiency that cannot appreciate difference at all. The political expression of this failure is found in fascism. It is of more than passing significance that Adorno's accusation of identity thinking concerning homosexuals' alleged inability to appreciate women itself operates out of an identity thinking that is

---

[31] Theodor Adorno, "Sociology and Psychology—II," *New Left Review*, no. 47 (January-February 1968): 96.
[32] Ibid.
[33] Adorno, *Minima Moralia*, 46.

incapable of grasping the wide diversity among homosexual men. This is perhaps explained in his identification of homosexuality with femininity; the "tough guy" behavior of cruel and brutal men disguises an "effeminate" interior, and the "male principle of domination," expressed in the objectification of "all without exception," renders itself "totally passive, virtually feminine."[34] The diverse humanity of both women and homosexual men is swallowed up within irrational and ideological prejudices whose function in the larger society is to justify the various forms of discrimination and oppression typically used against both groups. Irrespective of his intentions, Adorno's treatment of male homosexuals and women reinforces rather than criticizes the injustices to which they have been subjected throughout history.

Adorno's treatment of homosexuality does not indicate a mere "traditional bias," as one of his commentators remarks, perhaps in order to minimize the controversial nature of Adorno's views.[35] Adorno is guilty of theoretical incoherence—that is, incoherence within the logic of his own theory—in extending the dominating impulse of identity thinking to explain all expressions of homosexuality. Sexual orientation has nothing to do with the repression of difference or repudiation of otherness as such; people who love those of the same sex are not intrinsically impervious to perceiving and celebrating particularity or diversity. Likewise, heterosexuality is no guarantee in itself of either an inherent capacity to appreciate difference, or an inner tendency toward democratic politics. Adorno's remarks betray a highly undifferentiated, homogeneous (mis)understanding of homosexuality as a singular, psychologically monolithic phenomenon to which the individual sensibilities and practices of all individual homosexuals correspond. Insofar as his attitude is part of a larger, longstanding "traditional bias," Adorno would be the first to admit that all theorizing, including his, occurs within the shadow of alienation and is irrevocably marked by it. At the same time, this does not adequately excuse his own lapse into the violence of identity thought with regard to homosexuals.

---

[34] Ibid.
[35] Jay, *Adorno*, 93.

Adorno's entire way of theorizing could have resulted in a more nuanced view of homosexuality. If consistent with his own commitment to non-identity, this view might easily have concluded that individual homosexuals do not conform to standardized social preconceptions about homosexuality. Rather, preconceived social prejudices regarding homosexuality function as "cover concepts" that destroy the diversity among homosexuals and thereby undermine their humanity.

Adorno's theoretical inconsistency with regard to homosexuality reflects a similar undifferentiated attitude toward women, despite his moving celebration of the difference between the sexes. This can be seen in his pejorative association of homosexuality with "passive" femininity.[36] Adorno's remarks on homosexuality and women provide a clear example of the dynamics of identity thinking concerning the relationship between sex and gender, where sociocultural constructions of gender issue in a corresponding set of ontological and metaphysical assumptions about individuals on whom typified gender attributes are imposed. The character traits Adorno sees as shared by women and homosexual men indicate an unquestioned acceptance of the typical dichotomy that associates activity with masculinity and passivity with femininity, a dichotomy derived from Hegelian and Freudian traditions. Yet given Adorno's careful elaboration of negative dialectics and the depth of his critical insight into identity theorizing, it is impossible to conclude that his remarks on women and homosexual men reflect nothing more than unreflective prejudice.

Self-Perpetuating Victims of Patriarchy

A DISTURBING DISSONANCE APPEARS IN ADORNO'S THOUGHT, wherein his uncompromising focus on difference and ethical commitment to the preservation of particularity has a tendency to evaporate. This dissonance can be seen most fully in his treatment of women. Adorno's entire philosophical project of rethinking dialectics in order to articulate non-identity, to insist that objects cannot be totally

---

[36] Adorno, *Minima Moralia*, 46.

absorbed by concepts and that something distinct and unique always remains, no matter how damaged and distorted it may have become as a result of the violence inflicted on them by concepts—all of this fails or stops short when he considers women. The images of women that appear in Adorno's work are fashioned within an identity logic that nearly reduces them to willing collaborators in the general social alienation that is responsible for their dominated condition. In a passage that shows accurate insight into the responsibility of social arrangements and attitudes regarding women's oppression, Adorno, in a somewhat savage twist of argument, blames women themselves for their own misery:

> the continued existence of traditional society has warped the emancipation of women. . . . In big business they remain what they were in the family, objects. We should think not only of their miserable working-day, and of their home-life senselessly clinging to self-contained conditions of domestic labor in the midst of an industrial world, but also of themselves. *Willingly, without any countervailing impulse, they reflect and identify themselves with domination.* Instead of solving the question of women's oppression, male society has so extended its own principle that the victims are no longer able even to pose the question. Provided only a certain abundance of commodities are granted them, *they enthusiastically assent to their fate, leave thinking to the men,* defame all reflection as an offense against the feminine ideal propagated by the culture industry, and are *altogether at their ease in the unfreedom they take as the fulfillment of their sex.* The defects with which they pay for it, neurotic stupidity heading the list, help to perpetuate this state of affairs.[37]

The unrestrained cruelty that infuses the tone of this passage is unrelieved by Adorno's recognition that women are also victimized by patriarchal domination. Not merely "stupid" but "neurotically" stupid, women are completely bereft of critical capacity, enthusiastic collaborators in their own humiliated, dominated condition, devoid of all desire or ability to struggle against their fate in masculine society. They are damaged beings. An unmodified, unreflective, undifferentiated identification is made concerning the weakness, imbecility, and

---

[37] Ibid., 92–93; emphasis added.

defective character of women. This identification corresponds to their subjugated condition and suggests (although Adorno never directly states it) that women deserve their lot.

In a remark that betrays a stunning lack of critical awareness as well as manifesting the violence of the imperial conceptualizing agent criticized by Adorno throughout his work, he baldly proclaims that, "*Without a single exception* feminine natures are conformist."[38] Not a *single* exception? What does Adorno mean by "feminine natures"? What has happened to the philosophical conviction that underlies negative dialectics: that no object can be "wholly known," that "the concept does not exhaust the thing conceived," and that objects are not absorbed by their concepts "without leaving a remainder"?[39] Where is the "remainder," the cracks and crevices between concepts of woman and the rich diversity of each living particular woman, where the truth of their fundamental humanity may be finally grasped? For Adorno, women are mutilated creatures, distorted and deformed beyond all possible redemption and beyond hope.

The images of women that surface throughout Adorno's work bear a cold consistency that carries over and perpetuates those pejorative attitudes to female nature found throughout the Western intellectual traditions described in the previous chapter. Adorno appears to accept the Freudian view of woman as a castrated being, little more than an embodied psychological wound whose crippled state reflects the social mutilation inflicted on her by a historically sustained "patriarchal humiliation."[40] For Adorno, woman's physiological constitution corresponds to her social condition; reflection on the former allows her to see through the false idealism fabricated by society as a miserable compensation for her enslaved position. "The woman who feels herself a wound when she bleeds knows more about herself than the one who imagines herself a flower because that suits her husband."[41]

---

[38] Ibid., 96.
[39] Adorno, *Negative Dialectics*, 5–14.
[40] Theodor W. Adorno, *Prisms*, trans. Samuel Weber and Shierry Weber (Cambridge, Mass.: MIT Press, 1990), 82.
[41] Adorno, *Minima Moralia*, 95.

Adorno's promising insight into the cultural production of "femininity"—that the "feminine character, and the ideal of femininity on which it is modeled, are products of masculine society"[42]—is immediately blunted by the astonishing caricature of how "feminine" women act, "flashing their eyes, using their impulsiveness" to wreck emotional havoc on the "jealous male." Adorno portrays women as bereft of critical self-awareness; their "sheltered unconscious" remains "unmarred by intellect."[43] Not surprisingly, women have little interest in social affairs. Adorno's views of women reverberate with the Freudian indictment of femininity, where women emerge as hopelessly damaged and irredeemably mutilated.

The social conditions responsible for women's dependent state and corresponding psychological and intellectual weakness, however, carry more analytical weight with Adorno than with Freud. Adorno's remarks on women combine an acute awareness of the historical and social roots and dynamics of their oppression with a curious personal contempt that appears to be based on an aprioristic, uncritical identification of female "nature" with all individual women. This identificatory approach to women surfaces in Horkheimer and Marcuse as well, although Marcuse does not view women with the harsh negativity so prevalent in the others. In *Dialectic of Enlightenment*, Horkheimer and Adorno acknowledge the ruthless brutality inflicted on women throughout history; the physical difference in strength between woman and man becomes the basis of her subjugation and humiliation in a male-dominated society that regarded her and the natural world as "one immense hunting ground."[44] Yet two pages later they condemn women's efforts to change their condition by participating in the activities of the public realm. Their image of contemporary women who take part in social and cultural affairs descends effortlessly and without prior warning to a level of sneering caricature infused with hostility and derision. It must be quoted in full to be believed:

> The shrew, a fossilized survival of the bourgeois esteem of woman,
> is invading society today. With her endless nagging she takes revenge

---

[42] Ibid.
[43] Ibid., 96.
[44] Max Horkheimer and Theodor W. Adorno, *Dialectic of Enlightenment*, trans. John Cumming (New York: Continuum, Seabury Press, 1972), 248.

in her own home for the misery inflicted upon her sex from time immemorial. If sufficient deference is not shown to her, a cross old woman will continue her scolding outside the house, knocking off the hat of any absentminded individual who neglects to rise in her presence. That whatever happens, his head should roll, she has always demanded in her politics—whether in recollection of the maenadic era or outdoing man and his organization in her helpless fury. The blood-lust a woman displays in a pogrom outdoes that of a man. Subjected woman in the guise of a Fury has survived and still wears the grimace of mutilated nature. . . . If a girl in past ages bore her subjection in the form of melancholy mien and loving devotion—an alienated image of nature, and aesthetic chattel—the Fury has eventually hit upon a new female pursuit. She bustles about after cultural goals like a social hyena. Her ambition runs to honors and the limelight, but her feeling for masculine culture is not yet so well developed that, weighed down as she is by additional sorrow, she can prevent herself from stumbling, and betraying that she is still not at home in a man's world. . . . The last vestiges of female opposition to the spirit of a male-dominated society are engulfed in a morass of paltry rackets, religious sects, and hobbies. They find some outlets in the perverse aggressiveness of social work and theosophical chitchat. . . . In this wasteland, fellow-feeling for other living creatures expresses itself . . . in neo-Buddhism and in Pekingese dogs.[45]

Loss of the Family

THE IMAGE FRAGMENTS OF GROTESQUE FEMALE TYPES CONtained in the preceding paragraph are blatantly sexist in their simplified homogeneity. They might be dismissed as the result of the rhetorical excess of a pre-feminist epoch or perhaps a momentary lapse of bad temper on the part of the authors, were it not for the fact that they begin to make a deeper sense when further examined in the context of some key themes in critical theory. These themes include critical theory's analysis of the relationship between the family and society, and the society and the individual.

Portraits of women as "shrew" and "social hyena" are connected with Horkheimer's and Adorno's beliefs about woman's role in the

---

[45] Ibid., 250.

family and her impact on the psychic development of her sons, including her humanizing function that softens the disciplinarian educational actions of the strong bourgeois father. The mother's capacity for unconditional love and the father's insistence that the achievements or failures of his sons be ultimately accounted for in terms of individual (in)adequacy rather than social determinations are crucial factors in the psychological formation of critically minded, independent individuals.[46] The domination of the mother both within the family and within the larger society, although "nothing could justify it,"[47] nonetheless works to her son's developmental advantage. The mother is able to impart a humanizing influence on her son precisely because her traditional isolation in the home, along with the restrictions imposed on her that severely curtailed her social activities, served to protect her from being too emotionally marked by historically specific forms of social alienation. Her continued confinement to the domestic sphere in the bourgeois period insulated her from the worst effects of an acquisitive, predatory capitalist culture. As Horkheimer puts it, "The mother, cut off from the community of the males and despite an unjustified idealization being herself forced into a dependent situation, represented a principle other than reality; she could sincerely dream the dreams of utopia with the child, and she was his natural ally whether she wished it or not."[48]

As women leave their families to take up paid employment, they endanger the psychological development of their male children (female development within the family is never mentioned). No longer able to depend on their mothers' "unrestricted love," the sons become threatened in terms of their own potential for loving. Mothers who actively participate in social and professional life, or who choose to exercise their "profession" at home, open the way for the encroachment of instrumental rationality, which transforms the family into yet

---

[46] Inst. of Soc. Research, trans. John Viertel, *Aspects of Sociology* (Boston: Beacon Press, 1972), 141.

[47] Max Horkheimer, *Critique of Instrumental Reason*, trans. Matthew J. O'Connell et al. (New York: Seabury Press, 1974), 16.

[48] Max Horkheimer, "Authoritarianism and the Family," in Ruth Nanda Anshen, ed., *The Family: Its Function and Destiny*, rev. ed. (New York: Harper and Row, 1959), 390.

another functional organization in the service of the prevailing social authority rather than the protective "second womb" it once was. The mother's traditional position and role in the family situate her as the final bulwark against this process. If she succumbs to the lure of the larger community by engaging in a misguided imitation within the family of the work-oriented, profit-seeking male, then there is no further possibility for her or her son to dream their utopian dreams together.

Instrumental reason and the reification of the closest human relations encroach upon the daily life activities of the family as a result of the changes of women's traditional role within it. "The modern model mother plans the education of her child almost scientifically, from the well-balanced diet to the equally well-balanced ratio between reprimand and friendliness. . . . The spontaneity of the mother and her natural, unlimited protectiveness and warmth tend to be dissolved."[49]

Horkheimer and Adorno locate two key factors that contribute to the dissolution of the family in contemporary capitalist societies, a dissolution that itself contributes to the disappearance of the (male) individual and the emergence of the authoritarian personality. One factor involves the transformation of the mother's traditional role vis-à-vis her (male) children and husband. The other (and perhaps more significant) factor relates to the disappearance of the loving, powerful, and protective father in the golden age of the bourgeois family unit. Although the restricted, dependent role of the bourgeois wife and mother permanently marked her as an "unsatisfied," "spiritless" being, her former capacity for unconditional love structured the relations within the family; this structuring in turn strengthened the family to withstand and to some extent counter the "dehumanization of the world."

Following Hegel's description of the opposition between the family and the larger community, Horkheimer argues that the commitment of the family, and in particular that of the mother, to the happiness and well-being of its members "cultivates the dream of a better condition for mankind" that might one day be mobilized for the realization

---

[49] Ibid., 386, 389.

of a more humane world. The woman's role in the family represents an irresolvable contradiction. On the one hand, she educates her children to accept social authority and also "chains" her husband to the status quo as a means of protecting her own economic security and that of her children. On the other hand, the love that her children feel toward her may one day foster in them "the seeds of a lasting spirit of rebellion" as they come to recognize the unfairness of her dominated condition.[50]

The ambivalent relation of the family to the larger society—that is, both educating its members to support and adjust to the status quo, as well as fostering the potential for a critical attitude that might be mobilized against society—is largely rooted in the ambiguous position of the woman in the family. Her historical condition of dependency and subjugation within society and the family, which has remained "uninterrupted in civilized lands" since the overthrow of the mother-right, has produced in her a spiritual, intellectual, and psychological deformity that appears to mark women for all time.

At no point do Horkheimer and Adorno allow women to emerge as subjects in any sense, nor do they attempt to lend a voice to the suffering that they freely admit has been unjustly inflicted on women in patriarchal society. The most woman can offer man is the mute reflex of a maternal love that is directed more by given biological facticity than by ethical choice. Woman never rises above the level of an empty, abstract principle with Horkheimer and Adorno. Moreover, it serves the interest of men, both in the family and in society, that she remain locked within her maternal function for the sake of the psychological development of her sons. Although they do not say it explicitly, Horkheimer's and Adorno's entire treatment of woman suggests that her only value lies in self-sacrifice; any attempt by women to break out of the condition imposed on them by history is immediately repudiated and ridiculed.

If women represent an unconditional love that provides an important emotional source for the individual development of their sons,

---

[50] Max Horkheimer, "Authority and the Family," in *Critical Theory: Selected Essays*, trans. Matthew J. O'Connell et al. (New York: Continuum, 1972), 114–21.

the father represents educational authority and economic security and relates to his sons through an "intellectual interaction."[51] As with the mother, however, social and economic changes have also altered the role of the father. He has been transformed into the colorless entity of a paid "employee,"[52] with the result that he no longer "embodies the power, justice, and goodness, and above all . . . the protection, which the child had initially expected."[53] No longer the source of moral autonomy in the formation of his son's individuality, the father's "socially conditioned weakness" destroys his son's desire to identify with him. As a result, the male child seeks to incorporate the masculine images of power provided by fascism:

> Today the father tends to be directly replaced by collective entities, the school class, the sports team, the club, the state. The more family dependence is reduced to a mere psychological function within the soul of the infant, the more abstract and unspecific it becomes in the mind of the adolescent; gradually it tends to lead to a general readiness to accept any authority provided it is strong enough.[54]

The logical conclusion of such a point of view would mean that day care would also fall within the category of those "collective entities" that encroach upon and undermine the family, resulting in an institutionalized consciousness that provides fertile ground for the development of an authoritarian personality. Because human beings are subject to social and cultural influences from a very early age, it is crucial that those influences are modified within the family. There the mother's unquestioned love and the father's unassailable moral authority combine to form an independent individual with the capacity to realize himself as such.

Horkheimer's and Adorno's highly idealized and homogenous portrait of the bourgeois family, along with their analysis of the social and economic forces conspiring to undermine it, proceeds primarily at the expense of women. For all their insight into social alienation

---

[51] Horkheimer, "Authoritarianism and the Family," 390.
[52] Horkheimer, *Critique of Instrumental Reason*, 11.
[53] Institute, *Aspects of Sociology*, 141.
[54] Horkheimer, "Authoritarianism and the Family," 389.

and its effects on both men and women, their work exhibits an often not-so-latent bias that identifies women far more tightly with the damaging effects of capitalist society than men. The predatory spirit characteristic of capitalist economies is carried by men, whose intellectual abilities are actively mobilized in its service. Women, in contrast, appear to retain a certain passivity, whether they work exclusively in the home or as wage earners. No matter how alienated or distorted men's activities are, men nonetheless participate in history and society as subjects, whereas women do not. Consider Adorno's meditation on Thorstein Veblen's elaboration of the woman question, which says at least as much about Adorno as Veblen, and is in any event characteristic of most of Adorno's remarks about women:

> She rarely takes part as subject in historical development. The state of dependence to which she is confined mutilates her. This counterbalances the opportunity offered her by her exclusion from economic competition. Measured against the man's sphere of intellectual interests, even that of those men absorbed in the barbarism of business, most women find themselves in a mental state which Veblen does not hesitate to term imbecilic. Following this line of thought, one might reach the conclusion that women have escaped the sphere of production only to be absorbed all the more entirely by the sphere of consumption, to be captivated by the immediacy of the commodity world no less than men are transfixed by the immediacy of profit. Women mirror the injustice masculine society has inflicted on them— they become increasingly like commodities.[55]

The dichotomy of active masculinity over against passive femininity variously outlined by Hegel, Marx, Engels, and Freud is not only repeated and unchallenged in critical theory, it is sustained within it. As well, the further dichotomies that flow from this concerning men and women and their designated attributes—namely, woman/ nature, man/spirit, woman/feeling, man/intellect—are also reproduced in critical theory, as has been demonstrated. All the old prejudices are there yet not by necessity dictated by the theory itself. Adorno's careful elaboration of negative dialectics with its passionate concern for the preservation of particularity and difference (a concern

---

[55] Adorno, *Prisms*, 82.

shared by Horkheimer) could have been elaborated as a powerful emancipatory critique for theorizing the domination of women. If Adorno had thought to analyze the "woman question" within the logic of non-identity, he would have mounted a formidable challenge to cultural assumptions and political and social practices concerning women. Yet neither he nor his Frankfurt colleagues followed through on this but fell back into a crude form of identity thinking that their work consciously sought to dismantle.

It is indisputable that Adorno and Horkheimer construct an insightful and often deeply sensitive portrait of the oppression of women, elaborating the presence of sexism not only at the core of Western civilization, but woven throughout all its epochs. With this analysis, it becomes apparent that sexism is embedded within reason itself, insofar as reason seeks more instrumental, manipulative, and masterful techniques for dominating human and nonhuman nature. Yet Horkheimer's and Adorno's understanding of the complex dynamics of the domination of women, along with their realization of the integral relationship between the subjugation of women and the fabric of civilization, harbors antiwoman attitudes. These attitudes not only function to leave the oppressed condition of women intact, but further suggest that women are ultimately responsible for their repressed condition.

At the same time, Adorno and Horkheimer's uncompromising recognition of the imposed connection between women and nature that is a key element in the domination of both, along with their understanding of the operation of domination as it reverberates throughout the various levels of culture and society and how it affects women, requires that their work be seriously considered as an important resource for feminist critical theory. On the other hand, it cannot be overstressed that the way they theorize the depth and pervasiveness of women's subjugation involves their participation in it to the extent that they share uncritically in the biases toward women that they themselves expose in Western intellectual traditions.

How, if at all, can this more than contradictory perspective be explained? Is it worth explaining, or does an attempt at explanation risk producing what can be no more than a feminist apology for a hopeless and unredeemable sexist theory that is not only of no benefit to theorizing women's liberation, but can only undermine it? Why should feminist theorists even attempt to reconstruct Frankfurt theory in the interest of feminist goals when the theory is so heavily burdened by sexist prejudice? Or, are the negative images of women incidental to the theory in such a way that a feminist critique committed to utilizing the best elements of critical theory will be able to do so for its own purposes and thereby eliminate the sexism within critical theory? I will conclude this chapter by attempting to answer, however partially, some of these questions.

Toward Resolving the Sexist Problematic

THE ARGUMENT ADVANCED IN THE PREVIOUS CHAPTER CONcerning G. W. F. Hegel must also apply to the treatment of women in critical theory. That is, it is entirely inadequate and superficial to explain critical theory's collaboration in the domination of women in terms of the local *Zeitgeist*. Most people in most historical periods harbor all kinds of prejudices about women and other groups of people, yet it remains possible for some intellectuals to mount critiques of those prejudices in ways that challenge and undermine the prevailing cultural attitudes. To excuse critical theory's treatment of women with cheap appeals to prevailing attitudes not only misses the point, it does an extreme disservice to the theory itself.

To account for critical theory's treatment of women, one must look to the theory itself and consider some of its most urgent preoccupations. These rightly focused on the dehumanization and increasing barbarism of contemporary society, the extension of instrumental rationality into the most personal areas of human experience, and the destruction of the individual whom the critical theorists located as the last possible repository of an independent individual with some remaining capacity for resistance. These concerns, which largely framed the critical theorists' diagnosis of the human condition in twentieth-century capitalist societies, also produced a deeply ambivalent attitude toward women. Horkheimer's and Adorno's fear of the complete triumph of instrumental reason, along with the entrenchment of a totally administered society comprised of dehumanized, atomized entities, caused them to consider whatever possible counterforces and loci of utopian hope might still remain to a humanity drifting deeper into barbarism. Their concern with the decline of the family as threatening the disappearance of the only remaining social structure where humane relations are still possible forced them to consider the role of the mother. She, by virtue of her restricted isolation from the brutal world of capitalist accumulation and competition, was protected from the worst of its alienating effects. According to Adorno:

> With the family there passes away, while the system lasts, not only the most effective agency of the bourgeoisie, but also the resistance which, though repressing the individual, also strengthened, perhaps even produced him. The end of the family paralyzes the forces of opposition. The rising collectivist order is a mockery of a classless one: together with the bourgeois it liquidates the Utopia that once drew sustenance from motherly love.[56]

The association of the mother with utopia recalls a time of peace and gratification, the only moment of undistorted reconciliation with nature that humanity has ever experienced. The capacity for happiness originates in the harmonious, protective relationship between the mother and her infant; all subsequent experience of happiness is nothing more than an "after-image"[57] of that relationship. In his earliest encounter with his mother, the child knows unalienated pleasure and spontaneity as yet undeformed by the ordered, de-eroticized experience of mere physiological function that substitutes for genuine pleasure in a world under the sway of the performance principle or "work ethic." Although Herbert Marcuse developed this latter theme in greater depth than did Horkheimer and Adorno, they all share a view of the mother as representing perhaps the only humanizing influence left with the power to be suggestive of another form of life. She alone promises to negate the decline of individuals within an increasingly politically administered, culturally massified, and psychologically collectivized aggregate of isolated human beings. Although changing economic and

---

[56] Adorno, *Minima Moralia*, 23.
[57] Ibid., 112.

social conditions conspired to destroy the family as well as utterly transform the role of mother and father, the family could still assert its traditional Hegelian opposition to the larger world.

As far as Horkheimer and Adorno were concerned, the entry of women into the paid labor force signaled the annihilation of any hope of recovering that original experience and intimation of utopia in the protective unconditional maternal love that was also the ground of potential rebellion against the status quo. They acknowledged the possibility, more strongly believed in by Marcuse, that the memory of happiness and gratification experienced with the mother might be recalled and mobilized in political activity directed toward the realization of a humane transformation of society. A mother "pressed by other cares and occupations" is unable to lavish on her child the "dynamic friendliness, warmth and smile[s]" so necessary to the child's capacity for developing an undistorted relationship with "objects, men, and the world." If she is distracted by other activities so that she cannot focus her maternal energy properly on her son, she is in danger of producing "a cold character that is lacking in spontaneous impulses."[58] Whatever potential the male child has for retaining some measure of humaneness and resistance to the brutalizing, manipulating forces of the larger society depends on the quality of his relation with his mother and the experience of unconditional love only she can provide him.

Related to Horkheimer's and Adorno's concern for the decline of the family is their lament for the transformation of marriage from an intimate sexual love relationship to a more businesslike arrangement between business partners. Again, changes in women's social status and the enlarged field of activities open to them are seen as bearing a crucial responsibility for the loss of intimacy and romance characteristic of contemporary marriages. According to Horkheimer:

> The equal status of the wife, her professional activity, and the much speeded-up emancipation of the children have already effected a change in the atmosphere of the home. It is not rare for American fathers to feel left behind by their children. Like life generally, marriage is on its way to becoming more rational, utilitarian, and prosaic.[59]

---

[58] Horkheimer, *Critique of Instrumental Reason*, 8.
[59] Ibid., 97.

In the last interview of his life, Horkheimer condemned the birth control pill as heralding the "death of erotic love."[60] Not only Horkheimer but also Adorno and Marcuse understood that spontaneous sensual pleasure for the sheer joy and intimacy it brings contains a socially transformative power that could subvert the exploitative division of labor and soul-destroying effects of work in industrial societies. In a statement Horkheimer and Adorno might well endorse, Marcuse writes:

> The unpurified, unrationalized release of sexual relationships would be the strongest release of enjoyment as such and the total devaluation of labor for its own sake. No human being could tolerate the tension between labor as valuable in itself and the freedom of enjoyment. The dreariness and injustice of work conditions would penetrate explosively the consciousness of individuals and make impossible their peaceful subordination to the social system of the bourgeois world.[61]

Perhaps more than Adorno or Marcuse, Horkheimer strongly objected to what he saw as the rationalization of marriage, where husband and wife function more as impersonal partners than passionate lovers. In contemporary society the romantic spontaneity of erotic married love gives way to the prevailing rationality of society, and the "principle of equality" between men and women threatens to destroy the distinction between the private and social spheres. For Horkheimer this development meant the colonization of the family by the logic of exchange and instrumental rationality.[62]

Divorce is another example for both Horkheimer and Adorno of the triumph of the exchange principle, where human beings become reduced to the status of cheap, disposable consumer commodities. They write: "Marriage shrinks more and more into a relationship of exchange serving purely practical ends. . . . [It] is wholly undermined

---

[60] Max Horkheimer, *Die Sehnsucht nach dem ganz Anderen*, ein Interview mit Kommentar von Helmut Gumnior (Hamburg: Furche-Verlag, 1970), 74.
[61] Herbert Marcuse, *Negations: Essays in Critical Theory*, trans. Jeremy J. Shapiro (Boston: Beacon Press, 1969), 187.
[62] Horkheimer, *Critique of Instrumental Reason*, 24.

by the institution of divorce. The individuals become interchangeable here too as they do in business life, where one leaves a position as soon as a better one offers itself."[63]

Birth control, divorce, working mothers—all these social phenomena signal the ascendancy of the capitalist logic of exchange, where what is human is rendered into the status and function of an object. According to the identitarian logic of exchange, all difference and distinctness disappear within the fungible reduction of objects to commodities whose value—including that of human beings through wages—is determined solely by the drive for profit. The constitutive sameness necessarily imposed on objects when rendered into mere commodities whose primary value is determined by exchange pervades all spheres of human experience, including the most intimate areas of love, marriage, and the erotic life. Humanity now exists in a state of almost total reification, where the power of identity thinking renders the unlike into like, and where the principle of equality in fact levels all particularity into a social, cultural, and personal monochromic sameness. For Horkheimer and Adorno, this state of affairs meant that fascism as a social phenomenon, intolerant to all difference and committed to twisting everything into its own image, continued to exist in the administered democracies of the West.

The analysis of the destruction of the family as providing perhaps the only humanizing experiences left in an instrumentalized, administered, and massified world proceeds at the expense of women's full subjectivity. Yet Adorno's and Horkheimer's insights should not be hastily dismissed, however petty they may appear. Their lament for the passing of the bourgeois family with its protective, disciplinarian father, along with the ideal maternal presence who nurtures a humane and potentially rebellious spirit in her sons, neither derives from nor advocates a simplistic sexist demand that women return to the hearth while men reassert their former patriarchal glory. To read them in this way is to miss the dialectical structure of their critique, which recognizes the utopian potential within the family *and* recognizes that it exists by virtue of women's enforced restriction within the family unit. In similar dialectical fashion, they see that the emancipation of women

---

[63] Institute, *Aspects of Sociology*, 139.–40.

from their traditional domestic subjugation can only lead to a deeper, more thorough alienation where the achievement of "subjectivity" culminates in imitation of the aggressive, bustling business pursuits of men. Furthermore, both Horkheimer and Adorno hold grave doubts about the possibility of genuine individuality and subjectivity in a social context ruled by the hegemony of the exchange principle. As far as the emancipation of women is concerned, they do not object to women's liberation as such; rather, they raise questions about what forms freedom can take and at what price is it to be purchased under current conditions.

As there is no clear path to freedom, what Horkheimer and Adorno point out is that human efforts oriented toward emancipation occur within and through the alienation and distortion of what is. There is no location or standpoint beyond the existent that allows humanity to turn its back on it and move toward a new and better world. All human relationships, social arrangements, and institutional forms are embedded in and mediated by history and society; marriage, divorce, and birth control are thus also mediated practices that contain elements of instrumentality, fungibility, and efficiency. Adorno, and perhaps to a somewhat lesser extent Horkheimer, is asking that these realities be recognized, not necessarily that women be required to languish at home. To state the problem succinctly, Horkheimer and Adorno raise the prospect that although humanity yearns for a better world, the possibilities for freedom, autonomous subjectivity, justice, and human happiness may be illusory despite whatever temporary ameliorations from suffering may be achieved in specific circumstances.

Eclipse of the Individual

FINALLY, THERE IS THE QUESTION OF THE DECLINE OF THE individual. Horkheimer and Adorno fear such a decline guarantees establishment of a totally administered society. Their concern with the preservation of the individual—insofar as that preservation remains possible—does not arise out of an abstract, undifferentiated humanism so widely decried by contemporary postmodernism. Rather, the humanism of critical theory is concrete. It deconstructs false humanisms and reveals their political function as compensating individuals with the illusion that their dignity and worth are intrinsic to humankind alone, independent of inhuman social conditions.

Horkheimer and Adorno recognize the social nature of individuals and their historical situatedness. They are fully aware that the concept of "the pure individual in his ineffable singularity"[64] is an ideological construct devised to mystify the real and highly complex relation between individuals and society. They argue that the false reverence for individualism so widely proclaimed in Western capitalist societies conceals a disregard for concrete human beings, whose interests are negated and undermined by the prevailing social and economic order. They further argue that the realization of the individual is only possible within a "just and humane society."[65] Conversely, a "just and humane society" depends on the existence of intentional, independent human agents who, although socially mediated but not entirely socially derivative, harbor the critical capacity necessary to resist the irrationality of the social and political status quo. For Horkheimer, resistance "is always the core of true individuality."[66]

Critical theory's appropriation and reconstruction of psychoanalysis highlight the objectivity that resides in the subject, where social, cultural, and historical experience lies sedimented in the deepest layers of the human psyche. Adorno remarks that the psychology of individuals "points back . . . to social moments."[67] This means that theories of subjectivity necessarily devolve into objectivity until the social and historical experiences are revealed that both shape and distort the subject. Given the highly mediated but not identical relationship between the individual and society, and further given the potential of individuals for critique and resistance to domination, whatever countervailing forces or agencies still exist within the society must be fostered and nurtured in order to prevent the withering away of human beings into easily manipulated isolated social atoms. Once this concern

---

[64] Ibid., 41.
[65] Ibid., 46.
[66] Max Horkheimer, *Eclipse of Reason* (New York: Continuum, 1973), 161.
[67] Theodor W. Adorno, "Sociology and Psychology," *New Left Review*, no. 46 (November–December 1967): 73.

of critical theory is fully understood, the treatment of women becomes explainable, although never justifiable. With Horkheimer, Adorno, and even Marcuse, women are hidden behind the category *woman*. They do not possess full human significance, but are rather understood in terms of function or principle, always representing something other than themselves.

Restricted to the family and isolated from history, woman is protected from being deformed by the worst effects of the alienation and barbarism that grow deeper in the larger realm of capitalist acquisition and competitiveness. As long as woman remains a dominated and subjugated creature, she represents a refuge from a world marked by the inhumanity of instrumental reason and relationships driven by calculation and utility, an intimation of undamaged, benevolent nature and promise of future reconciliation with it. A still point in the turning world, woman offers men the last, if not the only, experience of unconditional love and authentic humane interaction, although she herself is not an actor. Primarily in her role as mother, woman provides her sons with possibly the only experience they will ever have of unalloyed peace, gratification, and utter security. This peaceful state might one day, if social injustice becomes truly intolerable, reemerge as a nonnegotiable demand for happiness, freedom, and the "reasonable conditions of life." Divorce, birth control, and a career outside the home threaten these future utopian possibilities because they undermine woman's humanizing effects, which become negated as she attempts to realize herself as an active human agent directing her own life.

The implication of this line of thinking is that woman abolishes herself as a potentially autonomous, free subject in order to function as an abstract ethical principle so that she may preserve her humanizing role and thereby provide the means through which the male may achieve *his* subjectivity. For the man to be born, the woman must not merely die—she is not permitted to come into existence. This explains at least partially the hostility and ridicule that characterize Horkheimer's and Adorno's portraits of women who struggle to take their place in a "man's world." It also accounts for their rather wooden views on marriage, divorce, birth control, and working women. Maintaining the Hegelian and Freudian opposition between the family and the larger society, Horkheimer and Adorno insist that however im-perfect, the family can be an oasis of warmth and mutual love that must be protected from the alienating, inhuman effects produced by the capitalist world. Woman is key to the preservation of the family and the utopian potential harbored within it. To abandon her traditional role is to risk foreclosure on future social transformation.

This perspective is reinforced by the conviction that there is no real freedom to be gained by entering the public realm either for women or for men, since the public realm is caught within the all-pervasive spell of the exchange principle and its corresponding identity logic. In their obstinate refusal to see any existential advantage for women in participating in social and cultural activities, Horkheimer and Ador-no betray the emancipatory impulse of their own theory by main-taining the incoherent thesis that social transformation and freedom may one day be achieved through the continued enslavement of half of humanity.

In spite of their inability to theorize women as fully human, Horkheimer and Adorno nonetheless provide contemporary feminists with a rich critical tradition whose main themes and analyses are of particular relevance for women's liberation. Adorno's reconstruction of the dialectic reveals the dominating and distorting power of concepts to mystify social reality. As well, his consistent efforts to sustain a philosophical commitment to difference and particularity produce a countervailing force that seriously undermines the ideology effects of identity thinking to deny suffering. The elaboration of negative dia-lectics and the paramount concern for the particular that run through-out Adorno's work not only anticipate central themes of contemporary feminism, they open to it creative directions toward the development of an open-ended, practical theory of women's liberation.

Current feminism's preoccupations with cultural, linguistic, and racial diversity among women and its expressed commitment to re-think and realign human relations with nature are to a large extent reformulations of the basic themes of critical theory, whether inten-tional or not. The concern with difference and non-identity theorizing have become especially important to feminist variants of postmodernist thought, although not in ways anticipated by Adorno nor in forms that he would likely endorse. Other developments in contemporary feminist theory, however, which share postmodernism's concern with difference and are also critical of identity thinking but do not follow postmodernist lines of argument, are more promising.[68] While Adorno's work does foreshadow some of the most creative developments in contemporary feminism and feminist postmodernism, it avoids the latter's more questionable elements. While a growing body of feminist literature embraces non-identity epistemology, that of the postmodernist type, in marked contrast to Adorno, jettisons most notions of subjectivity, a dangerous theoretical and political move that poses particular problems for feminism.

The repudiation of subjectivity in feminist postmodernism[69] in part arises out of an undifferentiated critique of philosophical theories

---

[68] For feminist critiques of postmodernism and the problems it poses for feminist theory, see Seyla Benhabib, "Feminism and the Question of Postmodernism," in *Situating the Self: Gender, Community and Postmodernism in Contemporary Ethics* (New York: Routledge, Chapman and Hall, 1992); Sabina Lovibond, "Feminism and Postmodernism," *New Left Review*, no. 178 (November–December 1989): 5–28; Toril Moi, "Feminism, Postmodernism, and Style: Recent Feminist Criticism in the United States," *Cultural Critique*, no. 9 (Spring 1988): 3–22; Rita Felski, "Feminism, Postmodernism, and the Critique of Modernity," *Cultural Critique*, no. 13 (Fall 1989): 33–56; Nancy Hartsock, "Postmodernism and Political Change: Issues for Feminist Theory," *Cultural Critique*, no. 14 (Winter 1989–90): 15–33; Marsha Hewitt, "Illusions of Freedom: The Regressive Implications of Postmodernism," in Ralph Miliband and Leo Panitch, eds., *Real Problems/False Solutions: Socialist Register* (London: Merlin Press, 1993), 78–91; and Marsha Hewitt, "Cyborgs, Drag Queens and Goddesses: Emancipatory-Regressive Themes in Contemporary Feminism," *Method and Theory in the Study of Religion* 5, no. 2 (1993): 135–54.

[69] Examples of feminist postmodernist theory based on a theoretical commitment to non-identity thinking whose inspiration derives more from French poststructuralism than from critical theory include: Linda J. Nicholson, ed., *Feminism/Postmodernism* (New York: Routledge, Chapman and Hall, 1990); Judith Butler, *Gender Trouble: Feminism and the Subversion of Identity* (New York: Routledge, Chapman and Hall, 1990); Jane Flax, *Thinking Fragments: Psychoanalysis, Feminism, and Postmodernism in the Contemporary West* (Berkeley: Univ. of California Press, 1990); and Donna Haraway, *Simians, Cyborgs, and Women: The Reinvention of Nature* (New York: Routledge, Chapman and Hall, 1991).

of subjectivity from René Descartes to the present, and presumes a more or less singular notion of the subject as an ahistorical, masterful cogitating entity that structures the entire epistemological tradition of the West. Such a perspective fails to take seriously the critical revisions of subjectivity and epistemology that have challenged such decontextualized approaches to knowledge and the corresponding relation between subjectivity and objectivity that also marks the Western tradition. Adorno's commitment to difference and particularity, although based on a critique of this dimension of Western concepts of subjectivity, does not lead to the repudiation of subjectivity altogether. His and Horkheimer's shared commitment to the preservation of the individual places their work in sharp contrast to present feminist theories that derive their critique of identity thinking from French poststructuralism.

I have discussed elsewhere the difficulties arising with non–identity epistemologies that actively promote the annihilation of subjectivity, and so I will not pursue the topic here. Horkheimer's and Adorno's concern for the preservation of the individual, however, should be carefully considered by feminists who are concerned with both the theoretical and practical liberation of women. Only subjective agents who have some degree of consciousness of themselves as such can possibly struggle for freedom, and only they can be held responsible for the activities they engage in. Adorno and Horkheimer are aware—and this is of the utmost importance for feminism—that the root of intolerance for difference lies in an "antifeminity" that "sets the pattern for the subsequent rejection of everything that is deemed 'different.' "[70]

Converse and related to this is Adorno's association of a "truly humane" consciousness with the recognition that the most powerful experience of difference is that between the sexes. While this insight needs to be purged of its antihomosexual bias, its value lies in pointing out the human, anthropological basis of difference that both structures and transcends race, ethnicity, class, and culture. Finally, the hope is again articulated by Adorno that the difference between men and women may one day be the source of their redemption:

> Hope cannot aim at making the mutilated social character of women identical to the mutilated social character of men; rather, its goal

---

[70] Horkheimer, "Authoritarianism and the Family," 393.

> must be a state in which the face of the grieving woman disappears
> simultaneously with that of the bustling, capable man, a state in
> which all that survives the disgrace of the difference between the
> sexes is the happiness that difference makes possible.[71]

Perhaps feminism may take heart from this expression of hope
and develop it in ways that Adorno was incapable of pursuing. Indeed,
this project has already been taken up by feminism in interesting but
not entirely unproblematic ways. The following chapters will examine
the work of some of the most creative feminist thinkers currently
writing in the field of what is basically misnamed "feminist theology."
Although these women—Mary Daly, Elisabeth Schüssler Fiorenza,
and Rosemary Radford Ruether—are academic theologians educated
in the Roman Catholic tradition, their thinking has developed along
lines that can no longer be properly understood as theology. Rather,
the feminist analysis that all three writers bring to bear on the theological tradition out of which they come has caused them to push
beyond the bounds of their own original disciplines to the point of
having surpassed the disciplines themselves. When looked at from the
perspective of Frankfurt critical theory, strong affinities, most often
unacknowledged, begin to appear. They allow for the emergence of
dimensions in the critique of these thinkers that might otherwise remain obscure. By arranging themes that mutually resonate between
both critical theory and feminist religious thought, interesting clari-
fications and directions begin to emerge, pointers toward a feminist
critical theory of religion.

Up to this point I have considered some of the most central preoccupations of critical theory. In the following chapters I will consider
further how these themes begin to surface in feminist religious thought
and what implications arise as the latter is examined in the light of
the former. Although strong resonances can be found between critical
theory and feminist religious thought, the treatment and appropriation
of themes of common interest by feminist writers also hold important
potential for revision of critical theory in accordance with feminist
goals. A feminist reconstruction of critical theory serves to realign

---

[71] Adorno, *Prisms*, 82.

critical theory more closely in accordance with its own emancipatory intent. At the same time some problems and limitations within feminist religious thought may be more adequately perceived and possibly remedied through a dialogical and dialectical encounter with critical theory.

While it would be impossible and pointless to attempt any form of theoretical synthesis or integration of feminist religious thought and critical theory, positioning them together as mutually enhancing constellations promises to illuminate both in ways conducive to a feminist critical theory of religion. What feminist religious thought and critical theory share is their commitment to utopia, that is, the strong belief in the possibility of a more humane future that will completely transform and negate the present. It is no accident that as critical theory articulates its hope for a different future, its language becomes explicitly religious, filled with intimations of the hope for a redeemed humanity. At the same time, as feminist religious thought sharpens its critique of Christian theological traditions and articulates possibilities for social and personal transformation, its language moves increasingly into the domain of critical theory.

Of further significance is the reluctance of both critical theory and feminist religious thought to follow through with their own insights. Thus critical theory pulls back from an explicit religious conclusion while feminists pull back from developing a thoroughly materialist religious theory by lapsing into standard theological discourse. In this respect feminist religious thought harbors its own contradictions that generate internal limitations. These limitations ultimately threaten to foreclose on feminist efforts, consciously or not, to negate, transcend, and preserve theology in a kind of Hegelian process of *Aufhebung*[72] or sublation that might reveal possible directions in a feminist critical theory of religion. If critical theory and feminist religious thought are brought together in a nonsynthetic way, however, the possibilities for mutual critical enhancement and illumination hopefully come into focus, with the effect that the limitations of both may begin to crumble.

---

[72] The noun *Aufhebung* derives from the verb *aufheben,* meaning "to pick up," "to preserve," "to dissolve," or "to cancel out." Hegel used the term to include all its meanings in order to describe the movement of *Geist,* which abolishes, cancels, preserves, and transcends epochs as it proceeds through history.

CHAPTER 4

Unreason and Revolution

Herbert Marcuse, Mary Daly, and Gynocentric Feminism

ANALYSIS OF DOMINATION MUST BE A CENTRAL CONCERN of any feminist critical theory if it aspires to be an adequate response to the subjugation of women. A comprehensive critique of domination is indispensable for feminism because the oppression of any social group occurs within a set of specific conditions that generate and support hierarchical structures of power. In the absence of hierarchy, there would be little possibility for the exercise of power over others. Presumably, social relations in a nonhierarchical world would be democratic and egalitarian, with notions of power transformed into the capacity of the community to empower its individual members, as opposed to exercising power over them. As women exist in social and historical contexts and systems of power, a feminist critique of the oppression of women must be, at its root, a critique of domination. Any attempt at a feminist rethinking of the dynamics of power and the hierarchical social relations that render women as its objects must ultimately account for domination in all its forms.

Feminist critical theory, then, seeks to comprehend the phenomenon of domination of which sexism is a part, along with domination's and sexism's directing roles in the development of Western civilization. In the absence of a thorough critique of domination, the dynamics of power that maintain women as the oppressed half of humanity cannot be adequately understood. As forms of domination reverberate throughout all dimensions of human experience, both internal and external, feminist critical theory must seek to penetrate and expose its hidden, invisible workings, which twist and distort our most private experience and which result in alienated relationships between people and with nature, and in distortions within the self.

Feminist critical theory also begins with the assumption that we have no standpoint outside of domination and alienation from which to theorize. We ourselves speak from within conditions of alienation already given to us, mediating not only our critical knowledge but our very mode of being in the world. If we accept this premise of a feminist critique, we must work with what is while struggling to transform it into what could be, given present conditions. If "what is" is understood as historically and culturally constituted, then this hope for transformation is rooted in concrete possibility rather than in metaphysics and ontology.

Resistance and Transformation

A COMPREHENSIVE FEMINIST CRITICAL THEORY OF DOMINA-
tion is, in part, an immanent critique of distortion, alienation, suffering, and injustice. Its explicit goal is not "the preservation of contemporary society, but . . . its transformation into the right kind of society."[1] What the "right kind of society" is, of course, ought not to be construed or prejudged because of the risk of imposing new regulatory strictures that require their own conformity to preconceived ideas. All efforts to theorize alternatives to "what is" can only repro-duce "what is" in a rearranged form, unless society and individuals are transformed sufficiently to make a real alternative future possible. Recall that negative critique is central to critical theory, finding its fullest, most sustained expression in Theodor Adorno's philosophy of negative dialectics. For Adorno, the true philosophical task was to expose this "untruth of identity," shifting philosophy's focus to reveal and sustain nonconceptuality, individuality, and particularity, which all previous philosophy had considered as transitory and insignificant.

---

[1] Max Horkheimer, *Critical Theory: Selected Essays*, trans. Matthew J. O'Con-nell et al. (New York: Continuum, 1972), 218.

Although differently cast than with Adorno, the theme of negativity is strongest in the work of Herbert Marcuse, for whom "the battle between negativity and positivity is the most consequential and decisive battle in the world."[2] For Marcuse, negativity reveals the hidden truth of things, dissolving and penetrating beneath their alienated, distorted surface to discover and release their inner authenticity. According to this view of negativity, every particularity contains within itself a contradiction. It is constituted by what it is and is not. Things exist in alienated form, and their inner truthfulness or authenticity is always in the process of breaking through its inadequate forms. For something to be what it authentically is, it must become what it is not. The process of negation of its given state of alienation leads toward the realization of its potentialities. All things must be grasped as transcending their appearance as "common sense," as "mere facticity," as containing the negation of their own negativity.

While Marcuse derived his concept of negativity from G. W. F. Hegel, he concentrated on the realization of potentiality within the historical realm of existence rather than some ultimate ontological sphere at the end of history. The progress of freedom out of unfreedom within history and society demands, in Marcuse's view, that thought, or reason, be understood as political, as "the shape of a theory which demonstrates negation as a political alternative implicit in the historical situation."[3]

Marcuse's version of critical theory stresses that historical negation takes place through political opposition, no matter how "fragmented, distorted, or hopeless"[4] social forms of opposition might appear at any given moment. Critical theory's role is to expose the unrealized possibilities contained within the social structure, "potentialities created by a gulf between prevailing human existence and human essence (the unfulfilled historically constituted abilities and capacities of human

---

[2] Richard J. Bernstein, "Negativity: Theme and Variations," *Praxis International* 1 (April 1981): 87–100.

[3] Herbert Marcuse, *Reason and Revolution: Hegel and the Rise of Social Theory* (Boston: Beacon Press, 1969), xiii.

[4] William Leiss, cited in David Held, *Introduction to Critical Theory* (Berkeley: Univ. of California Press, 1980), 224.

beings)."[5] Marcuse's stress on potentialities and the possibility of their realization was not shared by Max Horkheimer and Theodor Adorno, the focus of whose critical theory concentrated on reality in all its distortion and indigency. Only in a sustained negative critique might it be possible to intimate how things might appear otherwise. Unlike Marcuse, this is as far as Horkheimer and Adorno venture in thinking about alternative societies.

For Marcuse, reason, as "the power of negative thinking,"[6] is capable of generating its own self-negation; this is reason as domination, or instrumentality. At the same time, Marcuse allows for the possibility that reason contains the capacity for negating this negativity, since "reason alone, contains its own corrective."[7] The dialectical structure of reason allows for the possibility of freedom to emerge as an explosive shattering of the existent, since "unfreedom is so much at the core of things . . . the development of their internal contradictions leads necessarily to qualitative change: the explosion and catastrophe of the established state of affairs."[8] The history of reason in Western civilization in the form of domination could be overcome in a kind of apocalyptic negation that would unleash a new rationality of liberation and happiness that Marcuse came to associate with the "feminine."

Marcuse understood domination as assuming different forms in different historical periods. In advanced capitalist societies, domination "congeals into a system of objective administration"[9] that structures social institutions and systems of distribution in ways that appear to provide and preserve "the good life of the whole."[10] Maintaining the status quo thus becomes widely perceived as necessary and, with the vast increase of cheap consumer goods, even desirable. As near-total administration, domination becomes internalized within individuals,

---

[5] Ibid., 225.
[6] Marcuse, *Reason and Revolution*, vii.
[7] Ibid., xiii.
[8] Ibid., ix.
[9] Herbert Marcuse, *Eros and Civilization* (New York: Vintage Books, 1962), 89.
[10] Herbert Marcuse, *One-Dimensional Man: Studies in the Ideology of Advanced Industrial Society* (Boston: Beacon Press, 1968), 255.

resulting in the repression of "natural" human aspirations for freedom and happiness deep within the psyche. Drawing on and reinterpreting Freud's theory of instincts, Marcuse differentiated psychic repression as that which is necessary for the preservation of the achieved level of material conditions and "surplus repression," which functions to sustain social domination beyond the modifications of the instincts necessary for the continued life of the society.

Surplus repression functions in the service of domination *for its own sake,* and is so strongly entrenched throughout society that its complete negation can appear to be the "only truly revolutionary exigency"[11] open to humanity. Marcuse was well aware that the perception of domination as a unified totality was illusory and that the demand for its absolute dissolution could only produce an equally abstract, reified "revolutionary" negation incapable of changing "the Establishment." At this point I wish to distinguish "determinate negativity" from "reified" negativity, because both exist in an unresolved tension in Marcuse's work and at times weaken the emancipatory intent in his thought. Although Marcuse repeatedly insisted on the possibility of liberation as determinate negation of the existent, he also succumbed to a more reified, abstract, and finally metaphysical notion of negativity. This notion becomes most apparent when he explicitly associates it with a particular agent—woman. Marcuse's reified concept of woman as an abstract category or principle occupies an important place in his critical theory, constituting an irrational moment that tends to weaken both the critical nature and emancipatory potential of his social philosophy. Like critical theory in general, Marcuse failed at crucial points to see women as fully human, as active agents of history.

At the same time, Marcuse advances the theme of the transformative power of "the feminine" as part of a deeper, more significant insight that understands the necessity of human self-transformation as a nonnegotiable prerequisite for a liberated human future. For Marcuse, liberation includes social transformation as well as transformations in the psychic and emotional "infrastructure"[12] of human beings. The

---

[11] Ibid.
[12] Herbert Marcuse, *An Essay on Liberation* (Boston: Beacon Press, 1969), 4.

possibility of a free society depends on the formation of "a new sensibility [as] the medium in which social change becomes an individual need, the mediation between the political practice of 'changing the world' and the drive for personal liberation."[13]

To use an analogy drawn from Christianity, Marcuse is calling for the conversion of human beings from their present alienated state where their capacities for pleasure, happiness, and joy have been severely curtailed and repressed by the demands of a capitalist, techno-industrial society. Not religious conversion but psychoanalysis offers one possibility whereby individuals might consciously reclaim their desires for joyful life by relativizing and rethinking the role of commodity acquisition in their lives. For Marcuse, the need for commodities will give way to more authentic and humane needs for a more pleasurable and spontaneous way of life; this change in turn will require social and institutional changes that are more supportive of and conducive to transformations in the instinctual lives of human beings and their perceived needs.

Unlike Horkheimer and Adorno, Marcuse still believed in the possibility that such comprehensive transformation could be brought about through the conscious political actions of particular historical agents. Marcuse directs his critical theory to concrete subjects; this tends to distinguish him from his Frankfurt colleagues, who long ago abandoned any hope in the revolutionary potential of the industrial working class or of any other social group. Marcuse addresses his critical theory to those diverse, often isolated "militant minorities"[14] rather than to a united mass movement inasmuch as the possibilities and perhaps even desirability for constructing such a movement had long since passed away. Rather, Marcuse looked to scattered, politically committed groups whose varied practices of political resistance on a wide variety of fronts and challenges to the Establishment represent what he describes as the "Great Refusal to accept the rules of a game in which the dice are loaded."[15] Such militant groups exist in the

---

[13] Herbert Marcuse, *Counterrevolution and Revolt* (Boston: Beacon Press, 1972), 59.
[14] Marcuse, *Essay on Liberation*, 52.
[15] Marcuse, *Reason and Revolution*, x.

interstices and cracks within the social structure, where they are constantly seeking out possibilities to resist the forces of domination that push the status quo deeper and deeper into the most private recesses of human experience.

In a later essay, Marcuse began to associate the politics of resistance and potential transformation with a single movement, to which he referred as "socialist feminism." In so doing, he reduced feminism to a form of reified negativity that is the inevitable result of locating the role of revolutionary agency in any particular group or individual. Inevitably, Marcuse conceptualizes a feminist movement that would be the active vehicle for the historical actualization of feminine values and principles. In an exercise of sweeping identity logic, Marcuse articulates his hope in the promise of a socialist feminism that will become the "gravedigger" of "patricentric-acquisitive" societies; women dissolve into the universal concept of a "female counterforce," the negative power of historical transformation and ultimate salvation of humanity.

Marcuse visualizes this female counterforce in the image of French artist Eugène Delacroix's "Liberty," the bare-breasted woman who leads the people on the barricades, rifle in hand, promising to abolish unfreedom and inauthenticity through violent struggle.[16] Marcuse's imaging of "woman" in this way is indicative of a progressive reification in his thought that conceptualizes woman as an abstraction who is "naturally" linked with Eros, long repressed in Western civilization by the hegemony of distorted reason that he associates with patriarchal domination and destructive productivity. Unable to conceptualize concrete women in all their cultural, linguistic, class, or ethnic diversity as individuals who struggle against forms of domination specific to their historical location, Marcuse rather speculates on the notion of a Female-Eros that represents the power of negativity against the continued mastery of Male-Thanatos. This female counterforce promises to unleash the ascendancy of a new rationality and the emergence of a new sensibility with corresponding values and ethics of receptivity, peace, and justice that may in turn generate qualitatively new interpersonal relationships and social structures. There is something of an

---

[16] Marcuse, *Counterrevolution and Revolt*, 78.

eschatological dimension to this vision of liberation that undermines the subversive element of determinate negation by giving way to a more reified and abstract negativity that is both socially and politically ineffective.

However Marcuse images woman at any point in his work, she is always symbolic of that quasi-apocalyptic, negative power that shatters "mere factuality," breaking open the unalienated, transcendent potentialities locked within present conditions. At the same time, Marcuse expresses a lingering ambivalence concerning possibilities of transformation that causes him to vacillate between determinate negation, on the one hand, and reified negation, on the other. By reified negation I refer to Marcuse's tendency to locate the revolutionary possibilities for transformation of society and human individuals within an identifiable social group. The individual humanity of persons thus collapses into the group itself, which becomes hypostatized into a homogeneous force or instrument of transformation.

Marcuse was well aware that although late capitalist societies have attained a level of technological achievement that could be mobilized in the service of building a more comfortable, materially secure world for most human beings, such possibilities might never come to fruition. He expresses this ambiguity in the contradictory thesis that, "Advanced industrial society is capable of containing qualitative change for the foreseeable future," and that "Forces and tendencies exist which may break this containment and explode the society."[17] The inner contradiction of domination and liberation that is structurally embedded within contemporary capitalist societies cannot be resolved, however, by the activities of a single movement. In part this is because movements tend to operate along the lines of identity thinking, where all members are compelled to relinquish their own capacities for independent, critical thought and conform with the goals and values of the movement. When Marcuse postulates a particular vehicle whereby the explosive forces of transformation may be released in history through the redemptive power of an abstract feminine principle, he encourages this process whether intentionally or not. Furthermore, as

---

[17] Marcuse, *One-Dimensional Man*, xv.

"militant minorities" become absorbed into mass movements, determinate negation as a historical and political process is in danger of dissolving into reified negation, that is, negation of the concrete by the abstract.

Perhaps this dimension of Marcuse's thought represents the influence of Hegel, an influence that was far more profound in Marcuse than in Horkheimer and especially Adorno. Recall that Adorno's negative dialectics was aimed at refuting Hegelian idealism and at breaking the hold of the abstract over the particular. Marcuse exhibits a theoretical tendency to promote the universal at the expense of the particular; in part this accounts for his idealization of femininity into a reified principle with the power to drive and shape historical change. When this happens, theory totters on the brink of the ideology of messianism, which can only result in a cult form of political action that hypostatizes praxis and strengthens domination.

The theoretical ground for the reification of woman as feminine negativity was already laid in *Eros and Civilization,* Marcuse's philosophical reconstruction of Freud's theory of instincts. In Marcuse's historical account of the conflictual drama between Eros and Thanatos, the distortions each undergoes as a result of psychic repression are not irreversible, nor are they intrinsic to the process of repression itself. They are rather historically and culturally determined, and thus open to change. In the course of civilization, Eros and Thanatos split into mutually antagonistic forces, which resulted in the ascendancy of patriarchal Reason over repressed Eros. In advanced capitalist societies, the rule of Thanatos takes the form of the Performance Principle, which is the guarantor of alienated labor in class society.

Prior to their fragmentation, Eros and Thanatos existed in an immediate, natural union in the mother, in whom the son (Marcuse does not consider the daughter's role) experienced "Nirvana before birth," the "integral peace" of complete gratification and the absence of all need, desire, and want. This primal memory of security and peace experienced in the encounter with the Woman-as-Mother represents an alternative rationality to the domineering rationality associated with the father. As the embodied, "libidinal energy" of Eros,[18]

---

[18] Herbert Marcuse, "Marxism and Feminism," *Women's Studies* 2 (1974): 279–88.

the Woman-as-Mother is identified with an alternative, "pre-genital," "libidinal morality"[19] in which reason and sensuousness are reconciled, as was their original state prior to their violent separation that eventually resulted in the rule of the Male-Performance Principle.

Marcuse reinterprets the Freudian account of the Oedipal drama as the son's "sexual craving" for the mother not simply *qua* mother, but for the mother "*qua* woman—female principle of gratification."[20] According to this reading, the incest taboo is erected by the father to ensure against the son's achieving the total gratification he once experienced in the womb. If satisfied, the son's sexual craving for the Woman-as-Mother "threatens the psychical basis of civilization,"[21] the preservation of which depends on the continued hegemony of the Performance Principle and thus the sustained repression of desire. Marcuse's account of the history of the instincts is the story of two realities, of two rationalities structured around the polarities of domination (Performance Principle) and freedom (Pleasure Principle). The "return of the repressed" takes place through the release of critical remembrance, the mover of Eros: "Remembrance retrieves the *temps perdu,* which was the time of gratification and fulfillment."[22] Here, one cannot help but recall Georg Lukács's critique of Hegel's philosophy as "driven inexorably into the arms of mythology,"[23] which accurately describes this aspect of Marcuse's thought.

In his later work, Marcuse considerably modifies the Woman-as-Mother concept, finally realizing that such an identification is itself repressive in that it translates "biological fact into an ethical and cultural value and thus . . . [it] supports and justifies social repression."[24] Yet, instead of following through on his own logic and repudiating the Woman-as-Mother paradigm altogether, Marcuse rather intensifies the reification of woman, this time no longer as mother, but as a revolutionary "female principle" whose "natural" characteristics promise

---

[19] Marcuse, *Eros and Civilization,* 208.
[20] Ibid., 247.
[21] Ibid.
[22] Ibid., 213.
[23] Georg Lukacs, *History and Class Consciousness* (London: Merlin Press, 1971), 146–47.
[24] Marcuse, *Counterrevolution and Revolt,* 75.

social and individual liberation through the "femalization" of the male, a necessary precondition of a future socialist society.[25] The values Marcuse associates with the "natural" feminine are depressingly familiar—passivity, receptivity, care—all the culturally based feminine attributes that have become inscribed in the category of femaleness and as "natural" to women's being. "The faculty of being 'receptive,' 'passive,' is a precondition of freedom: it is the ability to see things in their own right, to experience the joy enclosed in them, the erotic energy of nature—an energy which is there to be liberated."[26]

Marcuse does not give sufficient critical attention to the unfortunate history of women's oppression that resulted from the imposition of feminine attributes on women as a means of regulating their lives. Indeed he cannot do so because of his idealization of women. At times he celebrates "feminine" characteristics as if they possess a life of their own that resides in some location beyond historical and political reality. Interestingly, the qualities of receptivity and passivity are not exclusively feminine, but are aesthetic qualities as well. Art intimates possibilities of an alternate reason and sensibility that is committed to "the reconstruction of society and nature under the principle of increasing the human potential for happiness."[27] The radical potential of art, with its promise for the transformation of the inward, subjective life of individuals, allows individuals to experience new needs for joy and happiness not to be found in the realm of exchange relationships, and coincides with the radical potential of the feminine. Marcuse treats art and the feminine in almost identical fashion as negative counterforces to both the status quo and the continued hegemony of the [male] Performance Principle. According to Marcuse, the beauty of woman and art, along with the happiness and reconciliation they promise in a future liberated society, is "fatal in the work-world of civilization."[28]

Marcuse describes the "radical qualities of art" as

> grounded precisely in the dimensions where art *transcends* its social determination and emancipates itself from the given universe of discourse and behavior while preserving its overwhelming

---

[25] Ibid.
[26] Ibid., 74.
[27] Herbert Marcuse, *The Aesthetic Dimension* (Boston: Beacon Press, 1978), 56.
[28] Marcuse, *Eros and Civilization*, 146.

presence. . . . The world formed by art is recognized as a reality which is suppressed and distorted in the given reality. This experience culminates in extreme situations . . . which explode the given reality in the name of a truth normally denied or even unheard. The inner logic of the work of art terminates in the emergence of another reason, another sensibility, which defy the rationality and sensibility incorporated in the dominant social institutions.[29]

Art unleashes the power of the imagination to glimpse the possibility of a new world, with a new social morality and new institutions of freedom within a "culture of receptivity," a "sensuous culture."[30] Here Eros finds expression in both the aesthetic and the feminine, combined in a utopian vision of a liberated society where beauty, pleasure, joy, and "nonrepressive," "desublimated" sexuality (no longer trapped within genitality as a form of sexuality most suited to alienated labor) mediate all human relations, including work. In a direct reversal of Sigmund Freud, Marcuse sees "polymorphous" sexuality as authentic to liberated human beings, the negation of the alienated sexuality of genital fixation that is co-opted in the service of maintaining exploited labor, oppressive bureaucracy, and technocratic specialization.

Woman and art meet in Eros, insofar as both partake in "the Beautiful," which is linked to the Pleasure Principle.[31] An examination of Marcuse's association of art, women, beauty, and pleasure suggests the possibility that underlying these connections is the concept of a deeper unifying link between woman and nature that is the root of the other associations. This idea is plausible insofar as Marcuse, like Horkheimer and Adorno, sees the possibility for a reconciliation with nature as occurring in art. Unlike them, however, Marcuse interconnects art, nature, sensuousness, and the feminine. His work includes the further suggestion that woman and nature are perhaps more intricately connected than are males and nature; he understands this connection as a virtue concerning women.

This rather schematic paradigm of the new society displaces—but does not entirely negate—the struggle for historical transformation

---

[29] Marcuse, *The Aesthetic Dimension*, 6–7.
[30] Marcuse, *An Essay on Liberation*, 89–90.
[31] Ibid., 62–63.

from the actions of human beings to a mythic world of higher forces locked in an epic struggle for control over the universe. As far as feminism is concerned, it is not living, suffering women who work for their liberation, but their surrogate, the revolutionary "female principle," the vehicle of the ascending Eros. Marcuse also acknowledges the struggle for social equality as an important goal in the women's movement, although he emphasizes the insufficiency of gaining equality alone. He urges that women seek a greater, more authentic freedom "beyond equality" on the grounds that "equality is not yet freedom . . . beyond equality, liberation subverts the established hierarchy of needs. . . . And this, in my view, is the radical potential of *feminist socialism*."[32]

Marcuse's insistence on going "beyond equality" is both understandable and reasonable, for the obvious reason that equality within alienation results in another form of alienation rather than freedom from it. This view was shared by Horkheimer and Adorno, who had no illusions that freedom is to be found in the world as it is. While they acknowledged the oppressed condition of women in their enforced historical confinement to the domestic sphere, they believed that in leaving the family for the world of paid work and participation in public affairs, women merely exchanged one form of alienation for a worse one. Similarly, many feminists are too well aware that the full liberation of women is to be found not in mere equality, but in the complete transformation of all aspects of human existence, both individual and social.

At the same time, equality is a necessary and unavoidable stage in the process of women's liberation, as Karl Marx fully recognized. Yet Marcuse is willing to concede that fuller equality between men and women in all aspects of life will require deeper changes in social structures, changes that will in turn effect the transformation of human relationships and inner psychic nature. A "transvaluation of values," then, cannot take place without changes in the existing social and political structures as well. In the words of the anarchist and proto-feminist activist and theorist Emma Goldman, "All existing systems of political power are absurd, and are completely inadequate to meet

---

[32] Marcuse, "Marxism and Feminism," 285–86.

the pressing issues of life."[33] While Marcuse recognized this, his enthusiasm for the "radical potential" of feminist socialism focuses less on its potential for concrete, political transformation because he insists on formulating it in terms of an ontological, metaphysical force.

Marcuse, in his celebration of traditional feminine attributes and their power to negate their masculine counterpart (understood as aggression, violence, competitiveness, and brutal ambition), and in his claim that feminine-specific characteristics are rooted in the natural difference[34] between women and men, contradicts the earlier position wherein he rejected the equation of "biological fact" with "ethical and cultural value." With this apparent reversal of his previous view, Marcuse leans toward a justification of a politics of biology that reifies gender difference into hypostatized categories in which no historical woman could possibly recognize herself or find political solutions adequate to address her situation.

Marcuse's grounding of the ethical values of receptivity and nonviolence in the female, who " 'embodies' them in a *literal* sense"[35] drives women back to the state of natural immediacy that is little more than a restatement of the Hegelian position regarding women.[36] At such points, Marcuse forgets his Marxian roots. For Marx, and for Marcuse, part of being human involves the necessary freedom from enslavement by unconscious natural forces. In the dialectic of history and nature, human beings surpass the condition of struggle for mere survival, which is a necessary part of the development of full human potentialities. Yet Marcuse could not quite include women in this process because of his inability to see them as historical agents; thus he participates in the Hegelian view of women and their association with the realm of nature. Although Marcuse recognizes that women's confinement to family and home was an important factor in their historical oppression, along with Horkheimer and Adorno he holds

---

[33] Emma Goldman, *Anarchism and Other Essays* (New York: Dover Publications, 1969), 199.

[34] Marcuse, *Counterrevolution and Revolt*, 77.

[35] Ibid.; emphasis added.

[36] G. W. F. Hegel, *Hegel's Philosophy of Right*, trans. T. M. Knox (Oxford, England: Clarendon Press, 1949), 114, pars. 165 and 166.

that women's isolation from civil society and paid work also functioned as a protection from the alienating effects of the Performance Principle, which was more destructive to the male.[37]

Mary Daly's Elemental Females

MARCUSE'S THESIS CONCERNING "NATURAL" FEMALE SPECI-ficity as an adequate basis for political praxis anticipates a theoretical expression in contemporary feminism that can be described most accurately as *gynocentrism*.[38] Although gynocentric feminism is differently nuanced in the work of various feminist authors, it can be described according to certain common features. In part, gynocentric feminism accounts for women's oppression in terms of the historical denial and exclusion of values and ways of thinking and relating that are traditionally defined as feminine. More significantly, gynocentric feminism presumes the existence of an ontological, metaphysical "stable subject of feminism"[39] who exists behind the sociocultural category of gender. The premise of an abstract, stable subject, woman, that grounds the characteristics and activities of individual women also provides the basis for the formulation of an equally abstract notion of "universal patriarchy"[40] that is the source and sustainer of women's oppression.

The notion of woman as the stable subject of feminine gender constructions functions as an underlying unity of all cultural, racial, class, and linguistic difference between women and in turn is seen as providing a basis for solidarity among women by virtue of their universal commonality. This position is closely related to Marcuse's. Further, the presumption of a stable subject encourages the designation

---

[37] Ibid.

[38] For a clear, concise, and fairly accurate description of gynocentrism, along with examples of feminist writers who are identified with it, see Iris Marion Young, "Humanism, Gynocentrism and Feminist Politics," *Women's Studies International Forum* 8, no. 3 (1985): 173–83.

[39] See Judith Butler, *Gender Trouble: Feminism and the Subversion of Identity* (New York: Routledge, 1990), for an interesting critique of the "stable subject" of feminism.

[40] Ibid., 3.

of a set of characteristics or attributes that are sex-specific, and "natural," which can be used to provide the foundation of a corresponding female-centered ethics. According to this theory, patriarchal societies value and promote male-specific qualities such as aggressiveness, assertiveness, and control at the expense of female-associated values, which are their potential negation and must therefore be subjected to a sustained repression and repudiation.

One of the most important theorists of contemporary gynocentric feminism is Mary Daly. The influence of her thought, especially in her later work, extends beyond the field of feminist religious thought.[41] Hers was not always a gynocentric feminist approach, however. Daly's first book, *The Church and the Second Sex* (1968), is a feminist critique of the treatment of women in the Catholic theological and ecclesiastical tradition. The tone of this book is strongly marked by the liberal spirit of the Second Vatican Council, which Daly briefly attended. In this work, Daly seeks to reclaim and articulate the emancipatory elements in Christianity that could be appropriated as "sources of further development toward a more personalist conception of the man-woman relationship on all levels."[42] In this respect, she is close to the feminist perspectives of theologians such as Rosemary Radford Ruether and Elisabeth Schüssler Fiorenza, although *The Church and the Second Sex* predates their major feminist work. In a spirit that anticipates the thinking of Ruether, Daly envisions a "real partnership" between men and women, in which they would struggle and work together in order to "at last see each other's faces, and in so doing, come to know themselves. . . . Men and women, using their best talents, forgetful of self and intent upon the work, will with God's help mount together toward a higher order of consciousness and being, in which the alienating projections will have been defeated and wholeness, psychic integrity, achieved."[43]

---

[41] See Bonnie Mann, "Gyn/Ecology in the Lives of Women in the Real World," "Appendix to New Intergalactic Introduction [sic]," in Mary Daly, *Gyn/Ecology: The Metaethics of Radical Feminism* (Boston: Beacon Press, 1990), xxxiv–xliii.

[42] Mary Daly, *The Church and the Second Sex* (New York: Harper Colophon Books, 1975 [1968]), 73; revised ed., Boston: Beacon Press, 1985.

[43] Ibid., 79; 223.

In her next book, *Beyond God the Father,* Daly's religious vision began to embrace a Tillichian "theism above theism" or "ground of being"[44] in a supersession of God reformulated as the "Verb of Verbs, Be-ing,"[45] including displacement of Jesus with the Goddess. Yet Daly still expressed the hope of human beings "becoming . . . androgynous human persons."[46] In her later works, she repudiates her view of androgyny as an adequate model of human wholeness, on the grounds that it conveys "something like the images of Ronald and Nancy Reagan scotch-taped together."[47] Even at the stage of *Beyond God the Father* her feminist critique and rejection of Christianity as one of the sources of the oppression of women had not yet taken the completely gynocentric turn that was to surface in *Gyn/Ecology* and *Pure Lust.* The perspective in these later works, although anticipated in the previous books, marks an extreme shift in Daly's thinking in her move toward an apparently militant gynocentric philosophy of women's liberation.

The feminist critical philosophy advanced in *Gyn/Ecology* and *Pure Lust* has its roots in the post-Enlightenment intellectual traditions of the West. It is perhaps better understood if read in the key of a Marcusean-Hegelian theme of being, negativity, and reconciliation. Daly's treatment of these themes bears a strong Hegelian influence (intended or not) that is largely modified by a Marcusean reading of Hegel. The kind of identification Marcuse made between negativity and the "feminine principle," or Eros, emerges as well in highly metaphoric fashion in Daly's later work. Daly is certainly familiar with Marcuse and refers to him several times in *Beyond God the Father* and *Pure Lust.* The similarities between Marcuse and Daly are deeper than scattered citations might indicate. This is not to argue, however, that Marcuse or Hegel exerts a direct influence on Daly's thought that shows her

---

[44] Mary Daly, *Outercourse: The Be-Dazzling Voyage* (New York: Harper-SanFransisco, 1992), 159.

[45] Mary Daly, *Websters' First New Intergalactic Wickedary of the English Language* (London: The Women's Press Ltd., 1988), 64.

[46] Mary Daly, *Beyond God the Father: Toward a Philosophy of Women's Liberation* (Boston: Beacon Press, 1973), 15.

[47] Mary Daly, *Pure Lust: Elemental Feminist Philosophy* (Boston: Beacon Press, 1984), 341. See also her autobiography, *Outercourse,* 160.

work to be a straight reconstruction of their philosophy. Rather, in situating or constellating Daly in relation to Marcuse and Hegel, it becomes possible to cast a particularly illuminating interpretive light on her thinking that brings out the deeper implications of some of her most important ideas.

In Hegel's philosophy, history is presented as a dialectical unfolding through which *Geist* or Spirit realizes itself in specific historical epochs and sociocultural forms before negating and transcending those forms to move onto the next stage of its movement. The teleological point of this dynamic movement or self-diremption of the universal *Geist* into external forms of self-alienation is the complete reconciliation of *Geist* with itself. Adorno criticized the Hegelian dialectic on the grounds that the relentless, inexorable drive of the universal toward self-realization occurs always at the expense of particularity. In Daly's thought, this Hegelian dialectic becomes reconstructed and extensively modified along feminist, exclusivist lines. For Daly, Spirit is the Background of authentic female Being, toward which specific women move in a dynamic process of casting off the alienated forms of femininity constructed and imposed by patriarchy, forms with which women are compelled to conform. Daly's idealist philosophical vision postulates a world of alienation against which women struggle in order to realize their inner psychic and spiritual creativity and integrity, which she describes as a journey or quest toward "Elemental participation in Being. Our passion is for . . . recalling original wholeness."[48]

This loosely constructed Hegelian reformulation of the dialectic of the phenomenological and the ontological is heavily laced with Tillichian and Thomistic resonances, where an authentic "ground of Being" forms the backdrop of the alienated phenomenological and existential world of daily existence. Women gain intimations of the reality of this Background world in recollective acts of memory, which aid them on their journey from alienation to the metaphysical ground of authentic Being. As an integral part of this journey, and as the condition of the possibility of "biophilic participation in Be-ing," women must negate or transcend the "forces of necrophilic negation"

───────────────

[48] Daly, *Pure Lust*, ix.

that make up the patriarchal world of the Foreground, "the perverted paradigm and source" of all social evil.[49]

Against the negative force of "Phallic lust" that spawns pseudo/sado-societies whose aim is to contain and control women's striving for the abundance of Be-ing, Daly counterposes Elemental Female Lust, the negation of phallic negation, an "intense longing/craving for the cosmic concrescence that is creation."[50] Women who consciously embark on this quest are blazing pathways to a "Background/homeland" from which they have been cut off but which they dimly remember. In overcoming the alienation of forgetting the source and end of their Elemental Be-ing, women move or "race" toward an ontological state of reconciliation, where female inner essence finally comes into unity with its original integrity, or Self. In achieving this ultimate reconciliation, women negate those forces that negated their potentialities, thus overcoming the alienated state of life in the Foreground in order to come into their "truth," finding groundedness and oneness in "Metabeing."[51] The dialectic between Spirit and history is reconceived by Daly as the dialectic between Elemental, Cosmic Female Being and the struggles of women to break through the patriarchal alienation that permeates and structures the existential realm. She is quite clear that this dialectic does not include males.

Daly's discussion of the journey to the Background/homeland that leads away from the alienated Foreground to participation in Metabeing to some extent parallels Hegel's idea of the movement of Absolute Spirit toward unity with itself, after having overcome and negated all previous forms of alienation. Hegel describes this movement, or "Becoming of Spirit," as a "coming-to-be of the whole." He writes, "It is in itself the movement which is cognition—the transforming of that *in-itself* into that which is *for itself,* of Substance into Subject, of the object of *consciousness* into an object of *self-consciousness*

---

[49] Ibid., xi, xii.
[50] Ibid., 1, 3. Since Daly uses such language over and over throughout this book, I will not note each reference when it is a matter of a phrase or term denoting either female power or male perversity.
[51] Ibid., 61.

. . . or into the *Notion*."[52] *Geist,* or Being, for Hegel, is Subject, whose "negativity" unfolds in *Geist's* "own restless process of superseding itself."[53] As all being is movement for Hegel, determinate being is not a separate metaphysical entity but part of the process through which all particular beings unfold into what they really are. Being-itself is the ground or substratum of all particular beings. According to Marcuse's reading of Hegel, "From this point, it was comparatively easy to take this most universal being as 'the essence of all being,' 'divine substance,' 'the most real,' and thus to combine ontology with theology. This tradition is operative in Hegel's *Logic*."[54]

This tradition is operative in Daly's logic as well, in her repeated claim to women's inherent capacity for biophilic participation in "Being" that occurs in the form of a restless negativity through and beyond progressive forms of alienation (both internal and external) that will culminate in the reconciliation of existence and Notion, of determinate female being and a cosmic, feminized "Be-ing." Daly's dialectic of the "male-centered and monodimensional" world of alienation, or "foreground,"[55] must be negated, overcome, and superseded in the process of women's movement to the Background, the state of complete reconciliation of women's being with Elemental Be-ing. As Hegelian philosophy posits a universal structure of all being, so does Daly, but whereas with Hegel all forms of particularity will be reconciled into Absolute Spirit, for Daly female particularity attains an analogous ontological reconciliation through the negation and exclusion of male particularity in all its manifestations. In order to come into their ontological and existential truth in the fulfillment of their inner potentialities, women must exorcise the false male-identified characteristics within, such as "male approval desire (MAD)," as well as aspirations toward "femininity," a "man-made construct" and "quintessentially" male attribute.[56]

---

[52] G. W. F. Hegel, *Hegel's Phenomenology of Spirit*, trans. A. V. Miller (Oxford, England: Oxford Univ. Press, 1977), 492, 487, 488.

[53] Ibid., 491.

[54] Marcuse, *Reason and Revolution*, 40.

[55] Daly, *Wickedary*, 76.

[56] Daly, *Gyn/Ecology*, 72, 68, 69.

Daly's uncompromising analysis of atrocities enacted against women in history, such as Chinese foot-binding practices, the Indian rite of suttee or widow-burning, the horrors of the gynecological profession, and her somewhat inflated account of the burning of "hundreds of thousands—probably millions—of women"[57] in the European witch-hunts, is an attempt to demonstrate beyond all doubt the gynocidal intent of patriarchy. The murderous drive of patriarchal societies is directed at destroying the female power or "divine spark"[58] that resides in women and is reflected in the divine cosmic power of the Goddess. The concept of negativity functions in Daly's work much as it does in Marcuse and Hegel, as a means for uncovering the latent truth implicit in forms of determinate being that could then be released and actualized. With Daly this represents a movement of women to wholeness and authenticity that is contingent on the negation of the male both within the female self and in external phallicist social forms, described by Daly in terms such as "phallocracy," "cockocracy," "boreocracy," "sadosociety," "Vapor State," "jockdom," "Daddydom," and so on. Daly's conceptualization of reconciliation departs from Marcuse and Hegel in the significant respect that it is not inclusive of all humanity inasmuch as all authentic being, including Be-ing,[59] is identified exclusively with the female element.

Spinning New Reifications

DESPITE THE FLAMBOYANT AND INTENSELY METAPHORIC language Daly uses in her later work, her underlying philosophical theory is steeped in the Western intellectual tradition in which she was formed. In like fashion with Hegel and those elements of critical theory that address the woman question, Daly also reproduces and sustains

---

[57] Ibid., 208.

[58] Ibid., 315.

[59] Daly writes, "On some level we have known with profound certainty that this has not always been 'a man's world,' and that reality in the deep sense— Elemental Be-ing—has never been such. For the man's world, patriarchy, is the Foreground." *Pure Lust*, 138. Daly is referring to the theories of matriarchy put forward by writers such as Elizabeth Gould Davis and Matilda Joslyn Gage.

reified, idealized concepts of "woman" that arise out of an identity logic that marks most of this philosophical tradition. The core structure of her feminist philosophy conceptualizes an authentic female Being to which all women ultimately correspond, but from which they have become alienated through the dominating and repressive practices of patriarchy. For Daly, the Goddess represents "the deep Source of creative integrity in women,"[60] which they may yet again uncover within themselves through recollection and the right form of consciousness. The Goddess symbolizes an ontological, metaphysical female identity that provides a unifying foundation or ground of the likeness of all women. Although Daly acknowledges differences between women, these differences are rooted in a deeper, "authentic likeness" that "Lesbians/Spinsters" share.[61]

She reinforces this philosophical view with historical claims about the existence of a universal matriarchal world that existed in prehistory, wherein Goddess religion prevailed prior to patriarchy. The origins of humanity were clearly gynocentric, with egalitarian and nonauthoritarian social structures; primary worship centered around a female deity. Although patriarchy has attempted to eradicate the Goddess in various forms of Goddess murder, She nonetheless lives on in a variety of manifestations yet is one cosmic substance.[62] Goddess murder occurs whenever the "divine life and creative integrity" of women are destroyed.[63] Daly formulates a correspondence between the divine feminine and an interior, authentic female nature that is contained in individual women. Thus with Daly, not women but "woman" functions as the underlying abstract subject or ontological principle to which individual women must correspond if they are to realize their Elemental Selves.

This is straight identity theorizing where unalienated, almost "pure" female-identified Being emerges as the standard or measure against which alienation on the particular level of concrete existence is defined. Her somewhat uncharitable discussion of the "painted

---

[60] Ibid., 111.
[61] Ibid., 382.
[62] Ibid., 90.
[63] Ibid., 130.

bird,"[64] that cosmeticized token and totally unreal agent of patriarchy whose purpose is to undermine natural, authentic women, indicates a dubious politics that separates the real women from the "fembots" and "totalled women" who participate in maintaining their own servitude.[65] According to Daly, "the painted bird functions in the anti-process of double-crossing her sisters, polluting them with poisonous paint."[66] Such women are cut off from their inner essence, an essence that can only be realized in the negative process of dissolving the patriarchy within. The painted birds of patriarchal distortion do not fit within Daly's identitary theory and have nothing to do with the "correspondence between the minds of Musing women and the intelligible structures of reality." These enemies of feminism and real womanhood are excluded from the "process of Realizing Elemental ontological reason" that can actualize the "natural, elemental relation between women's minds and the structures of our own reality."[67] In traditional theological terminology, it might be said that such women are damned, alienated from salvation, steeped in the sinfulness of collaborating with patriarchal evil.

The reality to which Daly refers is reminiscent of a similar kind of reality conceptualized by Marcuse, formulated as the hidden, latent truth of all things contained within the external forms of alienation from which they strive for release. She celebrates Elemental female capacity "to receive inspiration, truth from the elements of the natural world, the Wild, to which our Wild reason corresponds."[68] She refers to "Metamorphosing women" who are committed to the "consciously willed and continual affirmation of Ongoing Life that is Pure Lust."[69] For Daly, women's yearning "for experiencing our ontological connectedness with all that is Elemental implies a longing to mend, to

---

[64] For a different critical perspective on the "painted bird" as metaphor in *Gyn/Ecology*, see Ann-Janine Morey-Gaines, "Metaphor and Radical Feminism: Some Cautionary Comments on Mary Daly's *Gyn/Ecology*," *Soundings* 65 (Fall 1982), 347–49.

[65] Daly, *Wickedary*, 198, 232.

[66] Ibid., 334.

[67] Daly, *Pure Lust*, 163, 165.

[68] Ibid.

[69] Ibid., 347, 352.

weave together the Elemental realities that have been severed from consciousness."[70]

Daly's metaphoric descriptions of Elemental female being that signifies "ontological connectedness," or "gynergy," parallels Marcuse's concept of female-identified Eros, discussed above, although with greater intensity. As we have seen, Marcuse associates Eros with creativity and life forces, describing it as "the builder of culture."[71] We have also seen that Marcuse counterpoints Eros with the Performance Principle, identified with male-specific attributes that must be negated and transcended if society and individuals are to come into their own freedom and truth. Daly expresses a similar dualism in her dichotomy of Pure Lust and "Pure Thrust," the latter understood as "phallicism," or "phallocracy," "the basic structure underlying the various forms of oppression,"[72] in which all forms of domination are rooted. Daly cautions women not to forget that "racial and ethnic oppression, like the sexual oppression which is the primary and universal model of . . . victimization, is a male invention."[73]

Here we see a serious difficulty in Daly's thought, which claims reconciliation and participation in the flow of Being as its goal but which at the same time is rooted in the antagonistic dichotomy of woman against man that is both ontological and existential. This is a significant reversal of her earlier position of partnership and androgyny. For Daly, men have no place in the cosmic flow of creative Being; rather they represent its evil antithesis that seeks to destroy the female-identified life force. Women have an opportunity to overcome the alienations of existence imposed on them by patriarchal domination. For men, there is no redemption.

Daly directly acknowledges Marcuse's influence on her thought[74] and refers to his "useful concept of *repressive desublimation*,"[75] which she already found useful in *Beyond God the Father*. There Daly agrees,

[70] Ibid., 354.
[71] Marcuse, *Eros and Civilization*, 76.
[72] Daly, *Pure Lust*, 320.
[73] Ibid., 381.
[74] Daly, *Outercourse*, 157.
[75] Ibid., 252.

for example, with Marcuse's insight that a "relaxed sexual morality within the firmly entrenched system of monopolistic controls itself serves the system. The negation is co-ordinated with 'the positive.' "[76] Following Marcuse's line of thinking, Daly cautions women that lesbian sexuality under the oppressive conditions of patriarchy is not in itself any kind of authentic freedom, but must combine with a more profound expansion of "gynergizing connections between women" that has the power to negate the patriarchal status quo. Applying Marcuse's concept of "repressive desublimation" to lesbianism, she writes, " 'Liberated' women who are merely 'gay' remain bound libidinally to the institutionalized fathers. But if violation of the Total Taboo encompasses and transcends the sexual sphere and leads to 'refusal and rebellion' that is holistic and Elemental, guilt is indeed transferred to the fathers, and women can Touch and Move."[77] A female-oriented, lesbian sexuality contains an alternative set of values and demands that insists on a much deeper transformation of life than an alternative sexuality could foster on its own.

Daly also cites Marcuse's critique of Erich Fromm in *Eros and Civilization,* in which he objects to Fromm's articulated " 'goal of therapy' " as the " 'optimal development of a person's potentialities and the realization of his individuality.' " For Marcuse, this goal is unrealistic insofar as the "very structure" of the "established civilization" denies it.[78] For Daly, "Radical feminism, insofar as it is true to itself, is the Denial of this denial."[79]

Daly's main criticism of Marcuse is that he fails to direct his critique "*directly* and *essentially*" at sexual oppression."[80] While she agrees generally with his view that the "liberalization of sexuality provided an instinctual basis for the repressive and aggressive power *of the affluent society,*" she argues that it is "*the sexist society,*"[81] and not the "affluent society," that is aggressive and repressive. Daly charges that Marcuse's

[76] Marcuse, *Eros and Civilization*, 86.
[77] Ibid., 253.
[78] Ibid., 235.
[79] Daly, *Pure Lust*, 359.
[80] Daly, *Beyond God the Father*, 176.
[81] Ibid.

"social criticism does not go far enough" because he locates the "radical source" of social and individual alienation in capitalism,[82] whereas for her its real source is in sexism.

By replacing capitalism with sexism as the focus of critical social theory, however, Daly dangerously narrows the scope of domination and simplifies its dynamics, reducing it to a basic antagonism between male and female. In doing this she dismisses—without serious consideration—Marcuse's critical insights into the subtle and intangible workings of domination that have become so sophisticated in late twentieth-century industrial-technological societies as to be nearly invisible. Her critique of Marcuse's attempt at a comprehensive social theory tacitly repudiates the context of sexism in larger, more complex, and pervasive forms of domination. Sexism cannot be analyzed in isolation from other forms of oppression, but Daly appears uninterested in these if they do not directly focus on injustice to women. Her implication is that in eradicating male power over women, or at least rendering it ineffectual, women will have no problems whatsoever and will encounter no barriers on their journey to the Background/homeland of Elemental Be-ing. A comprehensive social theory of domination is irrelevant, as far as Daly is concerned, to understanding and addressing the subjugated condition of women.

Daly hardly addresses the question of the context of women's journey toward authenticity; where does it take place, in history or in some other realm to which only women have access? She writes of living "on the boundary," and of "creative boundary-living" that is "expressed and symbolized" by "whales and dolphins," the "tortoise," and "the hermit crab," whose main virtue is that she is "at home on the road."[83] Daly describes the hermit crab's "resourcefulness of . . . moving into the discarded shells of other animals . . . in which she comfortably travels while seeking larger shells to occupy as she increases in size." This is a loosely metaphoric expression of the Hegelian concept of negativity, where *Geist,* in the process of congealing into external forms that are momentarily adequate to its unfolding, must also continuously negate, discard, and finally supersede them.

---

[82] Ibid., 175–76.
[83] Daly, *Gyn/Ecology*, 394–95.

Daly's theorizing is here similarly vulnerable to Marx's critique of Hegel, which objected that the moving, creative force of history was not Spirit but human beings in their concrete laboring activity. As Hegel displaced human beings as the subjects of history, Daly exhibits a tendency in the same direction as she ontologizes femaleness and thus objectifies and reifies it with the result that living individual women all but disappear. It is not the activities of struggling, laboring women that contribute to the movement of history, but an ontological female Spirit that animates the cosmic creative life forces that underlie the patriarchal distortion of the phenomenal world.

Concerning Daly's exhortation for boundary living, it must be said that most women already live on the boundary of social existence and do not find it a poetic experience. However heightened many women's ecological consciousness may have become, it is both sentimental and absurd to offer hermit crabs and tortoises as symbolic models for how women might live alternative lives away from patriarchal oppression. What Daly proposes here is little more than a form of romantic escapism by driving women's revolutionary energy for social and personal transformation into esoteric realms of privatized experience. Her extended essays and detailed passages outlining the specific atrocities committed against women in various cultures and historical periods are actually lists of horrors devoid of any social analysis beyond the theoretically inadequate assertions of male perversity, evil, and gynocidal intent. Daly's exposition of crimes against women tends far more toward accumulative classification of brutalities than analysis of their root causes and sustaining conditions.

For all his inadequacies concerning his portrayals of the "feminine" as a kind of redemptive, transformative power of history, the value of Marcuse's social theory is that it offers profound and relevant insights into the complex dynamics of domination by examining its social and psychological mediations. Moreover, Marcuse's vision of a liberated, transformed humanity is profoundly humanist and inclusive. Daly's religio-philosophical vision is exclusivist and *antihumanist*. Not only does her philosophy exclude all men, it suggests that heterosexual women—"fembots," "painted birds," "totalled women"—are stamped with the alienation of patriarchy and collude in preserving its interests.

Gynocentric feminism, as represented by Daly and as a general theory of women's liberation, is self-defeating in that it rests on an identitary logic that generates a regulatory fiction of what true femaleness is by imposing a compulsory correspondence between a transcendental female subject and individual women. Daly's Elemental, Lusty, Racing Race of Women, Crones, Hags, Archelogians, Hag-Gnostics, Spinners, and Websters say little to women who daily struggle against domination in its nearly infinite variety of forms. Daly's A-mazing Amazons are mythological figures with which no woman can identify in ways that can open insights into oppression that may further lead to practical, emancipatory action. Daly is spinning new reifications of female nature, and her exhortations for living on the boundary drive revolutionary activity into imaginary esoteric realms that are mostly severed from concrete reality. In this, she shares in Marcuse's failure adequately to address women's oppression and construct an effective theory and practice of liberation. But Marcuse at least connected feminism with socialism, recognizing the need for a comprehensive feminist social theory that directly addressed women's condition in a way that opened up emancipatory possibilities for all humanity. Daly simply dismisses socialism and "its by-product, 'socialist feminism,' " as nothing more than a "bombardment of verbiage which often replaces/displaces any signs or acts of genuine biophilic concern."[84]

Daly's feminist philosophy at best is capable of providing only an abstract unity *among* women at the expense of the concrete differences that exist *between* women. Efforts to promote an abstract unity dissipate and atrophy revolutionary energy that addresses itself to the transformation of concrete conditions. Moreover, they all too easily result in oppressive politics of regulatory practices that exclude difference in the name of an illusory reconciliation only possible in a mythic utopia.[85]

---

[84] Daly, *Pure Lust*, 326.

[85] For example, see Audre Lorde's "An Open Letter to Mary Daly," in *Sister Outsider* (New York: The Crossing Press, 1984), 66–71. I agree with Lorde's main argument: that Daly implies that by virtue of being women, all women suffer the same forms of oppression. I do not think, however, that Daly's theory would be any more adequate if she also referred to African myths and legends in a search for "the true nature of old female power." In making such a statement, Lorde indulges in a reifying of women similar to Daly's.

Most disturbing of all, the political implications of Daly's theorizing are authoritarian and hierarchical; not only are males excluded from her unifying vision of reconciliation of existence and essence, but so, it appears, are those women who do not conform to her view of real womanhood, the criteria of which are defined by Daly alone.

For all the unreality and mythic quality to Marcuse's utopian vision of a pacified, liberated society governed by the new rationality of female-Eros, he did not propose that the feminist movement (or any other oppositional minority) merely reject the patriarchal status quo without first confronting it in a political praxis of determinate negation.[86] Marcuse claimed consistently that the possibilities for future liberation are contained in the present, and he even developed a set of criteria by which the rationality of a given historical effort for change could be evaluated: first,

> the transcendent project . . . must demonstrate its own *higher* rationality [in that] it offers the prospect of preserving and improving the productive achievements of civilization; (b) it defines the established totality in its very structure, basic tendencies, and relations; (c) its realization offers a greater chance for the pacification of existence, within the framework of institutions which offer a greater chance for the free development of human needs and faculties."[87]

---

[86] Richard Bernstein cautions that Marcuse's thinking shows a certain lack of "determinate negation" insofar as "What always seems to be missing in Marcuse is not 'Man' or 'human potentialities,' but *men*—or better, human beings in their plurality who only *achieve* their humanity in and through each other." "Negativity: Theme and Variations," *Praxis International* 1 (April 1981): 87–100. Bernstein makes this critique in part as a privileging of Jürgen Habermas's theory of communicative ethics over Marcuse's theory of social and individual transformation. While I think Bernstein has a point, my argument is that the real weakness of Marcuse's concept of determinate negation is linked to his incapacity to theorize women as concrete, historical agents of social and self-transformation. Bernstein's critique, it might be noted, contains references only to men.

[87] Marcuse, *One-Dimensional Man*, 220. See also xi, note 1, for Marcuse's definition of transcendence, which he uses in the "empirical, critical sense," as "overshooting" the "established universe of discourse and action toward its historical alternatives (real possibilities)."

Thus we can see in both Marcuse's critical theory and in Daly's feminist theory two somewhat contradictory concepts of negativity, one determinate and dialectical, the other abstract and reified. I associate humanist feminism with the former, and gynocentric feminism with the latter. Determinate negation was for Marcuse and must be for feminist theory a political, subversive power rooted in the concrete actions of real historical subjects. These are human beings opposed to actual suffering and injustice, who refuse to accept the existent state of affairs as well as refuse to relinquish their right to transcendence, "which is part of the very existence of [human beings] in history: the right to insist on a less compromised, less guilty, less exploited humanity."[88]

That Marcuse's notion of determinate negation collapses into utter reification when identified with "the feminine" attests to the general incapacity of the tradition of critical theory to conceptualize women as historical agents, and thus as full human beings.[89] Because of critical theory's failure to account for women as subjects of history, it could not articulate a theory of difference adequate to women's experience. This failure led to a further inability to formulate an ethics of intersubjectivity that is necessary for a reconstructed theory and practice of inclusive, pluralistic, and fully democratic politics. This failure of critical theory is reproduced more or less intact in gynocentric feminism. Because of their inability to comprehend women in human terms, the Frankfurt School thinkers could not fully theorize difference, they could only romanticize it. The following statement by Marcuse is perhaps the most moving illustration of the way in which critical theory understood relations between men and women: "All joy, and all sorrow are rooted in this difference, in this relation to the other, of whom you want to become part, and who you want to become part of yourself, and who never can and never will become such a part of yourself."[90]

---

[88] Marcuse, *An Essay on Liberation*, 71.
[89] For an earlier account of the notion of "woman" in critical theory, see my "The Politics of Empowerment: Ethical Paradigms in a Feminist Critique of Critical Social Theory," *The Annual of the Society of Christian Ethics* (November 1991): 173–92.
[90] Marcuse, "Marxism and Feminism," 287.

It is ironic that Marcuse could not sustain his analysis of the dynamics of alienation and domination within advanced capitalist societies when it came to understanding the oppression of women and the task of feminist politics. His concept of the negative power of the feminine prevented him from fully accounting for the historical forms and specific dynamics of the domination of women so that he could do no more than celebrate the women's movement as the vehicle of Eros triumphant and the new humanity, rather than formulate possible strategies for overcoming the negative condition of women in society. In many respects Mary Daly's thought harbors similar difficulties; her lengthy discussions of authentic female being spin new webs of reification of "woman" rather than formulating ways through which women may at least come to a greater understanding of the dynamics of domination within which their specific subjugated condition is located. Along with Marcuse, Daly engages in a reified negative theorizing that relies on abstract concepts to solve concrete problems. The identity logic that structures her philosophical feminism generates rigid correlations between Daly's conceptualizations of woman and what living women ought to be. She has replaced masculinity as the measure of the fully human with a metaphysical abstraction of femininity that is offered not as the negation of the masculine norm, but simply as its substitution. The social conditions and theoretical structures that postulate one class of humans over another as normative humanity remain, in Daly's work, untouched.

Marcuse, whose work holds rich potential for social transformation, nonetheless could not sustain his theory of determinate negativity because of his inability to comprehend women in any other terms than those of romanticized reification, and because of the recurring emphasis he placed on the future. Marcuse returned repeatedly to the theme of the "ingression" of the future into the present as the "depth dimension of rebellion"[91] and the redemptive power of the present. Marcuse's stress on the future and the possibility of reconciliation of human beings with their potentialities, including his attempt to picture what a liberated humanity in unalienated society could be like, lends a religious dimension to his critical theory.

---

[91] Marcuse, *An Essay on Liberation*, 89.

If it is to retain its negative power over against the present, the future can only be conceptualized in terms of absence, for that is where the truth lies. As Adorno wrote, the truth is the "unwhole." Efforts to conceptualize the future beyond this can only produce more alienation, because our ability to think, and even to imagine, is necessarily mediated by what is. Our commitment to a liberated future empowers our efforts to negate the present in the name of unrealized possibility, because we know that what is—the suffering, injustice, and misery experienced by most of humanity, and especially by women—must be brought to an end in the name of a just humanity that could be, and should be. The power of subversive negativity is located exactly there, in concrete struggles against the existent, against domination in all its manifestations. As domination congeals into ever more remote and less tangible forms, it becomes ever more the task of critical theory to expose them. As for the future, it must take care of itself. Marcuse's closing statement in *One-Dimensional Man* expresses what can only be the task of critical theory under the current state of affairs: "The critical theory of society possesses no concepts which could bridge the gap between the present and its future; holding no promise and showing no success, it remains negative. Thus it wants to remain loyal to those who, without hope, have given and give their life to the Great Refusal."[92]

Rather than constructing alternative visions of the future, attention might be focused on the past and the power of memory to reclaim stories of and the struggles of women against oppression, sifting through the historical debris to find traces of their activity in shaping the course of civilization. Although memory is an important dimension of Mary Daly's thought, she conceptualizes it as recollection of a female golden age that was overthrown but not totally destroyed by patriarchy. While she writes a great deal about an elemental, authentic background realm where women may rediscover their true selves, what the true female self is and how it is to reach its ground in elemental being remains extremely vague. It appears that Daly can only indicate what this metaphysical dimension is through a decisive separation from what it is absolutely not: maleness, and the patriarchal foreground.

---

[92] Marcuse, *One-Dimensional Man*, 257.

There is an elitist, antidemocratic strain to this line in her thinking that separates those women who are beginning to connect with their true selves from those women who seem irrevocably lost to patriarchal delusion; the former act as harbingers of a new age, while the latter are left to wallow in their demeaned state. Despite Daly's lengthy cataloging of the atrocities and brutalities committed by men against women throughout history, these memories of specific sufferings do not address the conditions and structures that continue to produce them.

Other possibilities exist, however, for understanding the power of memory and its role in reconstructing history in ways that allow deeper insight into the nature of domination in the present, ways that are capable of mobilizing women to take up political activities for social change. With respect to critical theory, the work of Walter Benjamin holds great promise as a theoretical resource for women who struggle to reclaim memories of suffering and the struggles against it. Insofar as feminist religious thought is concerned, the work of Elisabeth Schüssler Fiorenza resonates with Benjaminian concepts of memory, but builds upon and transforms them in ways that more adequately address the subjugated, marginalized condition of women both in the past and in the present.

In the following chapter, the work of both Benjamin and Schüssler Fiorenza will be arranged in such a way as to reveal how they illuminate each other with respect to the redemptive and political power of memory. The chapter will further probe the limitations that Benjamin shared with his Frankfurt colleagues with respect to women. At the same time, Benjamin's concept of memory reveals a deeper dimension to Schüssler Fiorenza's work than can be perceived otherwise. An examination of the work of Benjamin and Schüssler Fiorenza opens pathways that break through the limitations in the thinking of Marcuse and Daly on themes of memory and human liberation.

CHAPTER 5

Memory, Revolution, and Redemption

Walter Benjamin and Elisabeth Schüssler Fiorenza[1]

IN *THE BOOK OF LAUGHTER AND FORGETTING,* CZECH NOVEL-
ist Milan Kundera writes that, "The struggle of man against power
is the struggle of memory against forgetting."[2] This concept of memory as struggle against domination is thematically sustained throughout George Orwell's harrowing picture of the nightmare totalitarian
world of *1984,* where "the Party" exerts absolute control in its ruthless
and relentless measures to erase even the most private memories of
individuals. " 'Who controls the past,' ran the Party slogan, 'controls
the future: who controls the present controls the past.' "[3] Both writers
understand the intrinsic connection between memory and emancipation on the one hand, and forgetting and enslavement on the other.
They further realize that human beings bereft of the capacity for remembrance are helpless in the face of domination in any of its forms.

My intention here is to probe the dialectic of enslavement and
freedom, as well as the possibilities for human solidarity and social
transformation, in an analysis of memory and its implications for a

---

feminist critical theory of religion. I will situate the discussion within the philosophical and theological perspectives of Walter Benjamin and Elisabeth Schüssler Fiorenza.[4] While the theme of memory occupies an important place in the critical theory of Theodor Adorno, Herbert Marcuse, and Max Horkheimer, it is treated by Benjamin in ways that resonate more closely with specifically religious concerns. The religious elements within Benjamin's work, however, are by no means typically theological; they are both explicitly materialist and political.

Benjamin's preoccupation with history, memory, and social transformation situates him most closely with the work of Elisabeth Schüssler Fiorenza, who dwells on the same themes in ways that are remarkably similar to yet quite different from Benjamin's. Although Benjamin understood his approach to memory in terms of a reconstructed historical materialism, his focus tends at times to be less materialistic, in human terms, than that of Schüssler Fiorenza. As I will demonstrate in more detail later, this is in part because of Benjamin's greater emphasis on past cultural objects and discarded commodities and their potential to disclose redemption in their encounter with present generations through memory, rather than with human beings. As well, like that of the critical theorists of the Frankfurt School with whom he was associated, Benjamin's treatment of women is permeated with ambivalence. The images of women that appear in his work, be they nursemaids, prostitutes, or his own mother, are tinged with a curious mixture of idealization laced with a remote distaste that indicates an obliviousness to women as specific human beings with their own life histories and subjective experiences.

Schüssler Fiorenza, particularly in her more recent work,[5] focuses increasingly on the concrete and specific differences between women

---

[4] Although I will discuss the analysis of redemptive memory in a specifically Christian context, it must be pointed out that a similar discussion could be advanced with respect to Judaism. This is an implied part of my analysis, given the Jewish background of Walter Benjamin. Benjamin had a strong interest in the Kabbalah, and this plus his interest in wider themes in Jewish theology inform many aspects of his thought. An explicit discussion of possibilities for redemptive memory within Judaism, however, is the subject for another study. See note 15 below.
[5] See Elisabeth Schüssler Fiorenza, "The Politics of Otherness: Biblical Inter-

that resist and defy identitary[6] practices that aim at a false resolution of these differences in abstract, ideal categories. In her work, women are neither absorbed within inchoate categories of "the oppressed" or "suffering victims," nor do they function as devices for the speculations of a reflective consciousness, as often happens with Benjamin. Rather, Schüssler Fiorenza focuses on women in their historical specificity in ways that render them and the unjust conditions within which they live visible.

In the course of this discussion I will also refer somewhat more briefly to the German political theologian Johannes Metz, insofar as he provides a critical interface between the more directly theological aspects of Schüssler Fiorenza and the explicitly revolutionary dimension of Benjamin. The introduction of Metz's work into the Benjamin-Schüssler Fiorenza constellation makes it possible to see more clearly the political messianism of Benjamin on the one hand, and the more concrete focus of Schüssler Fiorenza on the other. In this respect Metz, whose work bears the influence of critical theory and Benjamin in particular, takes on something of an indirect yet important and relevant role in illuminating certain themes in both Benjamin and Schüssler Fiorenza in much the way "a glow brings out a haze."[7]

---

pretation as a Critical Praxis for Liberation," in Marc H. Ellis and Otto Maduro, eds., *The Future of Liberation Theology: Essays in Honor of Gustavo Gutiérrez* (Maryknoll, N.Y.: Orbis Books, 1989). In her latest book, *But She Said: Feminist Practices of Biblical Interpretation* (Boston: Beacon Press, 1992), Schüssler Fiorenza continues to develop and refine her feminist hermeneutic practice in terms of a heightened attentiveness to differences between women, especially in terms of color, language, and culture.

[6] As we have seen, Theodor W. Adorno uses the term *identitary* or *identitarian* thought as one way of describing the coercive nature of conceptualization that he critiques in *Negative Dialectics*. See his essay, "Subject and Object," in Andrew Arato and Eike Gebhardt, eds., *The Essential Frankfurt School Reader* (New York: Continuum, 1982), 497–511.

[7] The phrase is found in a novel by Joseph Conrad, *Heart of Darkness*, ed. Robert Kimbrough, 2d ed. (New York: W. W. Norton, 1971), 5. The image of a "glow bringing out a haze" indicates the kind of relation I am positing between Metz and Benjamin and Schüssler Fiorenza. Metz's work is not meant to explain the other writers in any systematic or analytical way but rather is brought to bear upon them insofar as it casts an oblique but significant light on their thinking in much the same manner as the illuminating power described by Conrad's narrator.

Although Benjamin's concept of memory directly influences Metz, and while Schüssler Fiorenza explicitly takes over Metz's understanding of "dangerous memory" in her feminist biblical hermeneutic and historical reconstruction of Christianity,[8] far more compelling theoretical resonances exist between Benjamin and Schüssler Fiorenza than between Metz and Benjamin, or Metz and Schüssler Fiorenza. My purpose here is to situate Benjamin and Schüssler Fiorenza in a critical-dialectical and dialogical interaction in order that each may progressively illuminate aspects of the other and contribute to an expanded feminist critical theory of religion and liberation. Again, it cannot be overemphasized that this encounter between Benjamin and Schüssler Fiorenza does not aim at any form of synthesis or integration concerning their theories of the redemptive power of memory. It rather seeks to position them within a tentative critical constellation that intimates new possibilities for a transformed human and humane future fashioned in solidarity with past (and present) generations of women.

What Benjamin and Schüssler Fiorenza share is a concept of memory laden with redemptive and emancipatory potentialities that are released when history is brushed "against the grain" of the false and falsifying perspective of the rulers' and oppressors' accounts of the world. The sparks generated by this brushing against the grain of hegemonic historical discourses in turn reveal as "authentic" history the history of the oppressed victims. Without their labors and struggles civilization would not be possible, yet they remain oppressed and unredeemed after death by being forgotten and erased from the historical record.[9] Benjamin and Schüssler Fiorenza resist this politically motivated historical amnesia by developing a concept of history that is materialist, theological, and deeply political in its own way. It is determined to break through the ideological veil of anonymity and obscurity that conceals the truth that the victims of history are also

---

[8] Elisabeth Schüssler Fiorenza, *In Memory of Her: A Feminist Theological Reconstruction of Christian Origins* (New York: Crossroad, 1984), 31–32.

[9] According to Benjamin, "the authentic conception of historical time rests wholly and totally on the image of redemption." Cited in Susan Buck-Morss, *The Dialectics of Seeing: Walter Benjamin and the Arcades Project* (Cambridge, Mass.: MIT Press, 1989), 243.

the *makers* of history. Unlike the other critical theorists, Benjamin and Schüssler Fiorenza believe that the past is not finished and done with. It remains open to the present in ways that redeem both, creating possibilities for political action that may lead to liberating social transformation.

Walter Benjamin and the Puppet of History

In his theologico-political *THESES ON THE PHILOSOPHY OF History,* written not long before he died (1940), Benjamin images history as a puppet—called historical materialism—inside of which sits hidden a "little hunchback"—theology—that dazzles people with its remarkable success in games of chess.[10] The political meaning of Benjamin's allegorical image indicates that the relationship between theory and practice, although dialectical, is not an integrated unity that dissolves the distinctive elements of either thought or action, but rather preserves them in a creative tension. The historical materialist, if he or she is to "win," cannot act alone, but requires "the services of theology"; otherwise, history is little more than a mere sequence of empirical events, locked within what Jürgen Habermas describes as "the mythical compulsion to repeat," which generates the "repeatedly same"[11] in the guise of "new" epochs, with the result that the dead are buried deeper in anonymity. Although theology must necessarily animate historical materialism, it "has to keep out of sight,"[12] or its truth will vanish.

What Theodor Adorno referred to as Benjamin's "radical, 'negative theology' " could only facilitate the redemption of history if thoroughly absorbed in materialism; otherwise, humanity becomes estranged from itself as the self-conscious agent of history,[13] through

---

[10] Walter Benjamin, *Illuminations: Essays and Reflections*, trans. Harry Zohn, ed. and with an Introduction by Hannah Arendt (New York: Schocken Books, 1969), 253.

[11] Jürgen Habermas, "Consciousness-Raising or Redemptive Criticism—The Contemporaneity of Walter Benjamin," *New German Critique*, no. 17 (Spring 1979): 39.

[12] Benjamin, *Illuminations*, 253.

[13] Buck-Morss, *Dialectics of Seeing*, 244–45, 235.

whose struggles transformation takes place. "My thinking relates to theology," Benjamin wrote, "the way a blotter does to ink. It is soaked with it. If one merely read the blotter, though, nothing of what has been written would remain."[14] A historical consciousness that is "soaked" with theology prevents the suffering and injustice inflicted on humanity from being reduced to a mere record of so many links in a historiographical chain. Theology allows the historical materialist to grasp the truth of past ages in "dialectical images" or "constellations" that seize history at a standstill, releasing objects and events from the sterile and illusory continuity of history as progress (which Benjamin sometimes referred to as a "dream"), in order that they may be comprehended as they will appear "in the light of Messianic fulfillment":[15]

> To articulate the past historically does not mean to recognize it "the way it really was." . . . It means to seize hold of a memory as it flashes up at a moment of danger. Historical materialism wishes to retain that image of the past which unexpectedly appears to man singled out by history at a moment of danger. The danger affects both the content of the tradition and its receivers. The same threat hangs over both: that of becoming a tool of the ruling classes. In every era the attempt must be made anew to wrest tradition away from a conformism that is about to overpower it. The Messiah comes not only as the redeemer, he comes as the subduer of Antichrist. Only that historian will have the gift of fanning the spark of hope

---

[14] Walter Benjamin, "Konvolut 'N,' " *The Philosophical Forum* 15, nos. 1–2 (Fall–Winter 1983–84): 18.

[15] Richard Wolin, *Walter Benjamin: An Aesthetic of Redemption* (New York: Columbia Univ. Press, 1982), 125, 96. For a fuller account of Benjamin's concept of messianic time and the roots of his theology in Jewish mysticism and the Kabbalah, see Rolf Tiedemann, "Historical Materialism or Political Messianism? An Interpretation of the Theses 'On the Concept of History,' " *The Philosophical Forum* 15, nos. 1–2 (Fall–Winter 1983–84): 71–104; Buck-Morss, *Dialectics of Seeing*, especially part 3, chap. 4; Charles Davis, "Walter Benjamin, the Mystical Materialist," in Howard Joseph, Jack Lightstone, and Michael D. Oppenheim, eds., *Truth and Compassion: Essays on Judaism and Religion in Memory of Dr. Solomon Frank* (Waterloo: Canadian Corporation for Studies in Religion, 1983); and Gershom Scholem, *Walter Benjamin, The Story of a Friendship*, trans. Harry Zohn (New York: Schocken Books, 1981), for a more general account of the theological and religious aspects of his thought.

in the past who is firmly convinced that *even the dead* will not be safe from the enemy if he wins. And this enemy has not ceased to be victorious.[16]

Benjamin sifts through the debris of the past—discarded commodities, cultural artifacts, literary and philosophical quotations—in order to rescue historical fragments by rearranging them not into concepts but into "constellations," where they are preserved in a redeemed form in the cracks and fissures of historical continuity. The historical materialist, like the present generation, has a responsibility for the dead and for past ages, upon which the redemption of both past and present rests: "To be sure, only a redeemed mankind receives the fullness of its past—which is to say, only for a redeemed mankind has its past become citable in all its moments."[17] The present generation redeems the past in an act of anamnestic[18] solidarity with all who suffered at the slaughter-bench of history. There is no possibility of redemption, neither for them nor us, if we allow the annihilation of their very memory:

> There is a secret agreement between past generations and the present. Our coming was expected on earth. Like every generation that preceded us, we have been endowed with a *weak* Messianic power, a power to which the past has a claim. That claim cannot be settled cheaply. Historical materialists are aware of that.[19]

Ours is a "weak" messianic power because only human efforts can usher in the messianic age, which for Benjamin is secularized in the "classless society." The *Theses* employs directly theological language for thoroughly materialist purposes.[20]

---

[16] Benjamin, *Illuminations*, 255.

[17] Ibid., 254.

[18] The word derives from the Greek *anamnesis*, which is a form of knowledge that is not derived from direct experience, but occurs in acts of recollection or remembrance. Remembrance allows later generations to enter into solidarity with the dead in acts of recollection that bring the sufferings experienced in the past to the light of contemporary knowledge.

[19] Benjamin, *Illuminations*, 255.

[20] Tiedemann, "Historical Materialism or Political Messianism?" 95, 82.

Benjamin did not propose that historical transformation would come about via an external, eschatological divine agency. Benjamin's concept of solidarity with the dead does not seek an empathy or identity with past generations; rather, Benjamin requires that the historical materialist initiate a "Messianic cessation of happening" that offers "a revolutionary chance in the fight for the oppressed past."[21] The "fullness of the past" is not recovered by efforts to integrate it into the flow of historical continuity, where it becomes absorbed by the totalizing power of master narratives (the narratives of the masters and victors) and thus falsified. Rather, redemption becomes possible when the historical continuum is arrested by blasting "a specific era out of the homogeneous course of history—blasting a specific life out of the era or a specific work out of the lifework."[22] The "re-awakening" of the past occurs through a cognitive shock that results when the horrors of past brutality and exploitation are made visible.

In Thesis IX, Benjamin images historical continuity and progress as "one single catastrophe" that piles up "wreckage upon wreckage" at the feet of the Angel of history, who "would like to stay, awaken the dead, and make whole what has been smashed,"[23] but is powerless to do so. The Angel, his back turned to the future—his eyes staring, his mouth open—is transfixed by the horror of the catastrophe produced by the wind of progress that blows him toward the future. While the Angel is powerless, human beings are not; humans may subvert the catastrophe of history and wrest tradition from the thrall of the exploiting classes by bringing it to a halt. This "Messianic cessation" that blasts history apart is "characteristic of the revolutionary classes at the moment of their action."[24] Benjamin invokes the avenging nature of the working class within a thoroughly politicized concept of messianism that completes "the task of liberation in the name of generations of the downtrodden."[25]

---

[21] Benjamin, *Illuminations*, 263.
[22] Ibid.
[23] Ibid., 257.
[24] Ibid., 261.
[25] Ibid., 260.

The historical materialist can only "get beyond the history of the oppressors" by holding on to "the history of the oppressed"[26] against the historical hegemony of the rulers who want to obliterate it. The historical materialist continues the struggle of the past against oppression by exploding the epic grandeur of the history of the victors in establishing history as "the discontinuum which it always has been as well."[27] In this way history from the perspective of the oppressors and the privileged is subverted by the authentic history of the victims, whose suffering and labor are the unseen condition of the very possibility of culture, "which owes its existence not just to the efforts of the great geniuses who fashioned it, but also in greater or lesser degree to the anonymous drudgery of their contemporaries. There is no cultural document that is not at the same time a record of barbarism."[28]

Emancipation and Absolving Soteriology

THE CONCEPT OF MEMORY AS A SUBVERSIVE AND REDEMPTIVE force informs Benjamin's early and later writings in the form of a theological expression with a thoroughly materialist meaning. Not surprisingly, his concept of history lends itself well to political theology. In particular it has influenced the work of Johannes Metz.[29] Unlike Benjamin, who invoked the idea of the Messiah only as an image and analogy,[30] however, Metz speaks of the "*memoria passionis,*

---

[26] Tiedemann, "Historical Materialism or Political Messianism?" 92.

[27] Ibid.

[28] Walter Benjamin, "Eduard Fuchs, Collector and Historian," in *One-Way Street and Other Writings,* trans. Edmund Jephcott and Kingsley Shorter (London: New Left Books, 1979), 359.

[29] See Johannes Baptist Metz, *Faith in History and Society: Toward a Practical Fundamental Theology,* trans. David Smith (New York: Seabury Press, 1980), especially chaps. 5, 6, 7, and 11. In a footnote Metz writes, "In my opinion the usage of the notion of 'redemption' in Adorno, and especially in Walter Benjamin, deserves closer theological scrutiny" (p. 134, note 9).

[30] Tiedemann, "Historical Materialism or Political Messianism?" 83. Because of this symbolic use of the term *Messiah,* Benjamin's concept of history is not soteriological, as Metz's is.

mortis et resurrectionis Jesu Christi" as the "dangerous memory of freedom" that anticipates the future as a "future of those who are oppressed, without hope and doomed to fail." In this way memory "breaks through the magic circle of the prevailing consciousness"[31] that sees significant historical meaning residing only in the actions of the rulers and politicians. According to Metz, memory of suffering forces us to look at "the public *theatrum mundi*" from the standpoint of the "conquered and the victims." This view in turn motivates us to establish "a new form of solidarity, of responsibility towards those most distant from us, inasmuch as the history of suffering unites all men like a 'second nature.' "[32]

In fashion similar to Benjamin, Metz is also careful to distinguish between memory as "false consciousness" that functions as an "opiate" of the present, and authentic or "dangerous memories" that in solidarity with the victims of the past anticipate "a particular future of man as a future for the suffering, the hopeless, the oppressed, the injured and the useless of this earth."[33] Although in more muted form, Metz also echoes Benjamin's notion of the proletariat as an "avenging class" whose "hatred and spirit of sacrifice . . . are nourished by the image of enslaved ancestors"[34] when he tells us, "Every rebellion against suffering is fed by the subversive power of remembered suffering."[35]

Liberation requires the redemption of past suffering if it is to be abolished in the future. Both Benjamin and Metz locate the history of suffering as "a medium" of redemption that breaks open future possibilities of freedom. Benjamin's immanent apocalypticism, which conceives of history in terms of "discontinuity" and "Messianic cessation," however, and Metz's concern to relativize emancipatory struggles within a soteriological framework[36] point in different ways toward

---

[31] Metz, *Faith in History and Society*, 90.

[32] Ibid., 105.

[33] Ibid., 117.

[34] Benjamin, *Illuminations*, 260.

[35] Metz, *Faith in History and Society*, 110.

[36] According to Metz, a "revolutionary theory of emancipation" is insufficient if not relativized within a soteriology that emphasizes the guilt of all human

a shared but finally untenable and undesirable political messianism. It threatens to be little more than an "impotent proclamation that salvation is indeed at hand in spite of all the barriers presented to it by actual conditions."[37] The idea of a revolutionary, avenging subject of history identified as a specific class or group (more prominent in Benjamin than in Metz) is highly problematic. It is by now inescapably apparent that no revolutionary subject exists, and that the only legitimate goal of emancipatory action is not vengeance, but transformation on the level of society and individuals.

Nonetheless, in several respects Benjamin's development of the concept of history remains less abstract than Metz's. In part this is because Benjamin does not need to legitimate struggles against injustice with an absolving soteriology, and because his more highly developed materialism focuses on concrete objects and events and differentiates between those who commit injustice by virtue of their position of class and power and those who suffer it. To state the difference between them in other words, Benjamin's theology is inextricably embedded within an explicit politically motivated social theory, while Metz's theology is ultimately more conservative in that it is less materialist and more abstractly spiritualist in a traditional theological sense than Benjamin's. However political Metz's theological perspective is, he escapes into soteriological guarantees that situate the ultimate outcome of the human condition in a realm beyond history and society.

Metz's references to the "history of suffering as the history of guilt,"[38] and his critique of the "Marxist version" of history that fashions a history "with no dirty laundry,"[39] have the effect (however unintended it may be and all disclaimers notwithstanding) of equalizing

---

beings, thereby preventing the emergence of a self-identified innocent, aggrieved class or group who struggle against an oppressive "enemy." This move to situate and legitimate revolutionary activity in history within soteriology, however, threatens to absorb historical struggles into an apolitical, abstract, and spiritualized realm that to some extent obfuscates and minimizes the experience of injustice and exploitation, in spite of Metz's intentions to the contrary. See *Faith in History and Society*, 126.

[37] Tiedemann, "Historical Materialism or Political Messianism?" 96.
[38] Metz, *Faith in History and Society*, 127.
[39] Ibid., 125.

the vanquished and the victors through a shared guilt that can only be redeemed "through God in the cross of Jesus."[40] Metz employs an ontological and spiritualized concept of guilt that tends to dehistoricize the actual, specific, and deliberate practices of injustice, exploitation, and slaughter that are perpetrated on innocent victims. The universalization of the concept of guilt obscures the crucial fact that the innocent victims of history are innocent exactly because their suffering was (and is) entirely without justification. Benjamin knew this in a more profound way than Metz, which is why he insisted on history as unfinished, thereby opening the possibility of redemption through anamnestic solidarity, so that the victims did not suffer for nothing.[41] Benjamin's work aspires to be a theory of history that "itself becomes historical praxis, a part of the class struggle."[42]

The concept of memory generally shared by Benjamin and Metz, despite the latter's tendency to greater abstraction, nonetheless reveals possibilities for what Helmut Peukert calls the "common depth structure" of historical materialism and theology. The common ground is anamnestic solidarity, forged in acts of remembrance and sustained recollection of the sufferings and injustices inflicted on past victims of oppression.[43] What unites repressed and suffering humanity across the generations is "the solidarity of the living with the dead."[44] Human beings struggling for justice and liberation in the present cannot break

---

[40] Ibid., 129.

[41] Benjamin's concept of the incompleteness of history was challenged by Max Horkheimer: "Past injustice is done and finished. Those who have been beaten to death are truly dead." Cited, with an excerpt of Benjamin's reply, in Tiedemann, "Historical Materialism or Political Messianism?" 77.

[42] Ibid., 79.

[43] Helmut Peukert, *Science, Action, and Fundamental Theology: Toward a Theology of Communicative Action*, trans. James Bohman (Cambridge, Mass.: MIT Press, 1986), 208. I disagree with Peukert's discription of Benjamin's concept of memory as "empathetic." The historical materialist does not enter into the continuum of history in an empathetic act of solidarity. To do so would be to support the continuity of history. See especially Tiedemann's discussion of Benjamin, cited above.

[44] Christian Lenhardt, "Anamnestic Solidarity: The Proletariat and Its Manes," *Telos*, no. 25 (Fall 1975): 151.

free from "the magic circle" that enslaves history within the self-serving perspective of the victors in the absence of remembrance. Historical amnesia generates a false consciousness that extends injustice and domination into the future, leaving human beings powerless to resist oppression because, in Metz's words, "their memories of the past are taken away."[45] In the absence of the memory of our anonymous ancestors, we have no hope for a redeemed present or future.

The Mother and the Whore

HISTORICAL MATERIALISM AND THEOLOGY MEET WHERE ELements of social reality from the past and the present may be rearranged to form a politically charged constellation of meaning that points toward new possibilities for social transformation. Probing the liberative potential of the "common depth structure" of historical materialism and theology is promising for feminist religious thought if it is reconstructed in the light of feminist goals. At the same time, a feminist approach to the redemptive power of memory is necessary for a more adequate and genuinely emancipatory concept of history than is found in Benjamin or Metz.

A feminist critique of Walter Benjamin is especially important for at least two reasons: first, to probe more deeply the abstract core of his historical materialism, which tends to situate victims of injustice within a general anonymous category of passive victims or "proletariat"; and second, to reclaim the emancipatory and materialist intent of his own thinking for feminist purposes. While it is doubtlessly true that Benjamin accepted "the cause of the oppressed [and] the class position of the proletariat, as his own,"[46] he was at times unable to differentiate the various levels and complex specifics of domination. This inability is apparent in his treatment of women. While Benjamin's approach to history is far less abstract than that of Metz, the inadequacies concerning women are key to uncovering some deeper contradictions in Benjamin's thought that work against his expressed intent to enter into solidarity with past victims.

---

45 Metz, *Faith in History and Society*, 110.
46 Tiedemann, "Historical Materialism or Political Messianism?" 92.

As Benjamin did not write in a systematic fashion, but rather in essays, images, citations, short paragraphs, and aphorisms, it is not possible to find in his work any concentrated or developed political theory of women, or "the feminine," as one might do with a Frankfurt theorist such as Herbert Marcuse. Rather, women tend to float in and out of his writings, often in enigmatic and ambivalent ways. In one of the most moving and vivid texts he wrote, "A Berlin Chronicle," Benjamin refers somewhat in passing to the prostitute in a tight-fitting sailor suit who haunted his erotic fantasies for years. Images recur of whores framed in doorways, encountered during his many walks through the city, less as human beings in their own right than as occasions of Benjamin's introspection:

> There is no doubt . . . that a feeling of crossing the threshold of one's class for the first time had a part in the almost unequalled fascination of publicly accosting a whore in the street. . . . But is it really a crossing, is it not, rather, an obstinate and voluptuous hovering on the brink, a hesitation that has its most cogent motive in the circumstance that beyond this frontier lies nothingness?[47]

For Benjamin, prostitutes appear as dialectical images representing the commodity as fetish, the salesgirl and commodity in one,[48] the "household goddess[es] of this cult of nothingness."[49]

Benjamin also offers ambivalent images of his mother, whom he blamed for his "inability . . . to make a cup of coffee" well into his adulthood.[50] He relates unhappy reminiscences of shopping excursions, where the young Benjamin was subjected to the "ignominy" of being forced to try on a new suit. After the ordeal had passed, he recalls the relief found in the sweet shop, which offered him escape from "the false worship that humiliated our mother before idols."[51] Benjamin's uncanny memory for the smallest detail unlocks strong sensations and feelings of a past always mediated by the present. He remembers with vivid clarity

---

[47] Benjamin, "A Berlin Chronicle," in *One-Way Street*, 301.
[48] Buck-Morss, *Dialectics of Seeing*, 221.
[49] Benjamin, *One-Way Street*, 301.
[50] Ibid., 294.
[51] Ibid., 327.

the noise made by the knife that my mother used to spread the rolls that my father took to his work in the morning, when it was scraped for the last time, to remove the butter still adhering to it, against the crisp surface of the cut roll. This signal preluding the labor of *my father's day* was no less exciting to me than, in later years, the sound of the bell that announced the start of a performance at the theatre.[52]

His memories of trips to the parks of Berlin contain descriptions of nursemaids and caregivers as "scatterbrained womenfolk."[53]

Given Benjamin's feelings of solidarity with the oppressed classes, his representations of women contain a poignant irony. Many of Benjamin's recollections are connected with women working, although he does not appear to perceive their activities *as labor.* For the adult Benjamin, the childhood memory of his mother making his father's lunch signaled the start of his father's work day, not his mother's. The possibility that shopping trips with young Walter might not have been so pleasant from his mother's point of view is never considered by Benjamin the man; insofar as she appears in these scenes, it is as the object of her son's consciousness, which unflatteringly remembers her as a "humiliated" consumer of commodity items. Laboring nurse-maids—obviously members of lower classes, and thereby recipients of the injustices inherent in class societies—are "scatterbrained," not apparently part of the working, exploited humanity with whom Benjamin saw himself in solidarity. Prostitutes are unreal representations of an almost mystical "nothingness," as well as objects of sexual awakening. Yet when Benjamin describes how he seeks to evoke memory in a way that seizes the past at a "dialectical standstill," or "now-time," he resorts to an utterly idealized, romantic image of the mother: "That which the child (and the grown man in his faint memory) finds in the old folds of the dress into which he pressed himself when he held fast to the skirted lap of his mother—that must be contained by these passages."[54]

As is obvious from these illustrations, women appear in Benjamin's writing as somewhat less than full human beings, lacking agency or

---

[52] Ibid., 325; emphasis added.
[53] Ibid., 296.
[54] Walter Benjamin, quoted in Buck-Morss, *Dialectics of Seeing*, 276.

subjectivity. He does not consider their experience or point of view. Benjamin moreover is aware of the limited male capacity to see "the female only under two simultaneous perspectives, as a whore and as an untouchable lover,"[55] as he writes in an early fragment on the nature of love and the relations between men and women. His treatment of women generates an unreality about them that adheres to many of his recollections. In Benjamin's intellectual world, women acquire a status that is much like the discarded commodities and cultural artifacts from former times, whose past reality persists as memory traces that fuse with the present in quasi-mystical ways. It is this inability to perceive women as concrete, specific, particular human beings that undermines Benjamin's historical materialist approach, thereby abrogating the political potential of memory to motivate change. As well, not only women, but the victims of history that he repeatedly invokes take on a certain abstractness because they are recollected through the commodities and artworks that survive them. The cultural products that render civilization possible are indeed the result of "the anonymous drudgery" of laboring humanity; however, the scandalous memory of their exploitation is preserved in the products of their past labors.

The Prophetic Power of Redemptive Memory

A VERY DIFFERENT TREATMENT OF HISTORY AS "REMEMbrance and memory"[56] that is both redemptive and liberating informs the feminist critical hermeneutics and liberation theology of Elisabeth Schüssler Fiorenza. Her work holds more promise for actual emancipation than we find in Benjamin's. For one thing, Schüssler Fiorenza reclaims women's concrete suffering in stories that emphasize their

---

[55] Walter Benjamin, "On Love and Related Topics (A European Problem)," in *Gesammelte Schriften*, vol. 6 (Frankfurt: Surkamp Verlag, 1985), 72–74.
[56] Elisabeth Schüssler Fiorenza, *Bread Not Stone: The Challenge of Feminist Biblical Interpretation* (Boston: Beacon Press, 1984), 114. Elements of the following discussion of memory in Schüssler Fiorenza are drawn from my article, "The Politics of Empowerment: Ethical Paradigms in a Feminist Critique of Critical Social Theory," *The Annual of the Society of Christian Ethics* (November 1991): 187–90.

agency. They are historical actors who fought and struggled (and continue to do so) against the injustices that marginalize them, exploit them, and render them historically invisible and silent. By redirecting her focus away from apocalyptic and soteriological concerns that tend to overshadow historical human agency, she avoids the tendency to political messianism implied in Benjamin and Metz.

Schüssler Fiorenza proceeds by initiating an "imaginative reconstruction of historical reality"[57] that searches historical records for redeemed traces and fragments of women's past that counter the prevailing androcentric interpretations of Christian origins. The friction generated by Schüssler Fiorenza's "paradigm shift"—which, among other things, allows her to ask "what it was like for a woman in Palestine to hear and be involved with Jesus and his movement"[58]— illuminates not only women's suffering at the hands of a patriarchal society and culture, but also their active struggles to transform it. Her effort to construct "new conceptual frameworks"[59] that provide contemporary women with a "usable past"[60] does not seek "empathy and identification with the dead"; rather, in anamnestic "solidarity with them,"[61] it translates into the political motivation necessary for the liberation of women in the present. Acts of solidarity in remembrance not only help to redeem the past, they also provide the political and moral empowerment that is necessary to sustain women's energy and courage in the process of transforming oppressive social relations and unjust political institutions.

In "brushing against the grain"[62] of prevailing androcentric historical consciousness and interpretation, Schüssler Fiorenza does not intend to "explode" history by "blasting" past epochs out of historical continuity in the sense meant by Benjamin. Nor does she subsume

---

[57] Schüssler Fiorenza, *Bread Not Stone*, 112.
[58] Schüssler Fiorenza, *In Memory of Her*, 151.
[59] Ibid., 84.
[60] Schüssler Fiorenza, *Bread Not Stone*, 9.
[61] Ibid., 115.
[62] Schüssler Fiorenza describes her "critical feminist strategy for dislodging texts from their patriarchal frame" in terms of "reading them against their kyriocentric, or master-centered, grain." *But She Said*, 35. Benjamin describes his historical method also as "brushing against the grain."

Jewish and Christian women's past into an absolving soteriology as put forward by Metz. Yet she shares Benjamin's particular concern to preserve and restore those utopian moments of tradition that remain as liberative traces and promises of redemption. With both Benjamin and Metz, Schüssler Fiorenza understands memory as politically dangerous in that it possesses a subversive potential that threatens the historical privilege and hegemony of the rulers and oppressors who would have us believe that history stands "on the shoulders of giants,"[63] thereby legitimating and perpetuating their own power and narrow self-interest at the expense not only of women, but of all those victimized by injustice. She writes:

> Christian feminists *reclaim* their [foresisters'] sufferings and struggles in and through the subversive power of the "remembered past." If the enslavement and colonization of people becomes total when their history is destroyed because solidarity with the faith and suffering of the dead is made impossible, then a feminist biblical hermeneutics has the task of becoming a "dangerous memory" that reclaims the religious suffering and engagement of the dead. Such a "subversive memory" not only keeps alive the suffering and hopes of Christian women in the past but also allows for a universal solidarity of sisterhood with all women of the past, present and future who follow the same vision.[64]

Schüssler Fiorenza's feminist hermeneutics of remembrance works to recover the traces of women's lives and the "faint echoes of their voices" from those "historical silences"[65] that render them invisible and mute or, at best, frozen on the margins of history. For example, her treatment of the Syro-Phoenician woman's debate with Jesus challenges the accounts found in Christian biblical texts by retelling the story from the woman's point of view. In this way Schüssler Fiorenza shifts the focus of the story, including its subsequent interpretations, from what Jesus meant in his insulting response to the woman; instead she considers the importance of the woman's action when contextualized within the early Christian controversy concerning the mission

---

[63] Christian Lenhardt, "Anamnestic Solidarity," 151.
[64] Schüssler Fiorenza, *In Memory of Her*, 31.
[65] Schüssler Fiorenza, *But She Said*, 101.

to the Gentiles. Through this kind of historical and textual analysis, Schüssler Fiorenza not only restores the Syro-Phoenician woman's subjective agency, she illuminates her contribution "to one of the most crucial transitions in early Christian beginnings." She makes the woman "visible again as one of the apostolic foremothers of Gentile Christians."[66]

When the visibility of women's role in the development of Christianity is established, contemporary women chafing under the heavy yoke of oppressive patriarchal theological and ecclesial practices become empowered in their struggles to redeem their humanity and realize their legitimate place as full Christians. The sense of empowerment gained in feminist rhetorical practices of reading biblical texts "against the grain" strengthens women in all aspects of their life by demonstrating the historical reality of their role as subjective agents in the unfolding of Western civilization. The political motivation that animates the *ekklesia* of women and their actions for social transformation in the world at large does not result in the construction of specific, detailed alternatives in the spirit of negative dialectics. Yet whereas critical theory tends toward abstraction and vagueness with respect to women, Schüssler Fiorenza focuses on their concrete condition. In contrast with Benjamin's historical materialism that renders women as momentary objects of male consciousness, Schüssler Fiorenza's feminist critical approach allows women's particularity to come through; she is more of a "historical materialist," in this sense, than is Benjamin. Moreover, her feminist critical hermeneutics of remembrance is itself a form of a political praxis of emancipation, given that "our reconstructions of the past shape present and future reality."[67]

The philosophical-theoretical orientation that informs Schüssler Fiorenza's approach rejects identity thinking. This means that women do not dissolve into abstract categories of "the oppressed," nor do they succumb to reification in being identified with female essence.[68] In Benjaminian terms, she "explodes" such categories, refusing passive

---

[66] Ibid., 97.
[67] Ibid., 101.
[68] Ibid., 9.

designations of women as mere victims of history in need of redemption. Through a subversive rhetorical practice of reading texts, she emphasizes women's agency and active struggle against oppression. Women have always struggled against injustice, and those struggles have had decisive historical consequences, as is evident in the Syro-Phoenician woman's challenge to Jesus' initial exclusionary ethnocentrism.[69] Schüssler Fiorenza insists that women's "theological heritage" is seriously misrepresented when interpreted mainly in the key of oppression; further, she insists that it must be reconstructed as "a history of liberation and of religious agency."[70] This point is especially important, because it confronts us with the historical and religious reality that women were (and remain) largely responsible for sustaining and preserving the "egalitarian currents" within early Christianity that were never entirely eliminated,[71] currents that may be restored to the Christian present through women's efforts.

Schüssler Fiorenza calls us to consider that women's conversion to Christianity must have intensified the contrast between the more egalitarian social relations within early Christian communities and the patriarchal world of Roman Hellenism. Women could experience a degree of freedom and respect in Christian circles denied them in the dominant cultural context. As well, women's active participation and leadership activities in both the household churches and the movement to evangelize the Gentiles were part of an initial "praxis of coequal discipleship" that included not only men and women, but also "slaves and masters . . . Jews and Greeks, Romans and barbarians, rich and poor, young and old [that] brought the Christian community in tension with its social-political environment."[72] The presence of women as active participants in the early Christian mission on the basis of coequal discipleship shows that a "nonpatriarchal Christian ethos" informs the root of Christian belief and practice, and that the "patriarchalization process is not inherent in Christian revelation and community but progressed slowly and with difficulty"[73] over a long period of time.

---

[69] Ibid., 162.
[70] Schüssler Fiorenza, *In Memory of Her*, 36.
[71] Ibid., 92.
[72] Ibid., 279.
[73] Ibid., 35.

Schüssler Fiorenza's focus on the primacy of relationships as the central focus of early Christian self-understanding[74] opens up possibilities for deeper insight into the nature of women's subjugation that includes but transcends the notion of patriarchy. In her most recent work, Schüssler Fiorenza utilizes the term *kyriocentrism*,[75] which she does not elaborate upon in great depth, but which nonetheless is potentially a far richer theoretical and political concept than patriarchy. The idea of *kyriarchy* or kyriocentrism acknowledges the complex interstructures of domination that include sexist practices and social arrangements but contextualizes and situates them within a wider scope of oppression. Kyriarchy is a more expansive notion than the more limited idea of patriarchy because it allows for a more comprehensive and diffuse critical analysis of the intricate structures of domination without which no adequate theory or practice of women's liberation is possible. Unless feminists begin to understand how the oppression of women functions within and serves the general condition of dominated humanity, it cannot hope to contribute to women's emancipation. The concept of kyriarchy exposes the embeddedness of the domination of women within the entire social and cultural fabric, further revealing that the subordination of women is crucial to its maintenance. Thus the liberation of women from all forms of alienation and subjugation will inevitably herald the death knell of domination as such.

Schüssler Fiorenza reclaims those dangerous memories of resistance and suffering buried deep within the Christian tradition in order to empower women in the present both politically and theologically in their struggle for change. Furthermore, by calling us to remembrance of those forgotten egalitarian Christian values that informed and shaped the praxis of coequal discipleship, Schüssler Fiorenza subverts those prevailing interpretations that excessively spiritualize and privatize the meaning of Jesus' ministry by severing it from its political and social implications. She reminds us that Jesus and his followers offered Israel an alternative interpretation of Torah that upset the established power structures by allowing everyone, in spite of their social

---

[74] Ibid., 345.
[75] Schüssler Fiorenza, *But She Said*, 122–23.

status, to experience the "all-inclusive love" of God.[76] The Jesus movement in Palestine focused on the people, not the political or religious hierarchy, as "the locus of God's power and presence."[77] It is significant that the image of God portrayed in the earliest Jesus tradition was perceived "in a woman's *Gestalt* as divine Sophia" whose child and prophet is Jesus, sent to proclaim that God is the God of the poor, the outcast, and the victims of injustice.[78] Although Jesus did not explicitly attack the power structures that create injustice and oppression, he "implicitly" subverted them "by envisioning a different future and different human relationships on the grounds that *all* persons in Israel are created and elected by the gracious goodness of Jesus' Sophia-God."[79]

As "paradigmatic remembrances,"[80] the Gospels show that Jesus' expanding sense of his own ministry was established largely through his relationships with women.[81] Schüssler Fiorenza points out that women were among the first non-Jews[82] to become members of Jesus' movement and that his parables take their images "from the world of women."[83] Unlike other religious leaders and teachers, Jesus associated freely with women, and he did not recoil from menstruating women, as illustrated in the story of the woman who hemorrhaged for twelve years, to whom he restored her "life-creating power" (Mark 5:25-34).[84] Not least of all, women were the first resurrection witnesses.

Memories such as these are redemptive for past and present generations of Christian women. In them, women remember their participation in all aspects of the earliest phases of Christianity, in which they took an active and central role. Such memories are a scandal to the present situation of many Christian women who continue to suffer the repression and subordination inflicted on them in the name of a

---

[76] Schüssler Fiorenza, *In Memory of Her*, 130.

[77] Ibid., 120.

[78] Ibid., 132, 135.

[79] Ibid., 142.

[80] Ibid., 102.

[81] Ibid., 137.

[82] Ibid., 138.

[83] Ibid., 121.

[84] Ibid., 124.

false theological consciousness that betrays their Christian origins. In acts of anamnestic solidarity with the dead, contemporary women may begin to realize—and here Schüssler Fiorenza fully reconnects with Benjamin—that history remains incomplete, always open to the possibility of redemption through recollection. In a statement that Schüssler Fiorenza might have written, Benjamin insists that, "What the science [history] has 'established,' recollection can modify. Recollection can make the incomplete (happiness) into something finished [and] suffering into something incomplete."[85] A forgetful humanity incapable of recollection and remembrance is without hope for the future because it abandons the dead and thus forecloses on the possibility of its own redemption. After all, it is only for their sake that hope is given to us.[86]

In reclaiming and restoring these and other dangerous memories to Christian women's history, Schüssler Fiorenza shatters not only the false memories that expel women to the margins and silences of history, but also the ideological interests that distort our theological traditions and rob them of their political power by directing them toward an accommodation with the status quo of sexist society and patriarchal-kyriarchal culture. The liberation of women from oppression within Christianity is requisite to the process of the restoration of Christianity to its own original emancipatory and inclusive intent; without the liberation of women, this restorative process cannot take place. The historical project of women's liberation is the very condition of the possibility for "the emancipation of the Christian community from patriarchal structures and androcentric mind-sets" that allows the gospel to "become again a 'power for the salvation' of women as well as men"[87]—and, I would add, for the preservation of Christianity itself. Christianity will either consciously embrace and promote the liberation

---

[85] Benjamin, "Konvolut 'N,' " 19.

[86] Cf. Walter Benjamin's often quoted statement, "It is only for the sake of those without hope that hope is given to us." Cited in Herbert Marcuse, *One-Dimensional Man: Studies in the Ideology of Advanced Industrial Society* (Boston: Beacon Press, 1968), 257.

[87] Schüssler Fiorenza, *In Memory of Her*, 31.

of women and all subjugated peoples, or it will wither away of its own historical irrelevance.[88]

What Schüssler Fiorenza fully understands, neither Benjamin, Horkheimer, Adorno, nor Marcuse could ever see: that without the liberation of women, human liberation cannot achieve even the status of a utopian dream. At the same time, Adorno's negative dialectics and Benjamin's theological materialism lend themselves to Schüssler Fiorenza's feminist critique in ways that not only resonate with her work but may contribute to it as well. The result is a mutual clarification and deepening that serves to expand the critical theories of both. As one commentator has written of Walter Benjamin, in words that are no less true of Schüssler Fiorenza, the "theological illumination that redeems past history, and [the] political education that condemns it, are one and the same endeavor."[89]

---

[88] I owe the specific formulation of this idea to the liberation theologian Leonardo Boff. See "Conservative Vision Threatens Tradition of Medellin and Puebla," *Prairie Messenger*, 27 May 1991.
[89] Buck-Morss, *The Dialectics of Seeing*, 245.

CHAPTER 6

The Radical Vision

Utopia, Socialism, and Humanist Feminism in Rosemary Radford Ruether

ONE OF THE MAJOR DIFFERENCES AMONG THE CRITICAL SO-
cial theorists concerns politics, and in particular the question of political
action. The theoretical perspectives of Max Horkheimer and Theodor
Adorno are rooted in a deep political commitment to the transformation of the human condition toward freedom, justice, and happiness. Both writers nonetheless resolutely refuse to engage in constructivist, programmatic hypotheses that would in any way give visible
shape to the outlines of a new world with its correspondingly transformed humanity.

As far as Horkheimer is concerned, neither philosophy nor theology is capable of defining reality in such a way that a concrete
alternative may be articulated. Nor is there any possibility of "telling
men how they are to act in order to halt the withering away of the
human." Indeed, for Horkheimer, all philosophy and theology may
do is to dwell on the "negative side" of the historical process in all its
"gruesomeness" and "injustice." They "cannot prescribe how people
are to escape from the charmed circle of the status quo; [they] can
only seek to give the charm a name." In a view that resonates with
the famous "Finale" of Adorno's *Minima Moralia,* Horkheimer will
only acknowledge the possibility that "perhaps an accurate grasp of
what is false in the situation will enable what is true and valid to force

its way through."[1] For both Horkheimer and Adorno, intimations of utopia, in which a transformed humanity has at last been able to achieve a certain degree of reconciliation among themselves and with nature, might become dimly apparent—but only through an uncompromising, negative critical theory of the existent. As Adorno remarked on more than one occasion, the critical theory of society is a theory of human relations insofar as it is able to theorize the *inhumanity* of those relations.

For Horkheimer, theorizing is itself a form of action, in that "activity is not to be regarded as an appendix, as merely what comes after thought, but enters into theory at every point and is inseparable from it."[2] While both Horkheimer and Adorno regarded negative thinking as both political and active, they did not embrace political activism; in fact, they deliberately refused to endorse it in any of its forms. In their view, liberation struggles not only occur within existing structures, they are marked by them, and historically so. In the words of Horkheimer, "It is folly, after all, to think that we can break off the hazardous developments in technology, family life, and all human relationships; all these developments are what they now are because of deficiencies at earlier points in the process."[3] The most that humanity can hope for, then, is to retain whatever capacity is left to it to think what is becoming increasingly unthinkable under current conditions. More than that is to reproduce domination and distortion because every act and every thought are implicated in the distortion and indigency of what is.

Although Herbert Marcuse embraced a similar commitment to negative thinking, unlike the others he allowed that the possibility of a reconciled state between human beings and between humanity and nature might become actual through historical struggle. Marcuse, it will be recalled, understood that every thing or concept contains within

---

[1] Max Horkheimer, *Critique of Instrumental Reason*, trans. Matthew J. O'Connell et al. (New York: Seabury Press, 1974), 32, 33.

[2] Max Horkheimer, "On the Problem of Truth," in Andrew Arato and Eike Gebhardt, eds. *The Essential Frankfurt School Reader* (New York: Continuum, 1982), 420.

[3] Horkheimer, *Critique of Instrumental Reason*, 33.

itself the contradiction of being constituted both by what it is and what it is not. As a result, all particularity must be seen as always in the process of transgressing its given forms, of negating its own negativity. In this sense all things exist in a dynamic state; all being exists as being-as-becoming, where the thing's potentiality negates its false actuality by overcoming its limitations and driving toward the realization of what it ought to be. In contrast to Adorno, Marcuse acknowledges the "critical potentiality" of concepts[4] to release the authentic objectivity contained within them.

In further contrast to Adorno, Marcuse did not disavow political activism and was very much in support of the social struggles engaged in by various socialist "militant minorities," such as the women's and students' movements of the 1960s and '70s. As has been seen previously, for Marcuse one of the purposes of social theory is to identify those oppositional tendencies that might open new paths beyond the existing state of affairs. In his view, utopia is no longer "no place," but rather that which is blocked from coming into being by the power of established social forms.[5] Thus Marcuse could support some of the activist social struggles and resistance movements of his time despite his recognition that no concepts can "bridge the gap between the present and its future." Marcuse went further and attempted to describe what a transformed society might look like, what sort of values it would be based on, and what kind of transformed relations could exist between human beings, men and women, and humanity and nature. Marcuse's elaboration of critical theory is both negative and to an extent constructivist, especially insofar as he locates and elaborates the possibilities for concrete historical transcendence within present conditions.

Christianity's Latent Emancipatory Power

IN THIS RESPECT MARCUSE'S THINKING RESONATES IN THE work of Rosemary Radford Ruether. She shares many of his perspectives, such as the hope for "the new society" of men and women

---

[4] See David Held, *Introduction to Critical Theory* (Berkeley: Univ. of California Press, 1980), 228.
[5] Herbert Marcuse, *An Essay on Liberation* (Boston: Beacon Press, 1968), 3–4.

"with new psyches"[6] for whom the experience of pleasure and enjoyment is perceived as a necessity of daily life. As well, it is possible to distinguish Ruether from Mary Daly and Elisabeth Schüssler Fiorenza in a fashion analogous to the distinction between Marcuse on the one hand and Horkheimer and Adorno on the other regarding the question of political involvement. Although similarities exist between Ruether's feminist critique and that of Daly and Schüssler Fiorenza, they are more incidental and superficial than substantive. What marks Ruether's work in contrast to the work of these other feminist theologians are (1) her comprehensive critique of domination that ranges far beyond specifically feminist issues, and (2) her articulated commitment to communitarian socialism. Although Schüssler Fiorenza's work contains some inherent socialist sympathies,[7] Mary Daly's feminist theory is explicitly hostile to socialism in any of its forms.

As well, Daly and Schüssler Fiorenza largely restrict their critical analyses within a feminist framework no matter what particular subject they are dealing with. In contrast, Ruether addresses her theoretical inquiries to a wide variety of issues that includes feminism but is not limited to it. Ruether is interested in human liberation, which she works out in terms of a sustained critique of domination in its multiple manifestations. Ruether's focus on whatever possibilities for human liberation might exist under current conditions precedes and transcends her interest in women's liberation, although she sees the latter as integrally connected with the liberation of all humanity. Her sustained and consistent preoccupation with understanding the dynamics of domination in all its concrete forms, along with her commitment to reveal and reclaim those subterranean emancipatory elements and impulses that persist in Western religious and intellectual traditions, situate her most closely and comprehensively in relation to the Frankfurt School than either Schüssler Fiorenza or Daly.

---

[6] Rosemary Radford Ruether, *Gaia and God: An Ecofeminist Theology of Earth Healing* (New York: HarperSanFrancisco, 1992), 172.

[7] I have explored the implicit socialist political implications of Schüssler Fiorenza's work elsewhere, and so I will not elaborate my argument here. See my "The Socialist Implications of Feminist Critical Liberation Theology," *Studies in Religion* 22, no. 3 (Summer 1993): 323–35.

Ruether's work engages in a creative effort to reconstruct and restore the emancipatory traditions of the West that have become repressed, discarded, or marginalized but still contain the critical potential to offer cultural and political lifelines to a humanity that is becoming increasingly bereft of hope and incapable of generating its own self-transformation. Ruether's analysis of the various forms of domination that pervade all areas of social, cultural, and personal life, along with her explicit commitment to a communitarian or libertarian socialist politics, marks her as the most radical feminist religious thinker writing today. Although the term *radical* is cliché-ridden and therefore empty, it is useful as it may be applied to Ruether in that it challenges the superficial view popular in some feminist quarters that describes Mary Daly as one of the most risk-taking, progressive, and revolutionary feminist religious thinkers to occupy the category.[8]

Furthermore—and this is one of the major points I want to emphasize—Ruether is the least theological of the feminist thinkers under discussion. As I will demonstrate in the final chapter, Ruether's work most closely approximates a feminist *critical theory of religion* rather than a feminist *theology*. At the same time, her continued use of theological concepts and discourse tends to limit the inner logic of her thought, which is clearly pushing toward a critical social theory of religion whose intent is both deconstructive and reconstructive in relation to one of the most important repositories of Western utopian thought: the Jewish and Christian religious traditions. For Ruether, these religious traditions contain emancipatory themes and impulses

---

[8] See Carol P. Christ's article, "The New Feminist Theology: A Review of the Literature," *Religious Studies Review* 3, no. 4 (October 1977): 203–12, wherein she classifies feminist theologians as either "reformist" or "radical." She classifies Ruether as "a radical reformist feminist theologian" (whatever that means) and herself as a "feminist revolutionary" (p. 206). For Christ, the criterion used to define a revolutionary as contrasted with a reformist has to do with whether one believes that Christianity has any liberating potential. Revolutionaries reject Christianity as containing any liberative possibilities for women, whereas reformers think that there is an "essential core" of Christian truth that is promising for the transformation of the subjugated condition of women. In my view, these classifications are nearly useless in any critical-analytical sense, as they overschematize and therefore simplify the differences and similarities among the various feminist theologians.

that resonate with nonreligious theories of human liberation.[9] Taken all together, they point toward the possibility of a transformed future that is contained in the present, awaiting release through human action.

To explain the distinction between theology and religious thought that is relevant to a fuller understanding of Ruether's "theological" vision and critical perspective, it is helpful to consider Horkheimer's and Karl Marx's views on religion. It must always be borne in mind that when Horkheimer and Marx (or any of the members of the Frankfurt School) write of religion, they are referring to Christianity, or what they understand to be the Judeo-Christian tradition.[10] In a statement that recalls Marx's formulation of the protest character of religion as the sigh of the oppressed creature and the longing for soul in soulless conditions, Horkheimer describes religion as "the record of the wishes, desires, and accusations of countless generations." What characterizes the religious impulse is the longing for "perfect justice," which in contemporary times animates many liberation struggles. Given that no such justice is possible, no matter how society might transform for the better, the idea of the existence of absolute justice that condemns the wretchedness of the human condition in the name of a more reasonable and humane future has become lodged within nonreligious political struggles that have long forgotten their utopian source in religion.

In the wake of the collapse of the classical theological systems and the increasing irrelevancy of ecclesiastical institutions, Horkheimer concludes that, "true discipleship . . . does not lead men back to religion." Rather, the traditional outward forms of religion become discredited and discarded, but the longing for and image of a perfect justice persists and motivates struggles for social justice. He writes,

> Mankind loses religion as it moves through history, but the loss leaves its mark behind. Part of the drives and desires which religious

---

[9] Rosemary Radford Ruether, *The Radical Kingdom: The Western Experience of Messianic Hope* (New York: Harper and Row, 1970).

[10] The term *Judeo-Christian* is problematic in that Judaism becomes collapsed into Christianity, as if Judaism did not exist as a distinct religious tradition out of which Christianity emerged. The use of the term in the present text reflects the views of the writers under discussion only.

belief preserved and kept alive are detached from the inhibiting religious form and become productive forces in social practice. . . . In a really free mind the concept of infinity is preserved in an awareness of the finality of human life and of the inalterable aloneness of men, and it keeps society from indulging in a thoughtless optimism, an inflation of its own knowledge into a new religion.[11]

A careful examination of Horkheimer's remarks on religion helps to illuminate Ruether's critical liberation theology. In many respects Ruether's work is a sustained protest against the current human condition as well as an articulation of a longing for and hope in the possibility of a future perfect justice within history. In a statement that is powerfully evocative of Walter Benjamin, she describes the resurrection as representing "my basic faith commitment that lies, violence and death will not have the last word in human affairs. Life will triumph over death; truth will win out finally against deceit."[12]

With respect to women, this hope that the violence and brutality inflicted on them throughout history will not remain unredeemed does not require or rest on false memories of an idealized past. Ruether has maintained a consistent critical skepticism toward developments in feminist spirituality that derive female dignity and power from a remote prehistory where women enjoyed high social status largely derived from worship of the Goddess. Although Ruether seeks a "new feminist religious culture" where women may "experience the divine in their own image,"[13] she has no interest in engaging in new mythologizations or reified hypostatizations of female "essence." Rather, her work seeks to reclaim the concrete life histories of actual women struggling within their religious traditions as well as to push the redemptive power of feminist spirituality and women-church to include

---

[11] Max Horkheimer, *Critical Theory: Selected Essays*, trans. Matthew J. O'Connell et al. (New York: Continuum, 1972), 129–31.

[12] Rosemary Radford Ruether, "Is There a Place for Feminists in a Christian Church?" in Daphne Hampson and Rosemary Radford Ruether, *New Blackfriars* (January 1987). (Reprint of their debate.) I wish to thank Professor Hampson for bringing this discussion to my attention.

[13] Rosemary Radford Ruether, "The Development of My Theology," *Religious Studies Review* 15, no. 1 (January 1989): 4.

the whole of humanity.[14] The critical force of feminist theology lies in its capacity to deconstruct the false universalism of patriarchal theologies in order to reconstruct a more genuine and concrete universalism that includes all humanity in its manifold diversity and difference. The significance of focusing on women's experience as a point of departure for theological analysis "explodes as a critical force, exposing classical theology, including its codified traditions, as based on *male* experience rather than on universal human experience."[15]

Ruether's critique of the patriarchal false universalism of Christian theology, with its attendant doctrines and ecclesial power structures, is aimed at uncovering the emancipatory potential that remains preserved, although somewhat defaced, within the Christian religion. In a statement that bears remarkable affinity with Horkheimer's view of the transition of religious longing into "conscious social practice," Ruether writes that the emancipatory potential of Christianity:

> could only be released in a post-Christian world, in a world where the monopoly of Christian society upon history had been thrown into question, where the dispensation of the historical church and the society it had founded had been relativized, thus releasing again the idea of a genuinely new event occurring in future history. While the Christian message implicitly carried a social revolutionary ideal, in practice, after the absorption of the apocalyptic message of the new age into the age of the church and the projection of the fulfillment of the gospel into an other-worldly heaven unrelated to future history, this potential could only be released through the secularization of society, the dethronement of the Christian establishment.[16]

As Christianity was forced to accommodate to the status quo through its theological and ecclesial traditions, it lost its redemptive power,

---

[14] For the life histories of women active in their religious traditions, see Rosemary Ruether and Eleanor McLaughlin, eds., *Women of Spirit: Female Leadership in the Jewish and Christian Traditions* (New York: Simon and Schuster, 1979); and Rosemary Radford Ruether and Rosemary Skinner Keller, *Women and Religion in America*, volume 2 (San Francisco: Harper and Row, 1983).

[15] Rosemary Radford Ruether, *Sexism and God-Talk: Toward a Feminist Theology* (Boston: Beacon Press, 1983), 13.

[16] Ruether, *The Radical Kingdom*, 17.

which derived from its "world negating" protest against the suffering and oppression inflicted on humanity by the status quo of whatever historical epoch. In the cleavage between "ultimate salvation" and the "available horizon of salvation" in history, the revolutionary thrust of the gospel became inaccessible to human beings. As a result, Christianity became another ideology of social conservatism in the service of the preservation of prevailing social forms.[17] Thus theological authority and traditions along with their political expression and guarantor, the church, function as the negation of the Christian religion with its message of liberation and demanding hope for a more humane world. Only in a world where established theology and ecclesial power have waned is it possible to reclaim and restore the liberative dimension of Christianity.

Ruether's idea that the emancipatory power of Christianity can only be redeemed in a "post-Christian" or post-Christendom world meshes with similar insights of both Horkheimer and Marcuse. According to Marcuse, "with [the] transubstantiation [of Jesus], his gospel too was transubstantiated; his deification removed his message from this world. Suffering and repression were perpetuated."[18] In a similar vein Horkheimer expresses "the hope that, in the period of world history which is now beginning, the period of docile masses governed by clocks, some men can still be found to offer resistance, like the victims of the past and among them, the founder of Christianity."[19] For Horkheimer, Marcuse, and Ruether, the spiritualization of the gospel, the severing of the notion of ultimate redemption from historical redemption, represents the domestication of the transformative power of Christianity and the loss of one of humanity's most important sources of utopian promise. While Horkheimer and Marcuse accepted this loss, Ruether refuses to do so. She believes that a feminist critical deconstruction of Christian theology will release its emancipatory potential, which has long been repressed but not destroyed.

---

[17] Rosemary Radford Ruether and Eugene C. Bianchi, *From Machismo to Mutuality: Woman-Man Liberation* (New York: Paulist Press, 1976), 113.

[18] Herbert Marcuse, *Eros and Civilization* (New York: Vintage Books, 1962), 64.

[19] Horkheimer, *Critique of Instrumental Reason*, 49.

If theology must die, as it were, so that the religious impulse to perfect justice may be released as a necessary condition for a redeemed humanity (that is, redemption in Benjamin's sense), then this longing or desire for justice realized in history requires a new location and vehicle if it is to be preserved. In several respects, this search constitutes Ruether's overall theoretical activity, although she cannot take the final step and abandon theological discourse altogether. Nonetheless she does provide for a new location whereby a possible reconciliation between the material (or concrete) and utopian dimension of the Christian hope in liberation may occur. She does this in part in her sustained focus on and commitment to a clear socialist political praxis. It informs her comprehensive critique of domination, which speaks in the name of the particular, that is to say, the particularly oppressed, be they women, Palestinians, Jews, or nonhuman nature.

As well, although she does propose certain constructivist visions and political directions that she thinks will open pathways to redeemed relations between human beings and humanity and nature, she does not lapse into false constructivist abstractions that appeal to mythic reifications of femaleness. Rather, Ruether offers a practical theory of human liberation that shares much in common with some of the basic themes and preoccupations of critical theory. An example is her expanded focus on domination as it reverberates throughout all areas of human experience, including economic forms, cultural institutions, interpersonal relations, and the treatment of the natural world. Her analysis of these phenomena is mediated by a definite and distinct political commitment. It is this dimension of Ruether's work that infuses her insights with critical power.

Ruether's interest in exposing the dynamics of domination and hierarchical power structures in contemporary society allows her a larger and more politically engaged perspective on a wide variety of issues that is somewhat unique in current feminist theological writing. She acknowledges this as she recounts her early political activities and interests and how they set her apart from other feminists. Recalling her experiences at Harvard Divinity School, she writes, "To be concerned about class and race was seen as distracting from 'pure' feminism. The influence of Mary Daly was evident here."[20] To be sure,

---

[20] Rosemary Radford Ruether, *Disputed Questions: On Being a Christian* (New York: Orbis Books, 1989), 53.

Mary Daly openly repudiates political engagement, especially socialist politics and theory of the kind espoused by Ruether. Daly prefers a more privatized and individualistic approach that promotes personal flamboyancy and outrageousness rather than public, issues-oriented struggle.

The case of Elisabeth Schüssler Fiorenza is quite different in that she consistently maintains that feminist theory can only derive its critical and transformative power from its location in a feminist movement. As indicated earlier, she has recently turned her attention to questions of race and has refined her own theoretical perspective. She has turned toward difference and particularity among women, resisting abstractionist tendencies within feminism that are grounded in reified conceptualizations of female being. In this way Schüssler Fiorenza shares Adorno's concerns with the preservation of the particular as outlined in his *Negative Dialectics*. Ruether, however, goes further even than Schüssler Fiorenza in articulating her vision of and commitment to a communitarian socialist politics that remains the only viable means whereby particularity and diversity may be enhanced and preserved.

Ruether's socialist political vision is thoroughly democratic, anti-hierarchical, anti-authoritarian, and anti-centralist. In the tradition of the late Marcuse and anarchist anti-statism,[21] Ruether calls for local communities that are self-managed and nonsectarian and that seek alliances with other politically engaged groups such as peace activists, local neighborhood organizations, environmental groups, the women's movement (especially as it relates to poor and working-class women), and labor unions.[22] As for the relationship between feminism and political action, Ruether shares Marcuse's commitment to socialist feminism, although without the idealized romanticism. Her articulation of socialist feminism is more concrete and more adequately

---

[21] Ruether's discussion of Jesus' teachings about the messianic age suggests a certain anti-statist perspective that informs her interpretation. She writes: "Jesus repudiates the nationalist-revenge mythology of much of the messianic tradition. The messianic age will not be a time when Israel will defeat its enemies and be installed in possession of a great Near Eastern empire through which it will rule its former masters. *Rather it will be a time when all structures of ruler and ruled are overcome.*" *Sexism and God-Talk*, 121 (emphasis added).

[22] Ruether, *Disputed Questions*, 87–89.

addresses the actual condition of women than Marcuse's; in this sense, Ruether's concern for women is closer to that of Engels and Marx. "Socialist feminists," she writes, "see the conflict between women and men as embedded in a hierarchical economic system that divides housework from paid labor and structures women as an unpaid and low-paid labor class at the bottom of both these systems."[23] More than Schüssler Fiorenza and certainly in contrast to Daly, Ruether consistently emphasizes the importance of class division as a factor in women's subjugated state. She also addresses the specific condition of women both in the home and in the world of wage labor. She exposes the interstructures of domination that infuse both realms, where women most typically perform the "shitwork" of menial jobs that merely extend the tasks of domestic labor into women's jobs in the workforce so that women's labor functions as an "auxiliary support system" for males.[24]

Ruether's interest in the transformation of family structures extends far beyond the freeing of women from domestic chores that is a precondition for the development of their full capacities. For Ruether, the transformation of humanity from alienation to freedom is inextricably linked to necessary changes in family life, where "new forms of gender parity" must be constructed through changes in parenting relations. In a passage that resonates with the psychoanalytic theories of Dorothy Dinnerstein, Nancy Chodorow, and Jessica Benjamin,[25] Ruether links the transformation of society with the transformation of family structures; without transformations in the family, the possibility of human liberation is at best remote. She writes,

> A genuine change in the pattern of parenting must be understood, not as a slight adjustment toward males "helping" females with

---

[23] Ibid., 132.

[24] Rosemary Radford Ruether, *New Woman/New Earth: Sexist Ideologies and Human Liberation* (New York: Seabury Press, 1975), 181.

[25] Dorothy Dinnerstein, *The Mermaid and the Minotaur: Sexual Arrangements and Human Malaise* (New York: Harper and Row, 1976); Nancy Chodorow, *The Reproduction of Mothering* (Berkeley: Univ. of California Press, 1978); Jessica Benjamin, *The Bonds of Love: Psychoanalysis, Feminism and the Problem of Domination* (New York: Pantheon Books, 1988).

childcare, but a fundamental reconstruction of the primary roots of culture, transforming the gender imaging of child-parent relations and the movement into adulthood for both males and females. This implies a reconstruction of the relation of the domestic core of society to the larger society. One must look at all the hierarchies of exploitation and control that emanate out of the family pattern of female mothering and domestic labor.[26]

Ruether places such importance and even urgency on the necessity of transforming family arrangements because of her view that "patriarchal family patterns" contribute to the socialization of males "into violence through mother negation."[27] Although this theme has been developed in the feminist psychoanalytic theories of Dinnerstein, Benjamin, and (particularly) Chodorow,[28] Ruether's line of argument does not take up their analysis. Rather it develops out of her critique of Goddess worship and feminist spirituality that hypostatizes maternal female power in such a way as to provoke resentment in males.

Ruether has been consistently critical of the Goddess spirituality movement that has become somewhat popular within contemporary forms of feminist religious practices and beliefs. Her contention that speculations on prehistoric matriarchies harbor a "psychological weakness" that "risk[s] developing the resentful male," however, is a recent development in her thinking. As far as Ruether is concerned, the quasi-mythological reconstructions of female power that some feminists suppose to have prevailed both sociologically and religiously in prehistoric times only contribute to existing masculine tendencies to negate women. Ruether suggests that men's sense of connection with the reproduction and sustaining of life is already somewhat tenuous because it is less immediate and therefore more of a socially constructed relation than that of women. Insofar as this is the case, it is important that societies "develop an adequately affirmative role for men, one that gives men prestige parallel to that of women but prevents their

---

[26] Ruether, *Gaia and God*, 171–72.

[27] Ibid., 172.

[28] Although Ruether refers to the psychoanalytic theories of Dinnerstein and Chodorow on the effects of female parenting on male and female children, she does not probe their views in any depth. See *Gaia and God*, 292, note 48.

assuming aggressive dominance over women."[29] In Ruether's view, feminist overvaluation of matricentric societies that might have existed in prehistoric times fails to recognize how "the matricentric pattern" of society itself fosters "the insecure, resentful male, who emancipates himself from his mother by negation of women."[30]

The Goddess Revealed

RUETHER'S CRITICAL ANALYSIS OF GODDESS WORSHIP IN CON-temporary feminism and ecofeminist spirituality, along with the historical truth claims that they rely on, is most fully but as yet incompletely developed in her latest work, *Gaia and God*. Ruether questions the validity and desirableness of the values and assumptions that animate Goddess spirituality; more important, she also confronts the problematic nature of its historical claims and in so doing raises significant issues that feminism cannot afford to ignore any longer.

Some years ago, Ruether began to identify several difficulties with contemporary Goddess spirituality that relate to a somewhat "tendentious use of historical material [that] reduces everything to one drama: the story of original female power and goodness, and the evil male conquest and suppression of the same."[31] More recently she has turned her attention to an analysis of some of the philosophical and archaeological materials that the feminist spirituality and ecofeminist movements have appropriated in their efforts to buttress their claims that in prehistoric times the prevailing mode of worship was centered around the Goddess and her priestess queens who wielded considerable power in their social environment. Goddess-worshiping societies were supposedly structured around ethical values that were sexually egalitarian, peaceful, and aesthetically well developed; women in these societies enjoyed a higher, more respected social and even political status than in subsequent epochs. These matricentric, sometimes matriarchal cultures flourished in a harmonious creativity that informed

---

[29] Ibid., 167.
[30] Ibid., 169.
[31] Rosemary Radford Ruether, "Goddesses and Witches: Liberation and Countercultural Feminism," *The Christian Century* (September 10–17, 1980): 843.

relations between people and with nature until they were destroyed by violent hordes of invaders. The invaders almost entirely wiped out the way of life and the cultural achievements of these cultures, replacing them with patriarchal and hierarchical social structures of domination and exploitation that have prevailed until this day.

Contemporary Goddess worshipers, Wicca adherents, ecofeminists, and members of feminist spirituality groups seek to restore elements of this matriarchal past and its corresponding gynocentric values within the present. Their hope is that domination between human beings and over nature will end, patriarchy will be overcome and abolished, and a new reign of harmony, peace, and loving mutuality will be ushered into history. The hope that such a transformation is possible is secured by the knowledge that human beings once lived this way and may be encouraged to do so again if the memory of prepatriarchal experience can be recalled. This is where efforts to establish historical truth concerning the gynocentric nature of prehistoric societies become important to the feminist spirituality movement. These historical truth claims, however, are extremely vulnerable and open to serious questioning. Ruether takes up this issue by confronting the main scholarly and popular influences on contemporary feminist spirituality: Marija Gimbutas, J. J. Bachofen, and (very briefly) Riane Eisler.

Ruether focuses primarily on the work of archaeologist Marija Gimbutas, and rightly so. Gimbutas's theories of the gynocentric structure of the cultures of "Old Europe" and their subsequent annihilation by patriarchal invaders continue to function as the main support of the appeal to historical accuracy that Goddess feminists repeatedly invoke to back up their views. Rather than provide a straight recapitulation of Ruether's critical arguments concerning the historical and theoretical bases of feminist spirituality, I will develop and extend them further than she does.

As well, I will offer a much expanded examination of her brief remarks on J. J. Bachofen, whose theory of Mother Right and the role of the feminine in history exerts a far stronger, if indirect, influence on contemporary feminist spirituality than perhaps Ruether recognizes. Bachofen's impact on Goddess spirituality is not immediately evident because his thought enters feminism via the work of Gimbutas, who refers to him directly only in passing. For anyone who has read Bachofen, however, it becomes readily apparent just how important his influence on writers like Gimbutas has been. It is also important to look more closely at Bachofen than Ruether does because of the profoundly antifemale structure of his thought. This bias appears to be quite unnoticed by feminists who uncritically adopt his theory of the primacy of the feminine principle in the unfolding of history as further legitimation for their own historical claims. Thus a more lengthy discussion of Bachofen than is provided by Ruether is indispensable to a fuller grasp of the contradictory implications of his thought for feminism.

The least will be said of Riane Eisler. Her popularist versions of the fall from gynocentric, "gylanic" cultures and partnership models of interaction into the patriarchal world of violence and hierarchical structures of social "dominator" relationships offer nothing significant beyond what has been written by Gimbutas. What is perhaps of greatest importance about Eisler for the purposes of this discussion is her influence on Gimbutas. Indeed, perhaps there is little more to say about Eisler than what Ruether has already stated in her one-paragraph description of Eisler's book, *The Chalice and the Blade:* "Unquestionably this story has powerful mythic appeal for people in the late twentieth century, deeply concerned by ecological and militarist threats to the earth; but is it really history?"[32]

Ruether's question about Eisler must also be applied to the general conclusions offered by Marija Gimbutas as a result of her archaeological researches into prehistoric societies. A critical examination of Gimbutas is mandatory in order to fully comprehend the deeper structural and conceptual difficulties of a feminist spirituality that strives to the level of history. A close critical look at Gimbutas's work is required in order to separate the elements of science (that is, archaeological research methods) from an excessive tendency in her thought to imaginative reconstruction bordering on fantasy. It is this curious mixture of careful research coupled with dubious interpretive conclusions that religious

---

[32] Ruether, *Gaia and God*, 151.

ecofeminists and Goddess adherents have unquestioningly appropriated. Unless the interpretive problems in Gimbutas's work are confronted, a critique of feminist spirituality claims is severely limited and therefore inadequate. Although Ruether challenges some of Gimbutas's more outlandish claims, she does so in too sketchy a manner. What follows here is an expansion of Ruether's line of argument that probes more deeply into the theoretical difficulties of Gimbutas's work. This probing begins to more seriously problematize the viability of Gimbutas's assertions.

A critical exposition of the weaknesses in Gimbutas's work is also valuable insofar as it provides women in the feminist spirituality movement with an opportunity to rethink (rather than abandon) some of their convictions. If the claims to the historical validity of a lost gynocratic, Goddess–oriented age can be questioned adequately enough, perhaps these feminists will reconsider their need for historical legitimation at all. Thereby they may achieve greater confidence in their religiosity as a valid form of spirituality in itself, whose symbols and images are understood as more authentic for women than the oppressive patriarchal theological systems from which they have broken free. While the issue of historical accuracy is problematic in a number of respects, Ruether's question about the very need for "proving" the existence of peaceful, egalitarian partnership societies in prehistory is the significant one, and her answer rings with plausibility. The effort to establish the existence of "a world before patriarchy . . . provides warrant for faith that such a society can happen again. The story affirms a faith in the nonessentiality of relations of domination."[33]

Patriarchal Invaders Revisited

GIMBUTAS'S MAIN HYPOTHESIS IS THAT IN NEOLITHIC TIMES, a highly developed, sedentary culture existed in southeastern Europe. It flourished without interruption until the invasions of mounted pastoralists from the Pontic Steppe region, known as Kurgan invaders, who destroyed these Old European cultures, plunging them into a

---

[33] Ibid., 154.

dark age. The societies of Old Europe were basically peaceful, sexually egalitarian, matrilineal and matrifocal, organized along the lines of a Goddess-worshiping theacracy presided over by a priestess-queen. Gimbutas interprets the high level of aesthetic production achieved by these societies as evidence of cultural superiority with respect to their patriarchal conquerors. She contrasts the "fine-quality ceramics"[34] of Old European cultures with Kurgan pottery, whose "stabbing and impressing technique is quite primitive and seems to focus only on one symbol, the sun."[35] The rich diversity of Old European symbols, in contrast, included multiple zoomorphic and ornithomorphic images of the Goddess and her animal companions. Gimbutas provides the following illustration of the sharp differences between the two cultures:

> In contrast to the sacred myths of pre-Indo-European peoples which centered around the moon, water, and the female, the religion of pastoral, semisedentary Indo-European peoples was oriented toward the rotating sky, the sun, stars, planets, and other sky phenomena, such as thunder and lightning. Their sky and sun gods shone "bright as the sky"; they wore starry cloaks adorned with glittering gold, copper, or amber pendants, torques, chest plates, and belts.[36]

While their pottery might have been "devoid of symbolic language and of aesthetic treatment in general," by Gimbutas's own account these Kurgans hardly seem devoid of aesthetic ability. Gimbutas appears to have little interest in acknowledging possible contradictions in her theory because she is constructing a singular interpretation of prehistory. This interpretation requires that the unquestioned cultural superiority of Old European Goddess-oriented theacracies was destroyed by a culturally inferior, aggressive, patrifocal people who were

---

[34] Marija Gimbutas, "The Kurgan Wave #2 (c. 3400–3200 B.C.) into Europe and the Following Transformation of Culture," *The Journal of Indo-European Studies* 8, nos. 3 and 4 (Fall/Winter 1980): 291.

[35] Marija Gimbutas, "Women and Culture in Goddess-Oriented Old Europe," in Judith Plaskow and Carol P. Christ, eds., *Weaving the Visions* (San Francisco: Harper and Row, 1989), 70.

[36] Ibid.

"indifferent to art."[37] Not surprisingly, she describes the Kurgans physically as a "steppe type," exhibiting a "certain facial flatness"[38] that seems to be in contrast to what she calls the "small statured, narrow faced" or "gracile Mediterranean" type they brutally subjugated.[39] The sudden displacement and disappearance of this Old European culture was not complete, however. Traces of their culture and religion persisted well into the Bronze and even Iron Ages, from where, according to Gimbutas, evidence of the Goddess and female power surface in Minoan Crete and in Etruscan culture.

In a brief introductory abstract to her essay "The Social Structure of Old Europe," Gimbutas writes that "archaeological, historic, linguistic, religious, and mythological evidence shows that pre-Indo-European (Old European) social structure was matrilineal and endogamous, with succession to the throne and inheritance in the female line. The society was organized around a theocratic, *socialistic* temple community."[40] That socialist political forms existed in the ancient world is an astonishing claim to put forward. It suggests a certain backward projection on Gimbutas's part that reads vastly different worlds too much in the light of our own. Any number of archaeologists and classicists caution against making such conclusions about prehistoric social structures; according to J. P. Mallory, "although there has been a vast amount of literature on the burial remains and ritual of the Pontic-Caspian Eneolithic cultures, we are still far from being able to pronounce authoritatively on the social structure of their communities."[41] As for the condition of women in prehistory, Sarah Pomeroy rejects postulating correspondences between goddess-worship and high female status in a given society. According to Pomeroy, because it is

---

[37] Ibid., 63.
[38] Gimbutas, "The Kurgan Wave #2," 291.
[39] Marija Gimbutas, *The Civilization of the Goddess*, ed. Joan Marler (New York: HarperCollins, 1991), 26.
[40] Marija Gimbutas, "The Social Structure of Old Europe," *The Journal of Indo-European Studies* 17, nos. 3 and 4 (Fall/Winter, 1989): 197; emphasis added.
[41] J. P. Mallory, *In Search of the Indo-Europeans: Language, Archaeology and Myth* (London: Thames and Hudson, 1991), 218.

impossible to draw any conclusions about social systems in prehistory in the absence of written documents from the time or with the archaeological evidence now available, then we must recognize that it is as foolish to postulate masculine dominance in prehistory as to postulate female dominance. The impartial scholar will be forced to confess that the question is open and may never be answered.[42]

Women of Stature: Minoan and Etruscan Cultures

THAT GIMBUTAS DOES NOT SHARE THESE QUALMS CAN BE seen from her treatment of Minoan Crete and Etruscan culture, which she claims illustrate the continued preservation of Old European social structures and matrilineal values well after those older societies had fallen to the Kurgan invaders. Gimbutas interprets the archaeological materials found at Crete, along with the frescoes, paintings, and pottery discovered in palaces such as at Knossos, as proof of women's elevated (even superior) status. She describes depictions of men in Minoan art "never as priests, kings or gods," but "usually engaged in subordinate occupations."[43] According to Gimbutas, the frescoes at Knossos reveal "beautiful, elegant women dressed in exquisite costumes . . . mixing freely with men in festivals, riding in chariots driven by female charioteers." Clearly, Gimbutas wishes to picture Bronze Age Crete as a matrifocal, harmonious, peaceful, creative society whose cultural achievements and social structure are inextricably connected with its veneration of the Goddess and her priestess-queen

---

[42] Sarah B. Pomeroy, *Goddesses, Whores, Wives, and Slaves: Women in Classical Antiquity* (New York: Schocken Books, 1975), 15.

[43] The section on the social structure of Minoan Crete in Gimbutas's latest book, *Civilization of the Goddess*, is a slightly revised version of her article, "The Social Structure of Old Europe." The description of males in Minoan art as engaged in "subordinate occupations" has been changed in the book to read, "a variety of occupations." As Gimbutas makes no reference to the article, nor mentions that it has been substantially reproduced in the later text, one can only presume that the revised description of male occupations from "subordinate" to "variety" reflects the influence of Riane Eisler's concept of gylany. Gimbutas explicitly applies this concept to the social structure of Old European cultures, where gender relations were "more or less" equal. Cf. 324.

representatives. The implication is that all Minoan women must have enjoyed the high status allotted to the theacratic nobility. But even granting the plausibility of her argument, does Gimbutas's portrait of Crete provide the whole picture?

Apparently it does not if one examines the work of archaeologist Peter Warren, whose excavations at Crete in the late 1970s and early '80s uncovered evidence suggesting practices of ritual sacrifice of children. Warren's examination of marks on the bones belonging to two children, aged approximately eight and eleven years old, reveal "clear evidence that their flesh was carefully cut away, much in the manner of the flesh of sacrificed animals." Warren hypothesizes that the children were not only slaughtered, but their flesh was cooked and "possibly eaten in a sacrificial ritual made in the service of a nature deity to assure the annual renewal of fertility." He goes on to discuss the "context adjacent to which the children's bones were found." He describes vessels "painted in the Marine Style with spray fronds, triton shells and double axes," designs used to decorate ritual vases with a "specifically religious connection."[44] Warren's examination of the children's bones discounts the possibility that they were victims of "ordinary murder" given the "elaborate cutting treatment" discovered on the bones. He also rules out the possibility that they were victims killed during a siege, as there is "nothing to indicate that this house, much less the city, was the object of a siege or battle." After reviewing a variety of possibilities as to how the children might have died and what significance might be attributed to their deaths, he writes:

> That child sacrifice was not totally unknown in Bronze Age Crete is suggested by a scene on a Late Minoan 1 ring impression recently published from Khania. It depicts a large seated female figure, probably a goddess, before whom stands a child in a skirt, most probably a girl. Over the child is what looks very much like a hilted sword, one poised for the kill.[45]

---

[44] Peter Warren, "Knossos: New Excavations and Discoveries," *Archaeology* 37, no. 4 (July/August 1984): 48, 51.
[45] Ibid., 53.

Needless to say, Gimbutas makes no reference to Warren's findings, which are put forward not in an intended negation of other interpretations, but in order to "amplify our picture of the Minoans' religious practices."[46]

Not only does Gimbutas not refer to Warren's work, she also denies that there is any evidence to suggest that warfare took place in Bronze Age Crete. Sinclair Hood, however, describes weapons found there, such as daggers, swords, and javelins. Hood takes a more tentative view of Minoan religion than does Gimbutas, admitting that "our knowledge of the . . . religion of Crete has been compared to a book of pictures without a text." Years before Warren's findings hypothesizing religious practices of child sacrifice in Crete, Hood anticipated his work with the suggestion that Minoan religion "like that of many early peoples may have had a dark side to it. Human sacrifice and suttee, the killing of a wife when her husband dies, were perhaps not unknown in Bronze Age Crete."[47]

Given these possibilities, along with the fact that our knowledge of Crete is limited to archaeological findings located in palatial sites, we can say little that is conclusive concerning the alleged privileged status of Minoan women in general. Nor can we conclude that Goddess worship in itself inevitably signifies the existence of peaceful, nonviolent societies and a concomitant reverence for life, as Gimbutas would have us believe.

Patriarchy Triumphant: J. J. Bachofen

FURTHER PROBLEMS CAN BE SEEN IN AN EXAMINATION OF Gimbutas's treatment of women in Etruscan societies. Her remarks on the status of Etruscan women paint a somewhat misleading picture of their so-called free lifestyle. To lend further support to her views, Gimbutas cites J. J. Bachofen, "who first noticed that the status of Etruscan women . . . was surprisingly high in comparison to that of

---

[46] Ibid., 55.
[47] Sinclair Hood, *The Minoans: Crete in the Bronze Age* (London: Thames and Hudson, 1971), 118, 131, 137.

Greek and Roman women."[48] Her reference to Bachofen somewhat enigmatically mentions his introduction to "The Myth of Tanaquil," with no further explanation. This is puzzling given the undeniable antifeminist tenor of his theories.

In the text cited by Gimbutas, Bachofen argues that succession to the Roman throne was facilitated by a woman. He offers this argument in support of his thesis concerning the "feminine origin of the supreme power."[49] For Bachofen, however, cultural periods of female power and social structures of matriarchy represent lower cultural stages[50] that are a necessary prelude to the establishment of a higher principle: patriarchy. The supersession of matriarchal societies by patriarchy represents the triumph of spirit over matter and history over nature. Moreover, matriarchy is the midstage between an earlier, more primitive "unregulated hetaerism"[51] and patriarchy. Bachofen states clearly that matriarchal cultures represented a "lower stage of existence"[52] yet were necessary for the victorious emergence of patriarchy. In patriarchy, he writes:

> Spiritual life rises over corporeal existence, and the relation with the lower spheres of existence is restricted to the physical aspect. Maternity pertains to the physical side of man, the only thing he shares with the animals: the paternal-spiritual principle belongs to him alone. . . . Triumphant paternity partakes of the heavenly light, while childbearing motherhood is bound up with the earth that bears all things; the establishment of paternal right is universally represented as an act of the uranian solar hero, while the defense of mother right is the first duty of the chthonian mother goddesses.[53]

This is the perspective from which Bachofen hypothesizes the "feminine origin" of monarchical succession that culminates in the

---

[48] Gimbutas, "The Social Structure of Old Europe," 206–8.

[49] J. J. Bachofen, *Myth, Religion and Mother Right: Selected Writings of J. J. Bachofen*, trans. Ralph Manheim (London: Routledge and Kegan Paul, 1967), 214.

[50] Ibid., 82.

[51] Ibid., 93.

[52] Ibid., 109.

[53] Ibid., 109–110.

Romanization and therefore civilization of Tanaquil, from an Asiatic king-woman to the virtuous, humanized, and historicized Roman matron, symbolized in Fortuna. Gimbutas says nothing of this, and yet she uses Bachofen in support of her thesis of the matriarchal and matrilineal structure of Old Europe. What in Bachofen is advanced with the denigration of women, Gimbutas appropriates as a celebration of femininity without comment concerning her reinterpretation of Bachofen's thesis. Without reference to his wider theory of matriarchy—which, by the way, is argued entirely on the basis of the mythological record—reliance on Bachofen's work is misleading for feminists. For Bachofen the "feminine principle" and all it implies are to be overcome, superseded in a higher form of human existence that leaves behind the lower realm of nature and the irrational. Bachofen would not be in favor of a return of the matriarchal age in any form. Yet Gimbutas has no hesitation using Bachofen's work as an authoritative source in support of her own views,[54] despite his unambiguous antifeminism.

Gimbutas's treatment of historical sources presents further difficulties. In support of her thesis about the freedom of Etruscan women, she cites fourth-century B.C.E. Greek historian Theopompus, who disapproves of their scandalous behavior. He describes how Etruscan women drink and socialize with men other than their husbands, seeming to prefer single motherhood to traditional family arrangements.[55] Although it may well have been true that upper-class Etruscan women enjoyed higher respect and status than their counterparts in early Republican Rome, Gimbutas fails to mention that Theopompus is not regarded as a reliable source of information and was "said to have had one of the wickedest tongues in antiquity." His portraits of the free lifestyle of Etruscan women included accusations of drunkenness and promiscuity; as for Etruscan men, they "felt no shame in committing the sexual act in public . . . enjoy[ing] homosexual more than heterosexual relations." According to one scholar,

> The evidence of the monuments amply demonstrates, however, that Theopompus' charges are no more than salacious gossip. Not only

[54] Gimbutas, *Civilization of the Goddess*, 324.
[55] Gimbutas, "The Social Structure of Old Europe," 208.

do the funerary inscriptions show a very strong pride in the family but a clear ideal of married love is expressed in the effigies of affectionate married couples, which we see on some of the sarcophagi.[56]

Gimbutas takes Theopompus' remarks on Etruscan women as historical proof of their freedom of lifestyle. In the process of using his work, however, she quietly transforms his disapprobation of Etruscan women into a celebration of their uninhibited freedom without mentioning that Theopompus' descriptions of the social activities of Etruscans were meant to discredit them.

Gimbutas's portrait of Etruscan women, like her portrait of Minoan women, is confined to selective representations of the upper classes that reveal nothing about the general condition of women, such as peasants and slaves. The status of women among the nobility and aristocratic classes, no matter how respected or free, does not mean that the wider population of women in those societies enjoyed anything similar. Gimbutas advances a restricted picture of women in ancient cultures that leads her to form singular conclusions that exclude alternative interpretations without consideration. Her argument that the cultures of Old Europe were gylanic (borrowed from Eisler), egalitarian, peaceful, and even "socialistic" assumes that a startling degree of cultural and religious uniformity existed throughout the societies of Neolithic Europe and was sustained over a long period. For Gimbutas, the "multiple categories, functions, and symbols used by prehistoric peoples to express the Great Mystery are all aspects of the unbroken unity of one deity"—the Goddess.[57] Her claims become dogmatic in their rigidity, and they are what have influenced contemporary feminist spirituality views.

---

[56] Ellen Macnamara, *Everyday Life of the Etruscans* (New York: Dorset Press, 1973), 169.
[57] Gimbutas, *Civilization of the Goddess*, 223.

Working Women: An Alternative View of Feminist Prehistory

RUETHER DOES NOT THINK, HOWEVER, THAT SPECULATIONS about women in prehistory are altogether irrelevant. On the contrary, Ruether looks to alternative feminist researches that offer different and more plausible interpretations of the activities and conditions of women in prehistory and that attempt to give them visibility as concrete human beings, insofar as this is possible. Ruether's consistent and sustained interest in the laboring activities of women in various historical epochs leads her to considerations of feminist readings of prehistory that attempt to show something of women's contribution to the development of civilization and preservation of the human species through work.

The theoretical archaeological work of Margaret Ehrenberg is an immensely interesting source of information that Ruether discusses as an alternative to writers such as Gimbutas. Again, however, a more extensive discussion of Ehrenberg's work is required than Ruether provides in order to give a fuller picture. Ehrenberg's research demonstrates what Schüssler Fiorenza consistently argues with respect to Christianity: that women have always been historical agents, active in shaping and directing human history no matter how ignored this fact has been. Once this is accepted, then it is reasonable to assume that women were active agents in prehistory as well. Along with Ruether, I too wish to argue that feminists need not disregard the issue of women in prehistory, nor do they need to ignore issues of how women came to be so thoroughly subjugated over time. Although it can never be known for certain how the domination of women came into being as a general crosscultural condition, the researches of feminists such as Ehrenberg offer a more balanced and realistic perspective for thinking about this issue than the quasi-mythic theories of Gimbutas or Bachofen.

Rejecting Goddess theories as necessary to her inquiry into the activities and status of women in prehistory, Ehrenberg attempts to find out what women were actually doing, the work they engaged in, and their material contribution to the development of civilization.

She suggests that Old and Middle Stone Age women likely enjoyed equal status with men, especially given their crucial contribution to food collection and preparation, which was essential to the survival of their group.[58] By the Neolithic period (6000 B.C.E.), farming was well established in southeastern Europe and southwest Asia, and women's primary role in food acquisition and production likely resulted in their inventing many farming tools and working out the principles of agriculture. As the techniques of farming grew more sophisticated, expanding into plough agriculture and stockbreeding, hunting was no longer important. As a result, men stayed at home and took over many of the main tasks of farming. Ehrenberg locates the change to male dominance in agriculture as taking place "at some time between the first stages of the Neolithic period and the advent of written records."[59] Changes in farming techniques, division of labor, and property ownership might also have involved more time spent in the production of "secondary products," such as spinning, weaving, and processing of milk into cheese, with the result that women became more involved in these activities, which could be more easily combined with child care. Developing this argument in some detail, Ehrenberg concludes that the social status of women probably began to decline in the later Neolithic period, when "men began to take over most agricultural work."[60]

Ehrenberg ranges over a number of cultures and historical periods looking for evidence about what women did, as opposed to how the "feminine" was symbolized and represented. Without having to contend with mythological goddesses and Kurgan invaders and our attention undiverted by stories of violent destruction of a matriarchal golden age by culturally inferior patriarchal belligerents, we see that changes in the status and condition of women took place gradually over long periods of time, involving complex technological, social, and cultural developments. We also see that women's subjugation and exclusion throughout history did not preclude their contributing to

---

[58] Margaret Ehrenberg, *Women in Prehistory* (London: British Museum Publications, 1989), 77.
[59] Ibid., 99.
[60] Ibid., 105.

all aspects of civilization; without women's work and active participation, civilization would not be possible. This is the history that feminists must strive to reclaim, along with the realization that female power involves the capacity for inventiveness, creative thought, and action.

Nor have women's activities always been directed toward peace. Ehrenberg tells us that Celtic women in the Iron Age and their children accompanied men to the battlefield, where they engaged in a variety of activities, such as carrying supplies, tending the wounded, and guarding prisoners. They also fought on occasion and participated in peace negotiations, with the result that early historians remarked on their reputation for "unreproachable fairness."[61] Celtic women included tribal chiefs and warrior queens, such as Boudica, who led the Iceni people in revolt against Roman oppression in Britain in 60 C.E.

All of this indicates that women, no matter how marginalized or silenced in the historical record, were active participants at the center of history, not only as its innocent victims, but also as agents who participated in directing its course.

The Human Face of Feminism

RUETHER'S ATTEMPT TO RECOVER THE ACTUAL HISTORIES OF living, concrete women and her focus on their laboring or political activities arise out of her socialist political perspective and her commitment to a humanist feminism that envisions a transformation of human beings themselves as well as social institutions and relationships. Ruether's refusal to embrace the remythologizations of woman and divinization of female attributes that are so prevalent in Goddess spirituality indicates a deeper repudiation of identity thinking that annihilates and devours the lived reality of diverse women. In this sense Ruether's humanism shares in the tradition of critical theory that rejects false, abstract humanism so that the actual condition of real human beings might become visible. As critical theory understands that idealizations of abstract humanity function to maintain oppressive

---

[61] Cited ibid., 164.

and unjust conditions by offering illusory compensations for the experience of misery, Goddess spirituality may also be criticized analogously, as offering a false compensation to women that undermines their motivation to public, political struggle. In both cases, the existent condition of suffering and domination remains untouched and to some extent obscured by celebrations of once denigrated "female" attributes.

This is not to suggest that there is nothing for women to celebrate about themselves and their contribution to the development of civilization and the preservation and enhancing of life. Rather, the question is, *what* is to be celebrated and how does it contribute to the liberation of women? As was argued in the discussion about Mary Daly, glorification of female attributes and values mobilizes identity thinking that imprisons women once again within the walls of rigid conceptualizations that foreclose on the mystery of individual being in all its diversity and difference. No matter how positive these conceptualizations may be, how flattering or complimentary, individual living women come under pressure to conform to these conceptualizations and if they do not, they risk the kind of derision and rejection typified in Daly's pejorative label, "fembot."

Further, forced correspondences between female attributes and female "Being" or "Essence" that fail to fully comprehend the social, cultural construction of such attributes result in their assumed naturalization. The somewhat incoherent result is that the despised attributes of femininity are dismissed as the product of patriarchal prejudice, while the glorified attributes of femininity are understood as authentically intrinsic to femaleness as such. This is one of the irresolvable contradictions at the heart of feminist Goddess spirituality theories, and it needs to be squarely addressed. Ruether does this in her critique of the treatment of history and archaeological data, concluding that,

> However good such [feminine] values may seem for us today, to project them on an ancient Neolithic people and to presume that these must have been their values and their understanding of both "woman" and "nature," on the grounds that they had a "goddess-dominated" culture and society, is very questionable. The stereotypic linking of these qualities with "women" and "nature" together is also problematic.[62]

---

[62] Ruether, *Gaia and God*, 152.

Another reason why Ruether seeks out a usable past for women by focusing on their laboring activity rather than indulging in quasi-mythic speculations on prehistory has to do with her commitment to humanist feminism, that is, a feminist critical analysis that is oriented toward the liberation of all humanity. A feminist religiosity that escapes into idealized and romantic valorizations of the "feminine" refuses to confront the necessity of struggling to resolve "the male-female conflict in society."[63] In the absence of the resolution of this particular conflict, no liberation is possible, either for men or for women. Unless feminists are prepared to confront the questions of domination and hierarchy *in all their forms* and struggle to overcome them *in all their forms,* the liberation of women is impossible. Not only is the liberation of women impossible, the chances for rescuing nature from the slow death that humanity is inflicting on it are destroyed.

Ruether's socialist and humanist feminist analysis is crucial to understanding the complex interconnectedness of hierarchy and the further interconnectedness between social justice, interpersonal justice, and eco-justice. Ruether argues that an ecological ethics that does not take account of this fact is woefully inadequate and can only function in ways that are aestheticist, personalist, and escapist.[64] Furthermore, a retreat into lifestyle ecologism services capitalism in that it acts within the logic of consumerism that feeds off attempts to alter personalistic modes of lifestyle changes that shift attention from the social and political realm of existence. What Ruether proposes is an ecological ethics that refuses to separate social and eco-justice issues; to do so is to continue in the prevailing mode of life.

> Converting our minds to the earth cannot happen without converting our minds to each other, since the distorted and ecologically dysfunctional relationships appear necessary, yet they actually support the profits of the few against the many. There can be no ecological ethic simply as a new relation of "man" and "nature." Any ecological ethic must always take into account the structures of social domination and exploitation that mediate domination of nature and prevent concern for the welfare of the whole community in favor of

---

[63] Ibid., 171.
[64] Ruether, *Sexism and God-Talk,* 85.

the immediate advantage of the dominant class, race, and sex. An ecological ethic must always be an ethic of eco-justice that recognizes the interconnection of social domination and domination of nature.[65]

Ruether's comprehensive analysis of the interconnected structures of domination that mediate both social relations and the human relation with nature, including her emphasis on the link between the domination of women and the domination of nature, echoes the critique of domination advanced by Horkheimer and Adorno in *Dialectic of Enlightenment*. Their grasp of the connections between the domination of men over men, men over women, men over nature, and the nature in themselves is shared by Ruether and informs her entire work. At the same time, she corrects their assumption that the subjugated condition of women provided a protective insulation that prevented their becoming alienated to the same extent as men,[66] with the result that their capacities for love and nurturance remain stronger. This truncated vision of women's ethical state, which is shared by gynocentric feminist theories, can inadvertently render into a virtue what is completely unjustifiable: namely, the domination of women in any form, under any circumstance. As well, feminist views that elevate femininity as a repository of values superior to those associated with masculinity risk ending in a dualistic reversalism and therefore impoverished mimesis of the status quo, leaving intact the conditions that produce

---

[65] Ibid., 91.

[66] Ibid., 105. Ruether, however, is somewhat ambivalent on this point. In her earlier book *From Machismo to Mutuality*, she argues that although women are victims, they are "aggressors as well." There are no "good" women who need to escape from "evil" men. This is the kind of view she condemns as a form of "moral absolutism" (cf. pp. 115–16). Yet in her later book *Sexism and God-Talk*, she asserts that women are not as responsible for evil as men because of women's lack of historical opportunity. "The monopolization of power and privilege by ruling-class males also means a monopolization of the opportunities for evil" (p. 150). The only way to account for this apparent ambiguity is to look at the general tenor of her thinking, which clearly identifies women and men as *both* capable of evil, on the grounds of their common humanity. For Ruether, femaleness is not inherently morally superior to maleness. As well, her insistence on women as fully human social agents mitigates against reading such conclusions into her work.

dualism, hierarchy, and domination. What Ruether suggests is that feminism develop a full humanist perspective and corresponding politics which affirms that "all humans possess a full and equivalent human nature and personhood, *as male and female*."[67]

Ruether's socialist and humanist feminist vision leads her to rethink human relationships in terms of relationality, understood as a deeply democratic, intersubjective way of being in the world *with* others and with nature. The liberation of women is a necessary precondition of human liberation; at the same time, women must be aware that without the liberation of all humanity, there is no possibility to realize their own emancipation. "Women, as the denigrated half of the human species, must reach for a continually expanding definition of the inclusive humanity: inclusive of both genders, inclusive of all social groups and races."[68] Ruether defines the "critical principle" of feminist theology as the affirmation and the promotion of the full humanity of women; when consciously embraced, this critical principle opens possibilities for right relations between men and women and with the divine. Feminist theology claims this principle for women who "name themselves as subjects of authentic and full humanity."[69] The struggle against sexism is not just a struggle to promote the full equality of women, it is also a process of "humaniz[ing] the world" because sexism cannot be challenged without the "dethronement of the cultural universe" that distorts both female and male humanity.[70]

The indivisible connection between feminism and humanism is the basis on which Ruether criticizes separatist tendencies in the so-called radical feminism of thinkers like Mary Daly, whose concept of the male as "generically evil" is dehumanizing both to men and to women. "The dehumanization of the other," Ruether writes, "ultimately dehumanizes oneself."[71] The liberation of women is inextricably connected with and takes place through the realization of their full

---

[67] Ruether, *Sexism and God-Talk*, 111.
[68] Rosemary Radford Ruether, "Feminist Interpretation: A Method of Correlation," in Letty Russell, ed., *Feminist Interpretation of the Bible* (Philadelphia: Westminster, 1985), 116.
[69] Ibid., 115.
[70] Ruether, *Sexism and God-Talk*, 191–92, 178.
[71] Ibid., 284, note 16; 231.

humanity, which is possible only in a just and humane world. This idea is of decisive importance, not just in Ruether's work but for feminism as well. Yet a truly humane world is only possible if the concrete, material conditions are sufficiently transformed so that people have the opportunity to recover the fullness of unalienated being. For Ruether, the establishment of a socialist society is the necessary means whereby such transformation can take place:

> Socialism . . . must recover those dreams of liberated creativity which Marx shared with the utopians and anarchists: the vision of a society in which the basic necessities of life have been conquered to such an extent as to free all persons for a life with room for celebration, free creativity, the reintegration of mind and body, the de-alienation of work, the overcoming of the split between work and pleasure.[72]

The parallels between Ruether's socialist, humanist feminism and Marcuse's views on socialist feminism are remarkably strong. Both Ruether and Marcuse envision the possibility that a new human future may emerge out of the concrete possibilities contained in the present. The "pacification of existence" means that the material conditions necessary to the sustaining and enhancement of life allow for the experience of joy, pleasure, happiness, and peaceful relations between people and with nature as part of daily life. A "democratic socialist society" will not come into being through some cataclysmic, apocalyptic event, but over time as people struggle to "work on pieces of the vision separately,"[73] to probe the cracks and interstices of society where domination and exploitation have failed to penetrate.

Ruether's "liberation communities," like Marcuse's "militant minorities" or even Horkheimer's "numerically small groups of men," are self-directed, cooperative base communities who work for change wherever it is concretely possible. Examples include the creation of communal child-care units, alternative energy systems, and the transformation of work from employer-owned and directed to self-managed production, where work becomes more of an expression of human creative capacities rather than the means whereby profit is

---

[72] Ruether, *New Woman/New Earth*, 182.
[73] Ruether, *Sexism and God-Talk*, 232–33.

acquired for the benefit of ruling elites. Such communities are critical cultures that renounce power over others for the empowerment of all, who live according to a flexible, open-ended "rule of life" rather than by "a set of laws fixed in stone."[74] For Ruether, these liberation communities represent "authentic Church" where clericalism is abolished in order that new forms of empowering ministry may emerge, where ministry means service and the sharing of "the unique gifts of each person." Ministry as service, sharing, and mutual empowerment reflects the gospel concept of ministry and is the only form of ministry appropriate to democratic, socialistic, and humanist communities:

> [M]inistry means exercising power in a new way, as a means of liberation of one another. Service to others does not deplete the person who ministers, but rather causes her (or him) to become more liberated. Ministry overcomes competitive one-up, one-down relationships and generates relations of mutual empowerment.[75]

Ruether's feminist liberation theology engages in a critical deconstruction of the Christian theological and ecclesial tradition in order to reclaim the emancipatory power of the Christian religion that itself is partially a continuation of the Hebrew prophetic emphasis on knowledge and love of God as doing justice. Ruether constantly returns to the Hebrew prophets, stressing their emphasis on justice over cultic practice and their insistence that God sides with the poor and the needy. She quotes Amos 5:21-24: "I hate, I despise your festivals, and I take no delight in your solemn assemblies. Even though you offer me your burnt offerings and grain offerings, I will not accept them. . . . But let justice roll down like waters, and righteousness like an everflowing stream."

In Ruether's view, women need to claim the "prophetic principle" of liberation for themselves, realizing that "women too are among those oppressed whom God comes to vindicate and liberate."[76] Jesus ministered in the prophetic tradition while transforming it by deepening and extending it to repudiate all forms of hierarchy and domination, stressing the model of interpersonal relations most pleasing

---

[74] Ibid., 212.
[75] Ibid., 207.
[76] Ibid., 24.

to God as one of service. "Jesus, the homeless Jewish prophet, and the marginalized women and men who respond to him represent the overthrow of the present world system and the sign of a dawning new age in which God's will is done on earth."[77] In this sense Jesus represents the negative of the Christian theological tradition, which, in the words of Horkheimer, "has always tried to reconcile the demands of the Gospels and of power. In view of the clear utterances of the founder, enormous ingenuity was required."[78] It is this effort to accommodate Jesus' teachings with the prevailing social and political power structures that Ruether wishes to negate, meaning that authentic church must "cease to be the sacralization of the powers and principalities." The church of Jesus, then, is a liberation community of resistance against domination and of struggle for "perfect" justice,

> where the good news of liberation from sexism is preached, where the Spirit is present to empower us to renounce patriarchy, where a community committed to the new life of mutuality is gathered together and nurtured, and where the community is spreading this vision and struggle to others.[79]

Although Ruether uses explicit theological language, she does so more as a vehicle that expresses her utopian vision of an alternative socialist, humanist, and feminist society than as a direct attempt to reformulate substantive theological claims. She raises the question of theodicy and of the meaning of life in the face of brutality, injustice, and human despair. In answer to questions that inquire into the meaning of "the whole tragic drama of human history," Ruether responds in a way that resonates with Adorno and Horkheimer—with agnosticism. Not only can we never know the "meaning" of life, the question itself is irrelevant, and not even religious teachings should dwell on it. As Adorno articulates the decisive ethical question as that which demands the end of hunger and torture, as the unavoidable command to abolish once and for all the conditions that make the existence of

---

[77] Ibid., 138.
[78] Horkheimer, *Critique of Instrumental Reason*, 36.
[79] Ibid., 213.

an Auschwitz even thinkable, Ruether concludes that the ethical responsibility of all human beings is to "use our temporal life span to
create a just and good community for our generation and for our
children." Neither does Ruether have any interest in standard theological doctrines of immortality or in what happens to individuals after
death; as far as she is concerned, death is nothing but "the final relin-
quishment of individuated ego into the great matrix of being."[80] Like
Marcuse, Ruether is more concerned with the quality of life and the
quality of death, that human beings should die as a peaceful, natural
result of the life process itself, not as the result of violence, starvation,
or sheer lack of the necessities that sustain life.

Ruether's analysis of specific forms of oppression and injustice
takes place within a utopian vision of transformed humanity in right
relation with itself and with nature. This vision is articulated in
symbolical theological language that is at the same time distinctly
nontheological. Ruether's religious sensibility echoes Horkheimer's
longing for the "wholly other" that has left theology behind while
preserving the traces of the religion that produced it. The negation of
theology is the shattering of the illusions that sustain and legitimate
suffering; through this negation of theology, the liberating power of
religion has a chance of being released, not directly as religion, perhaps,
replete with doctrine and ritual, but as utopia realized in concrete
history. Thus Horkheimer's dialectic of infinity and finitude most
closely describes the underlying conviction of Ruether's "theology,"
and bears repeating here: "In a really free mind the concept of infinity
is preserved in an awareness of the finality of human life and of the
inalterable aloneness of men, and it keeps society from indulging in
a thoughtless optimism, an inflation of its own knowledge into a new
religion."[81] Horkheimer's words describe the point of intersection between Ruether's feminist religious thought and critical theory, and
open the way to thinking about what a feminist critical theory of
religion might look like. This is the task to which I now turn.

---

[80] Ibid., 258.
[81] Horkheimer, *Critical Theory*, 131.

CHAPTER 7

Toward a Feminist Critical Theory of Religion

Toward the end of his life, Max Horkheimer remarked that a "politics that doesn't, even in very unreflected ways, preserve theology in itself remains, however cleverly it is done, at the end mere business."[1] Although enigmatic, the meaning of this statement becomes clear in the context of Horkheimer's other remarks on religion and the longing for absolute justice that motivates the religious sensibility.

Beyond Theology

HORKHEIMER'S VIEW OF RELIGION RESTATES THE MARXIAN notion that describes the central impulse or "vital reality" of religion as a protest and longing for better conditions, for heart in a heartless world, the unquenchable yearning for a just world. The "vital reality" at the heart of religion became repressed and weakened through the historical process of theology's accommodation to the prevailing power structures and political forces within which the churches sought their institutional self-preservation. This historical accommodation with the social status quo required the negation of the rebellious and liberating message of Christ through its complete spiritualization. As

---

[1] Max Horkheimer, *Die Sehnsucht nach dem ganz Anderen: Ein Interview mit Kommentar von Helmut Gumnior* (Hamburg: Furche-Verlag, 1970), 60.

a result, Christianity was compelled to a large extent to forfeit its prophetic action as counterforce to the experience of misery and suffering that marks the material conditions of most of humanity.

At the same time, the impulse to earthly justice and liberation from oppression contained within Christianity did not completely disappear, but over time became dislocated from specifically religious forms and theological systems. If Christianity is to reclaim its original emancipatory impetus, it must then transcend the traditional theological forms in which it has been embedded, forms that have become historically exhausted in their capacity to motivate and support efforts for social and personal transformation. As far as Horkheimer is concerned,

> It is a vain hope that contemporary debates in the church would make religion once again the vital reality it was in the beginning. Good will, solidarity with wretchedness, and the struggle for a better world have now thrown off their religious garb. The attitude of today's martyrs is no longer patience but action; their goal is no longer their own immortality in the after-life but the happiness of men who come after them and for whom they know how to die.[2]

Although the theological forms must be abandoned for the full release of an active pursuit of justice in a world drifting deeper into barbarism, the emancipatory traces of the Christian religion are not abolished in the struggle for a better world, but are rather transformed. What lingers in these residues is both the protest against an unjust reality and the longing for a more humane, happier world. The hallmark of a world transformed in such a way is reconciliation—that is, reconciliation among human beings and with nature. This is the utopian impulse that resides at the heart of religion although traditional religious and theological external forms have attempted, consciously or not, to negate the utopian thrust of the Christian message. When Horkheimer speaks of the necessity of preserving a theological moment in all politics, he is affirming that all strivings for a just world must

---

[2] Max Horkheimer, *Critical Theory: Selected Essays*, trans. Matthew J. O'Connell et al. (New York: Contiuum, 1972), 130.

be motivated by the utopian hope in and longing for humane conditions.

It is this commitment to freedom and happiness that marks the ethical character of politics, because its goals are directed to promoting the welfare of all human beings. The animating rationality behind this understanding of politics presumes that human beings are ends in themselves, not means to be utilized in the realization of nonhuman ends. If politics does not preserve this utopian ethical dimension, it aligns itself with the instrumental logic and practice of business whose primary concern is with the accumulation of profit for its own sake rather than the well-being of humanity as such. The preservation and release of the utopian yearning for a better world, which Horkheimer locates at the origins of the Christian religion, are predicated on the negation of its theological and ecclesial traditions. Authentic discipleship with the gospel message and solidarity with suffering humanity do not, in Horkheimer's view, lead human beings back to traditional or classical religion, but rather away from it. As protest against the status quo and hope in a future free from all forms of alienation and misery, the utopian-political and thoroughly humanist impulse of religion can only fully emerge with the death of theology and church as they have been known in history.

In several significant respects, Mary Daly, Elisabeth Schüssler Fiorenza, and Rosemary Radford Ruether are exploring Horkheimer's somewhat cryptic and suggestive dialectic of theology and religion in their feminist critiques of the Christian theological and ecclesial tradition. In doing this, they strain against the boundaries of traditional theological disciplines by engaging in a kind of sublation or process of *Aufhebung* that cancels, negates, preserves, and transcends various elements of Christianity. The overriding theoretical concern of all three feminist thinkers is with the liberation of women from alienating religious forms and practices that have played a key role in the larger domination of women throughout history. Their feminist critiques of the Christian tradition not only focus on the actual subjugation of women in the church and in theological systems, but are also directed toward uncovering the ways in which Christianity has been co-opted in the service of sustaining and legitimating the domination of women in the larger social cultural context.

Schüssler Fiorenza and Ruether engage in both deconstructive and reconstructive critiques of Christianity that recognize within it certain latent emancipatory forces that can be reclaimed and restored in the service of contemporary women's struggles for liberation. Neither of them is interested in formulating a Christian apologetics that seeks to justify the tradition on the grounds that it has been badly misinterpreted and distorted by the vicissitudes of historical and political factors. Rather, they are more interested in reading the emancipatory subcurrents within the tradition in a critical light in order to stimulate a reconstruction of its utopian potentiality in accordance with women's needs and strivings for liberation in present contexts. The demands of contemporary women who are struggling to realize their full freedom and humanity in present conditions take precedence over any interest in the preservation of theological orthodoxy. In many respects, neither Schüssler Fiorenza nor Ruether is as interested in articulating a new theology—even a feminist theology—as she is committed to preserving a theological or religious moment within a practical, political, feminist critical theory of women's liberation.

While Daly develops an explicit post-Christian feminist philosophy that has unequivocally repudiated the Christian theological tradition as holding no emancipatory potential for women, she does re-create a kind of theology along feminist lines. Ultimately this theology has little to offer women who are actively engaged in liberation struggles. What began as a deeply insightful and potentially subversive feminist critique of Christian theology and church power in *The Church and the Second Sex* and *Beyond God the Father* spins out into theoretical galaxies of political impotence and social irrelevancy in Daly's later works. One of the reasons for this is that Daly's ontologization and sacralization of elemental female being functions as little more than a feminized mimesis of the patriarchal theological traditions she rejects.

Nonetheless, many aspects of Daly's initial critique remain important for feminist theorizing of the oppressive, political nature of the Christian theological tradition, despite their embeddedness in feminist reversalism. For example, her relentless exposure of the fusions of power and domination that structures the patriarchal theological apparatus of the Catholic church retains much of its original value not only for women who are attempting to transform the Christian theological and ecclesial traditions, but also for those women who struggle against hierarchy and oppression in various dimensions of social life. She repudiates Christianity as a major source of the domination of women within and beyond the church; this repudiation arises out of a critical reasoning that seriously challenges the infantilism of a theological tradition that literally engenders the sacred and establishes a tight ecclesial hierarchical power structure that justifies its exclusively male character on the grounds that the incarnation took place in the male bodily form. The legitimation of a male priestly caste based on appeals to the maleness of Christ represents the triumph of brute, anatomical facticity over reason. Daly quips that in a world where god is male, then the male is god; this remark explosively illuminates the reciprocal interstructures of sexist domination on the sociological and theological levels. Her basic insights into the subtle and not-so-subtle dynamics of power that destroy women's capacities for unalienated, free, and creative existence remain an invaluable resource of critical inspiration for feminist theory.

When Daly's feminist philosophy is examined in more depth, and particularly in the light of negative dialectics, the authoritarian dimension of the structure of her thinking becomes apparent. Daly's philosophical approach is thoroughly informed by an identity logic or reasoning process that operates within her negative critique, counterpointing her conception of authentic female being against the alienated femininity of patriarchal society and culture. Having situated her in relation to Herbert Marcuse helps to bring this aspect of her work into focus. As Marcuse conceptualized an authentic, more truthful reality at the core of all phenomena that engages in a continual struggle against its own outward alienated form, so does Daly theorize the presence of an authentic femaleness that resides in women and is located as well in an ontological, metaphysical Background to which women have access and which empowers them in the discovery of their inner genuine Self. She constructs a somewhat dualistic schematic framework that contrasts the foreground, phenomenological world of alienated patriarchy against a cosmic, metaphysical realm of Being that grounds authentic, elemental femaleness.

The struggle against patriarchy and domination requires that women actively move toward the discovery and recovery of their original spiritual and psychic integrity that has been repressed and distorted by the manifold expressions of patriarchal control. Daly exhorts women to exit from patriarchal alienation by refusing to collude in maintaining the status quo and to find ways of living "on the boundary" where they may forge new possibilities for genuine self-realization. No matter how carefully one reads Daly, however, her exhortations to women to enter into their deep authenticity remain vague and insubstantial. Consider one of her descriptions about the surge of creativity inspired and nourished by her relationship with a woman friend, creativity that contributed to her writing her book *Gyn/Ecology:*

> It was in the rich, ecstatic, powerful Aura (O-Zone) of that connectedness that my writing flowed and sparkled, deep into the Hag-Time of night and early morning. In the Time before sunrise the landscape/seascape/skyscape of this book opened up to me, as I was Heard into the right words by the Sparking and Spinning of that Boon Companion who arrived in Tidal Time.
> Doorway after doorway of my imagination was flung open as I raced through the Labyrinthine passages of my own mind, Facing and Naming the myths and actual atrocities of Goddess-murder all over this planet and their interconnectedness—and A-mazing the masters' mazes in order to Dis-cover and celebrate Gynocentric Ecstasy.[3]

This passage, like so many others in Daly's later work, is rich with poetic metaphor and imagery that vividly convey the enthusiasm of the writer when she is in full creative power. Daly is also giving us an example of the sparking explosive energy that becomes released when women identify with women in all areas of life; lesbian identity, both spiritual and physical, represents for Daly the most authentic relations, opening "the way for Re-Calling Original Integrity." While sexual love between women does not in itself indicate a self-transformation and opening up to one's elemental being, it offers possibilities for new intuitions and insights into "Elemental Integrity."[4] Daly

---

[3] Mary Daly, *Outercourse: The Be-Dazzling Voyage* (New York: HarperSan-Francisco, 1992), 211–12.
[4] Ibid., 145, 144.

conceptualizes a notion of true female being that is highly poetic yet inevitably vague; her repeated use of a metaphoric, metaphysical, and personalist language of female authenticity that is divorced from concrete social analysis and considerations of the diversity of women collapses into a feminist jargon of authenticity whose aspirations to liberation are more illusory than real.

More significantly, Daly's notion of female authenticity is informed by an identitary logic that privileges the subject over the object so that individual women become compelled to correspond feature by feature with her subjectivist idea of what a "real" woman must be. Otherwise they are denounced as "fembots," painted birds, plastic and/or totaled women—those deadened, spiritless perpetrators of "fembotitude" who are the willing slaves and collaborators of patriarchy. Not only is Daly's philosophy exclusivist insofar as it relegates maleness to the realm of primal evil and gynocidal politics, it excludes entire groups of women as well, and can say little to heterosexual feminists and women. Rather than seeking reconciliation with otherness, Daly chooses to perpetuate and sharpen conflict and antagonism from the ontological to the existential. Not all women who wear makeup and style their hair are necessarily dead, expressionless, or without creative powers.

The compulsion to identity that is contained in Daly's feminist philosophy carries with it a set of disquieting political implications that value conformity to preconceived ideals and that can only undermine the diversity, particularity, and multiple differences among living women. The inner structure of Daly's thought is both authoritarian and antidemocratic, promoting a pure feminist theory and practice constructed by her, to which only "real" women adhere. The others are condemned to a status of double-otherness, where they are the others of patriarchy as well as the others of true feminism.

Negating Oppression

WHILE THE IDENTITARY RATIONALITY OF THE PHILOSOPHY OF Mary Daly results in new mythologizations and hypostatizations of authentic female being that correspond to the cosmic feminine nature of the Goddess, the feminist critical theory of Elisabeth Schüssler Fiorenza and Rosemary Radford Ruether moves in very different directions. It attempts to account for the concrete dynamics of domination of women in its multiple manifestations. Schüssler Fiorenza's feminist hermeneutic and historical reconstruction of women's activities in early Christian times have unfolded into an explicit negative theory of non-identity that seeks to empower women's present struggles against oppression by making their past efforts visible. The aim of her reconstructive project is to articulate the subjugated condition of women as "the subordinated others" who have also refused the definition of patriarchal politics attributed to them as unequal and dehumanized.[5]

Her move toward elaborating a subversive, emancipatory feminist rhetorical interpretation of biblical texts problematizes traditional readings and theological practices by presenting early Christian history as "a struggle that is still going on."[6] Her critical reconceptualization of the history of women in the Christian tradition, wherein she aspires to give voice to the "vanquished of history,"[7] mirrors Adorno's conviction that the condition of all truth is the articulation of suffering. Schüssler Fiorenza's appropriation of current feminist debates in literary theory and philosophy has led her to a serious consideration of the multiplicity of feminine identities that are located in a variety of class, race, linguistic, and cultural contexts. This approach in turn informs her readings of the past, where women do not disappear in some abstract, homogeneous category of "the downtrodden victims" but who fight and struggle on a variety of fronts against the oppression of their time. A differentiated, heterogeneous reading of women's history undermines totalizing, systematic interpretations that impose artificial correspondences by the reading subject and the object in the text. She thereby brings to light the reality of women's experiences and shows further that "women are and always have been historical subjects and agents," despite the colonizing practices of patriarchal

---

[5] Elisabeth Schüssler Fiorenza, *But She Said: Feminist Practices of Biblical Interpretation* (Boston: Beacon Press, 1992), 92.

[6] Ibid., 95.

[7] Ibid., 33.

domination.[8] Schüssler Fiorenza's commitment to lending a voice to those silenced by the hegemony of the rulers' point of view aims at a differentiated feminist theory that accounts for the variety of forms of oppression inflicted on women. Unlike Mary Daly, Schüssler Fiorenza does not construct a "universalist feminist position"[9] that situates the condition of women as a monolithic experience of victimization by patriarchy.

On one hand we have a feminist theory that operates from the logic of non-identity in order to do justice to the diversity and multiple particularity of women and their experiences; on the other hand we have one that mounts a singular, universalist, and ultimately abstract account of women as the sheer subjugated "others" of patriarchal violence. The distinction between the two is rooted in political differences that generate equally divergent political implications. In sharp contradistinction to Daly but in similarity to Ruether, Schüssler Fiorenza is consistently clear that feminist theory is inseparable from (although presumably not identical with) an emancipatory women's movement. The highly mediated relationship between theory and practice that informs Schüssler Fiorenza's work recognizes that theory, no matter how oppositional, proceeds from within given conditions rather than from some privileged transhistorical, transcultural perspective and that as such, feminists must theorize liberation out of the existent, no matter how distorted or indigent. As the story of women throughout the history of the Christian and biblical traditions is not one of pure victimization, so the development of Western civilization is not simply the unfolding of uncontested domination.

As Horkheimer and Adorno diagnose the history of reason as a progressive degeneration into purposive instrumentality, they are able to criticize this development through the use of reason itself, thereby exposing the contradictory tension of a rationality that is always working against itself. In similar fashion, Schüssler Fiorenza confronts the internal contradictory nature of the intellectual and political traditions of the West that both generate oppression, domination, and human misery on a vast scale and provide the means for the negation of those

---

[8] Ibid., 86.
[9] Ibid., 10–11.

negations from within these traditions themselves. According to Schüssler Fiorenza, feminist theory must "reappropriate emancipatory elements of the past so that it can *speak from within* Western society and biblical religions, although it simultaneously questions and indicts their patriarchal discourses."[10]

As the "emancipatory vantage point" of feminist critical theory resides within Western society and culture, feminists must look to those "democratic and humanistic discourses of freedom, self-determination, justice and equality"[11] that are also a part of the Western moral, political, and philosophical traditions of modernity and reclaim them for women in the light of their current conditions and needs. The recognition of the dialectic of freedom and domination that structures the Western traditions leads Schüssler Fiorenza to embrace a historically engaged politics of resistance and struggle against all forms of domination as they are encountered in specific contexts. In taking this position, she clearly rejects the political ambivalence and impotence of postmodernist discourses that offer rootless relative pluralisms which cloud the political ethical frameworks that mediate struggles for social transformation.

Although Schüssler Fiorenza's political vision resonates with the communitarian socialist perspective of Ruether, she does not name her politics in the same kind of specific detail. Schüssler Fiorenza's political theoretical stance calls for the overcoming of the Western logic of identity and its corresponding authoritarian political practices of compulsion and conformity with the "logic of democracy" that is also contained in Western traditions of modernity. A feminist critical theory that consciously operates out of a non-identity logic such as that advocated by Adorno inevitably issues in a nonauthoritarian and heterogeneous democratic political praxis that values particularity and difference and promotes and enhances their well-being. The liberation of women from all forms of alienation and subjugation will inevitably be the deathblow of domination as such, since the full liberation of women requires a complete "transvaluation of values" that promises

---

[10] Ibid., 91.
[11] Ibid., 92.

the liberation of the whole of humanity and nature. Without the liberation of women, human liberation and the liberation of nature from exploitative control and manipulation are not possible. Schüssler Fiorenza's differentiated notion of patriarchal and "kyriarchal" power is more adequate to feminist theory than the concepts of patriarchal power such as those advanced by Daly, which foreclose on a more comprehensive analysis and critique of domination and authentic insights into the interconnectedness of all human and nonhuman life.

Schüssler Fiorenza's notion of kyriocentrism leads to a politics of resistance and struggle from below, one that seeks to abolish all forms of centralized control that dictate people's lives and enforce conformity to preconceived rules. In this sense Schüssler Fiorenza's feminist critical theory intersects with that of Rosemary Radford Ruether, especially regarding their shared concept of ministry. In the view of the former this needs to be reconceived in terms of an "equality from below" and enacted in a democratic praxis of solidarity "with all those who struggle for survival, self-love, and justice."[12]

The political approaches of Schüssler Fiorenza and Ruether tend to diverge at the point of Ruether's programmatic constructivism, where she articulates what a socialist, humanist society will look like. In this respect, the feminist critical theory of Rosemary Radford Ruether may appear to be more satisfying than that of Schüssler Fiorenza, who does not engage in constructivist theorizing in the way Ruether does. Schüssler Fiorenza's *ekklesia of women* is meant to constitute a "practical center and normative space"[13] for women engaged in critical rereadings of the Bible as an act of empowerment in the struggle for their liberation. These feminist communities are discursive and intersubjective spaces of provisional emancipation where women rediscover and reclaim their active place at the center of the Christian tradition, where they have always been and where their activities have been crucial in the formation of the tradition.

Schüssler Fiorenza's feminist rereading of the encounter between Jesus and the Syro-Phoenician woman becomes a model for subversive rhetorical practices designed to bring women's contribution to history

---

[12] Ibid., 73.
[13] Ibid., 75.

back into visible focus. When the visibility of women's role in the development of Christianity is clearly established, contemporary women suffering under oppressive patriarchal theological and ecclesial practices become empowered in their struggles to redeem their humanity and realize their legitimate place as full Christians. The sense of empowerment gained in feminist rhetorical practices of reading biblical texts "against the grain" strengthens women in all aspects of their life by demonstrating the historical reality of their role as subjective agents in the development of Western civilization. The political motivation that animates the *ekklesia* of women and their actions for social transformation in the world at large does not result in the construction of a detailed program spelling out specific alternatives and lifestyle practices that will undermine the status quo. All it can—and should—do is point toward or intimate future possibilities of a more humane, just world.

Both Schüssler Fiorenza and Ruether engage in a deconstructive and reconstructive critique of Christianity that seeks to reclaim and refashion its emancipatory impulses in the context of women's current condition and needs. Ruether, however, goes much further than Schüssler Fiorenza in outlining what a future society transformed along the lines of justice, freedom, and happiness might look like. Ruether's critique of domination is far more comprehensive than Schüssler Fiorenza's; it addresses the interlocking and interconnected structures of domination that manifest themselves in sexism, anti-Semitism, imperialism, nationalism, militarism, class antagonism, and the domination and exploitation of nature. As Ruether turns her attention to all these phenomena, it is almost inevitable that she will, in Marcusian fashion, develop as comprehensive as possible a political analysis that is explicitly socialist, feminist, and humanist and that looks to concrete present possibilities out of which an alternate future may be forged.

Although Schüssler Fiorenza engages with nontheological disciplines in order to construct a politically committed feminist hermeneutical, rhetorical, and historical reconstructive methodology that gives voice to the sufferings and struggles of women throughout the development of the Christian tradition, she does not exhibit an explicit political orientation in the way Ruether does. Schüssler Fiorenza maintains her focus on interpretations of biblical texts in order to interrogate the ways in which they create and sustain "oppressive or liberating theoethical values, sociopolitical practices and worlds of vision."[14] Besides her strong affinities with Walter Benjamin regarding anamnestic solidarity and the emancipatory potential of memory for present and future generations, Schüssler Fiorenza is closer to Adorno in her approach as a sustained negative critique of the interpretive practices of biblical Christianity out of which emerge alternative images of resistance and subjective agency of women. In this way, fragments of the particularity and diversity of women in the past become visible to present generations, where they become capable of exercising an explosive force that shatters the distortions and repressions that continue to reinforce and sustain the enslaved condition of women.

While Schüssler Fiorenza describes her political orientation as democratic and located in an active, concrete feminist movement, she does not offer any specific outlines of a new society. Ruether does. Although Ruether also operates from a logic of non-identity that recognizes and respects the rich diversity of cultural and social realities of which women are a part, she articulates a fairly detailed vision of a new humanity in a transformed future where all human beings are able to live in right relation to each other and to nature. As Ruether spells out the contours of an egalitarian, communitarian socialist world, she moves from non-identity to identity thinking. Despite her best intentions, she moves also into the realm of instrumental reasoning with all its compulsions to conformity and homogeneity that inevitably issue in various modes of assertion of power over humans and nature rather than empowerment of them.

At this point, a remote similarity begins to emerge between Ruether and Daly regarding the structure of their thinking. Although Ruether and Daly represent vastly different and distinct feminist theories, their theoretical perspectives begin to intersect when Ruether conceptualizes alternative possibilities in concrete terms. That Daly's feminist philosophy is fashioned within an unequivocally identitary mode of reasoning is indisputable; she constructs an idealist metaphysics of an ontological feminine principle that grounds the specific concrete reality

---

[14] Ibid., 46.

of women, to which they must conform unless they are to be condemned never to free themselves from the manifold workings of patriarchal alienation. Disavowing all interest in social analysis or socialist politics, Daly theorizes an ethically hierarchical, dualistic worldview of maleness and femaleness along with their corresponding values and attributes where sexism and its patriarchal practices are identified as the source of women's oppressed social condition and emotional and psychological disfigurement.

Daly's politics implies the formation of homogeneous, "closely bonded" feminist in-groups that appear to display a remarkable degree of agreement with each other as well as mutual support.[15] Such groups are quite different from Marcuse's "militant minorities" who are active in a variety of political struggles that seek to establish pockets of freedom within the crevices of capitalist hegemony over most areas of human life. Ruether's interest in the work of local groups to establish child-care co-ops, alternative energy resources, or to work with the poor and in a variety of other political activities resonates with Marcuse's militant minorities and not at all with Daly's "Tigers." Ruether manifests tenuous connections with the identity theorizing of Daly only when she too begins to formulate how people ought to live and can live in a transformed world. While Ruether's vision of an alternative future is profoundly humanistic and democratic, it unavoidably utilizes the imperialistic logic of identity, forming concepts that compel their objects to conformity and unity.

Even if it cannot be said that she actually does this—and certainly she does not do it in the manner of Daly—Ruether's constructivist, programmatic politics inevitably contains what Adorno called "the rage" that is inherent in all idealism. Whereas this rage is explicit and open in Daly's work, in Ruether it is significantly more muted and latent. Nonetheless it is present; it constitutes the tragedy of thinking that does not consciously commit itself to sustained negativity. A relentless, uncompromising negative critique and non-identity thinking that dwells on the injustice and gruesomeness of the human condition might reveal crevices and fractures in the existent where the light of transcendence may briefly appear, in a flash of illumination

---

[15] Daly, *Outercourse*, 137.

that suggests intimations of a transformed future. Programmatic, constructivist theories extinguish such intimations of utopia as soon as they are formulated because they harbor demands for unity and general assent, demands that in turn generate regulatory practices that must be adhered to for a defined way of life to be realized.

In this way the logic of instrumentality and strategic, tactical thinking takes precedence over utopian thinking. The highest achievement of utopian thinking is reached in its capacity to think against thought, to think that which, in a world governed by the principle of exchange and organized along the increasingly strangulating lines of administration, is deemed to be unthinkable. While Ruether, like Marcuse, is able to sustain utopian thinking to a large extent in her theorizing, she undermines it when the negativity of her critique turns to the positivity of programmatic action.

Schüssler Fiorenza, on the other hand, suggests the contours of an *ekklesia gynaikon* as a discursive community of multiple, polyvalent voices and egalitarian relations without providing specific modes of action or ways of life. At the same time, her feminist critical theory is more restrictive in its analysis of domination than Ruether's and does not penetrate its complex dynamics with the same degree of comprehensiveness and depth. It is also important to note that Schüssler Fiorenza does not address ecological issues, which are indispensable components in the whole apparatus of domination and with which women have a particular relation.

Intimations of Utopia

WHAT ALL THREE FEMINIST THINKERS DO SHARE WITH EACH other, and with critical theory, is a profound interest in reconciliation, although the notion of reconciliation is treated quite differently by each. In the work of Mary Daly, reconciliation emerges as the telos of a-mazing women racing toward self-actualization in the rediscovery of their authentic being and its ultimate source in a cosmic female principle. Women who are consciously embarked on this ontological and spiritual journey become reconciled with each other in a quasi-religious solidarity that empowers them in their search for a metaphysical reconciliation with the background world of elemental female being. The notion of reconciliation in Daly operates strictly within the bounds of an identity theorizing that at the same time excludes men and those women not committed to the same goal as she. It is a reconciliation of sameness with itself that also generates antagonisms with all otherness—that is, otherness that does not reside within the parameters established by Daly.

Ruether seeks a reconciliation of human beings with each other and with nature that is flawed by its inability to resist the temptation of imagining and portraying the "completely reconciled condition,"[16] thereby lapsing into identity thinking and delimiting the integrity of particularity. More than Daly and Ruether, Schüssler Fiorenza is able to escape such premature and false reconciliations because of her consistent focus not only on the diversity among women, but the manifold variety of oppressions inflicted against them. In this respect she is closest to Adorno, whose negative dialectics is rooted in a firm commitment to a genuine reconciliation that neither resorts to "false equations" nor truncates difference.[17]

The critique of constructivist theories and programmatic politics, however, may be countered by the charge of quietism and political paralysis that colludes in the maintenance of domination and injustice by its somewhat elitist intellectualist avoidance of "getting one's hands dirty." It may well be argued that the attempts of theorists like Ruether and Marcuse to articulate a future world that has overcome alienation and exploitative relations between human beings and with nature are vital to present efforts to abolish injustice and human misery. As the title of the opening chapter of this book indicates, the point is to change the world, not merely to interpret it.

One of the main disagreements between the German student movement of the 1960s and Adorno's critical theory concerned his refusal of political involvement or formulation of specific tactical programs. Many of Adorno's most important critics, whether sympathetic or hostile, conclude that his understanding of the mediations between

---

[16] Fred Dallmayr, "Critical Theory and Reconciliation," in Don S. Browning and Francis Schüssler Fiorenza, eds., *Habermas, Modernity, and Public Theology* (New York: Crossroad, 1992), 130.

[17] Ibid., 124.

political and theoretical practice is vague and abstract and further fails "to provide a theory for revolutionaries."[18] Even Marcuse, despite his support of student protest movements and portraits of a transformed humanity through a socialist feminist political praxis, acknowledged the negativity of critical theory that can provide no conceptual link between the present and its future. At the same time, one of critical theory's primary themes concerns the relation between theory and practice, which it conceives of as mutually mediating and interrelated but not identical. The suggestion runs throughout critical theory that thought itself is a practical activity, much in the spirit of Karl Marx, where thinking and reality dialectically interpenetrate when theory turns to the questions of the concrete human condition and attempts to articulate it from a conscious position of solidarity with the oppressed. Despite its commitment to bringing about more reasonable conditions of life, "critical theory has no specific influence on its side, except concern for the abolition of social injustice,"[19] as Horkheimer acknowledged in the early phases of critical theory. This concern for the abolition of social injustice is the single motivating factor in feminist critical religious thought, including most forms of liberation theology as well.

In many respects the inability—or, perhaps stated more accurately, the refusal—of critical theory to articulate the specific outlines of a transformed world parallels the absence of a systematic, detailed ethics in the Christian Bible that correlates with the subsequent tradition of Christian ethics. Unlike the Hebrew Bible, which contains a rich repository of ethical formulations concerning living a life that is faithful to the divine command and that sustains the covenant forged between Israel and its God, the Christian Bible offers no such clearly delineated program for a religious, ethical code of conduct. Exhortations to behavior in church aside, the Christian Bible requires the community to engage in an ongoing hermeneutical activity, constantly interpreting the love command of Jesus and various suggestions to do the good

---

[18] Michael Sullivan and John T. Lysaker, "Between Impotence and Illusion: Adorno's Art of Theory and Practice," *New German Critique*, no. 57 (Fall 1992): 88.
[19] Horkheimer, *Critical Theory*, 242.

and to live as best as one can.[20] Christian biblical ethics reflects a kind of "situational ethics" where teachers such as Paul addressed concrete problems in specific situations.[21] The differences between specific contexts, however, mean that there can be no fixed, stable, detailed ethical program that Christians in all epochs and cultures can unerringly follow.

This kind of necessary vagueness of Christian ethics is not dissimilar to the vagueness of critical theory's commitment to "the right kind of society" and happiness, freedom, and justice for all humankind. Christian demands to love one another, to be good to and to care for one another, can only take concrete form in particular contexts. Even then there is a necessary provisionality and tentativeness to doing good to others given the open-ended nature of historical change.

The same must be said for political theories and actions that resist oppressive and dominating practices of societies that have never realized the humanist traditions of the West in relation to concrete human beings, and that betray them by subjugating them to instrumental practices that deny their humanity. Utopian promises of the future possibility of a more just, humane, and unalienated world and transformed humanity are preserved and nurtured in the minds of men and women of good will only if they remain vague and partial. When the utopian yearnings for absolute justice become formulated in political programs, the logic of instrumentality and identity thinking takes over. Strategies and tactics are devised for the implementation of different courses of action that inevitably operate within the existent structures. While modifying and changing them, these actions leave them substantially intact. Perhaps this explains Horkheimer's early conviction that "the future of humanity depends on the existence of the critical attitude."[22]

At the same time, it would be morally indefensible to abandon political struggles for justice and the abolition of the material conditions

---

[20] See Paul Lehmann, *Ethics in a Christian Context* (New York: Harper and Row, 1963), 26–29.
[21] Ibid., 32.
[22] Horkheimer, *Critical Theory*, 242.

that cause human misery. Ruether's wide-ranging critique of the interstructures of domination that produce global hunger, warfare, racial prejudice, sexism, and the slow destruction of the planetary ecosystem requires sweeping changes in lifestyles and worldviews that can result in the amelioration of human misery and prevent the annihilation of nature. Whether it is her commitment to women's free access to birth control and abortion or her call for the creation of base communities where democratic, egalitarian, and reciprocal human relations can emerge and be sustained, these political goals are deeply embedded in a humanist and socialist politics without which their realization is impossible. If her work motivates women and men to struggle together for the establishment and implementation of such goals, she has been partially successful in her feminist liberationist project.

However important it is to strive for the amelioration of human suffering, it must be realized that whatever gains accrue in that direction do not signify the kind of transformation Ruether envisions. Amelioration of specific and limited forms of suffering in particular contexts, such as North America and Europe, ultimately serves the preservation of the status quo because of the profound capacity of capitalism to absorb and accommodate change, as commodity production changes rapidly and constantly. As long as the overall social, economic, and political structures are not threatened, reform is always possible. While reforms are always taking place, the majority of humanity sinks deeper into poverty, starvation, violence, and despair.

Similar observations can be made with respect to Schüssler Fiorenza and Daly. The subversive, emancipatory hermeneutical practices devised by Schüssler Fiorenza challenge the prevailing values of the Christian theological and biblical tradition and empower women to take their rightful place within it. These changes remain marginal, however, insofar as no major transformations have yet occurred within mainstream Catholicism concerning the liberation and advancement of women. This is partially borne out by Schüssler Fiorenza's complaint that her scholarship, which continues to make an invaluable contribution to biblical studies, is not referred to by male scholars.[23]

---

[23] Schüssler Fiorenza, *But She Said*, 86.

Despite its serious limitations, Mary Daly's work also makes an important contribution to feminist theory insofar as her critique of structural sexism within Christian theology raises fundamental questions about the very possibility of women finding any opportunities for emancipation within the Christian theological and ecclesial traditions. The depth of antiwoman perspectives that reside at the heart of many theological concepts and doctrines, which Daly has effectively exposed in her earlier work, lends her post-Christian stance a great deal of legitimacy and a plausibility that feminist religious thinkers must seriously confront.

Ruether has provided the most extensive critical analysis of Christian theological concepts and premises, including anthropology, ecclesiology, nature, sin, Christology, and even eschatology. Her analysis has opened new paths for a complete rethinking of the tradition from an explicit emancipatory and humanist interest.

Yet however inspiring and empowering the work of all three feminist thinkers may be, they can only point toward future utopian possibilities by dwelling on the present condition of women in all its negativity and disfigurement. Whatever changes may occur in women's religious vision and practice as a result of their influence—such as the institution of feminist liturgies, inclusive language in prayers and hymns, feminist retelling of biblical narratives, or the creation of women-church communities—it is necessary to remember that these changes take place within and are generally tolerated by the same forces and structures of hierarchy and domination that occasioned these reforms in the first place. When oppressive conditions become so acute that people begin to resist and devise alternative life arrangements, they do so within whatever spaces and cracks remain uncolonized by prevailing power structures and social systems. Human beings may begin to forge emancipatory spaces for themselves and their communities that allow for glimpses of future justice and reconciliation, but they must not mistake their successes for a genuine transformation of social relations and our relationship with nature.

Whatever steps we may take toward ameliorating the misery of existence, we must always recognize that they are partial, provisional, tentative, and therefore always demand sustained critical reflection.

Thus there can be no preconceived plans, no social blueprints or programs that can lay out the specific moves and actions and tell us how to journey from the present to the future we must achieve if humanity and the planet supporting us are to survive. To do otherwise is to reinscribe and reinforce the compulsive logic of identity that enslaves and devours its objects, thereby flattening and foreshortening the mystery and integrity of the other's being in violent acts of conceptual digestion within the self-enclosed parameters of subjective thought.

Yet we cannot abandon politics altogether, thereby leaving the wretched ones of the earth to their own devices. Rather than formulating constructivist political programs that inevitably dictate what the new society will be and how it will be achieved, we need to reconceive politics in terms of sustained critical negativity that dwells on reality and the conditions that render it intolerably painful for the vast majority of human beings. If critical theory is correct in its diagnosis that in the times of late capitalist development "alienness becomes an anthropological category,"[24] then detailed socialist political programs and strategies are inadequate to negating and transcending the present human condition.

Rather than committing ourselves to the constructivist, positive socialism of Rosemary Radford Ruether, we should consider instead a kind of negative socialism alluded to by Jürgen Habermas when he remarked, "Socialism primarily means: to know what you don't want, what you want to liberate yourself from."[25] This remark is one that feminist critical thinkers and religious theorists must ponder carefully. If feminism is to follow through on its own insights into the coercive power of identity thinking that functions as an indispensable cultural component in sustaining and preserving the domination of women, then a feminist critique that aspires to adequate articulation of women's suffering is by necessity negative. A negative feminist critical theory

---

[24] Max Horkheimer, "Egoism and the Freedom Movement: On the Anthropology of the Bourgeois Era," *Telos*, no. 54 (Winter 1982–83): 49.

[25] Jürgen Habermas, *Die neue Unübersichtlichkeit* (Frankfurt: Surkamp-Verlag, 1985), 73. The English translation omits this sentence and the paragraph that follows it. See Jürgen Habermas, *Autonomy and Solidarity: Interviews with Jürgen Habermas*, rev. ed., ed. Peter Dews (London: Verso 1992). The missing paragraph would have appeared on page 143.

of religion must resist premature reconciliations with any aspect of present reality. In the absence of a complete transformation of society and humanity, reconciliation can be nothing more than accommodation.

At the same time, a feminist critical theory of religion must refuse analogous accommodations with an imagined salvific reconciliation beyond history that severs the ethical demands of the gospel for a new humanity from the concrete reality of an alienated, distorted humanity and the material conditions that produce and preserve it. By refusing false reconciliations with the world as it is and with illusory projections of salvation beyond history, all that a feminist critical theory of religion can do is preserve intimations of utopia in a relentless, uncompromising focus on the present that is also informed by the memory of history's innocent victims.

This is where critical theory and feminist religious thought intersect: Both traditions are repositories of the utopian hopes of humankind, longings for a better world, for comfortable, reasonable conditions of life and for humane, right relations between human beings and with nature. In this respect, critical theory and a feminist critical theory of religion are mutually enhancing and interdialectical theories. As critical theory dwells on the indigency, the distortions, and the "gruesomeness of it all," its language becomes explicitly religious rather than theological, its focus on suffering humanity. As feminist critical religious thought dwells on the misery and oppression inflicted on women throughout the history of Christianity, it utilizes the language of social and political theory, language that intensifies as it delves deeper into the dynamics of domination. Feminist religious thought transcends theology insofar as its interest is with the material sufferings of concrete women both living and dead. The untheological quality of feminist religious thought is expressed in the agnosticism of Ruether and the "negative theology" of Schüssler Fiorenza, who recognizes that "all language about the divine is incommensurate with divine reality."[26] Something similar can be said about utopian language: Although it may cast the light of transcendence on the darkness of

---

[26] Schüssler Fiorenza, *But She Said*, 6.

present reality, it is commensurate neither with transcendence nor the redeemed future intimated by it.

A feminist critical theory of religion must seek ways of preserving the utopian hope of an absolute justice that is uncompromising in its sustained indictment of those forces that drive into further misery and oppression not only women but all humanity and nonhuman nature. Like critical theory, feminist religious thought must relentlessly cultivate and sustain a negative character, where "dialectics confines itself to the (determinate) negation of existing ills and divisions," thereby functioning in the service of reconciliation; that is to say, reconciliation as the loving acceptance of diversity and difference no longer feared as hostile or threatening to subjective reason.[27]

This is an emphatic notion of reconciliation that is anticipated in a determinate negative critique that never turns its focus from the immanent conditions of suffering rather than indulging in speculations on what a transformed future world would look like. A sustained and courageous negative critique of the current human condition is humanity's only possible hope against a perpetual reproduction of the destruction of otherness that is inherent in thought itself, when thinking seeks the coercive and false reconciliation of annexing the object to its subjective conceptualizations. "If the thought really yielded to the object," writes Adorno, "if its attention were on the object, not its category, the very objects would start talking under the lingering eye."[28] Perhaps in this way, humanity and nature may begin to appear as they may one day look in the "messianic light."

---

[27] Dallmayr, "Critical Theory and Reconciliation," 130.
[28] Theodor W. Adorno, *Negative Dialectics* (New York: Continuum, 1983), 27–28.

Adorno, Theodor W.
  constellations, 82
  critique of Hegel and, 81,
    83, 130
  femininity and, 92
  identitarian thinking and,
    149 n.6
  negative dialectics, 78
  non-identity thinking and,
    78, 99, 216
  pure identity, 84
  women and, 89-91
  See also Dialectic of
    Enlightenment
Anamnestic solidarity, 153
  n.18, 158, 163, 169, 219
Analytical-referential discourse,
  7–8
Antitheological character of
  critical theory, x

Bachofen, J. J., 185–86, 192–
  94, 196

Benjamin, Walter
  dialectical images and, 152
  dialectical standstill and, 161
  debate with Horkheimer
    and, 158 n.41
  constellations, 152, 153
  historical materialism of,
    151, 152, 159, 162, 165
  Theses on the Philosophy of
    History, 151–54
Boundary living, 138, 139, 212

Commanding self, 27, 28
  self-denial and, 22
Constellation, 4 n.3, 5, 82, 112,
  149, 150, 152, 153, 159
Critical theory
  attitude to women and, 39,
    117, 142
  domination of women and
    nature and, 35
  hope in future and, 33
  individual and, 105–106
  theory of human relations
    as, 19

Critique, immanent, 114

Daly, Mary
  androgyny and, 129, 136
  antihumanism of, 139
  authoritarianism of, 141,
    211, 213
  background and, 130, 131,
    138, 222
  Be-ing and, 129, 132, 133
  elemental female being and,
    131, 136, 222
  goddess and, 129, 133, 134
  identity logic/thinking and,
    134, 143, 199, 211, 213,
    219
  importance for feminism
    and, 226
  Marcuse and, 129, 135, 136–
    38, 139, 140
  memory and, 144
  negativity and, 133, 142, 211
  pure feminism and, 180
  reification and, 140, 143
  rejection of socialism and,
    140, 181, 220

Dialectic of Enlightenment, 19–27
  critics of, 29–34
  domination of nature and,
    19, 20, 22, 27
  domination of woman, 24,
    35, 92
  mastering ego and, 21
  performative contradiction
    of, 30, 32
  renunciation of feminine
    and, 23
  sirens and, 21–22

Ehrenberg, Margaret, 196–98
Ekklesia, 165, 217, 218
Engels, Friedrich
  destruction of proletarian
    family and, 55
  domination of women and
    class society and, 58
  women as industrial workers
    and, 54
Enlightenment, self-betrayal of,
  19
Exchange principle, 84, 105,
  108

Fembot, 135, 139, 199, 213
Feminism
  autonomy and, 16
  critical theory as, 16, 114,
    216
  critical theory of religion as,
    3, 4, 35, 36, 148, 150,
    228, 229
  metacritique as, 38 n.2
  negativity and, 227, 229
  religious thought and, 3, 4,
    112, 159, 223, 228, 229
  stable subject of, 127
  subjectivity and, 15–16, 109–
    10
Freud, Sigmund
  Dora case of, 72–75
  Civilization and Its
    Discontents, woman in,
    68–69
  Femininity, 64–68
  true femininity and, 71

Gender identity, 18

Gimbutas, Marija, 185, 186,
    188–93, 194, 195, 196
Goldman, Emma, 125
Gynocentric feminism, 127,
    142, 201
    Mary Daly and, 128, 140

Habermas, Jürgen, ix, 20, 28
    n.59, 29, 30, 151, 227
Hegel, G. W. F.
    woman in the family and,
        43–45, 48
    woman and education and,
        46
    woman and marriage and,
        47, 48
    woman and universality and,
        48
Horkheimer, Max
    divorce and, 103–104
    emancipation of women and,
        104–105
    humanism and, 11–12
    religion and, 176, 207, 208
    *Traditional and Critical
        Theory*, 8–10, 11, 18, 19
Humanism
    abstract and concrete, 17,
        198
    humanist feminism, 142

Identity thinking, 84, 87, 88,
    120
Ideology
    distinct from theory as, 11
Irigaray, Luce, 75

Jay, Martin, 12 n.21, 19

Justice
    absolute, 207, 224, 229
    longing for, 176, 180, 208
    perfect, 205

Kurgan invaders, 187–89, 197

Labor
    alienation and, 54
    manual/mental division of,
        22
    Marx and, 51, 52
    ontological category as, 51
Lifeworld, 20
    system and, 29
Lukács, Georg, 122
    reification and, 50 n.28

Mallory, J. P., 189
Marcuse, Herbert
    negation determinate and
        reified, 117, 119, 120,
        121, 141
    negativity and, 15, 115, 116,
        143, 173, 223
    socialist feminism and, 119,
        125, 126
    surplus repression and, 117
    woman and Eros, 119, 124
    woman, receptivity and,
        123, 126
Marx, Karl
    divorce and, 60, 61
    ideology and, 11
    materialist approach to
        women and, 51, 57
    nature and, 53
    religion and, 176
    Theses on Feuerbach, 5–6

woman and factories, 54
woman as humanizing
    principle, 49, 57
Memory, 145
    struggle against domination
        and, 147
    See also Elisabeth Schüssler
        Fiorenza
Metz, Johannes, 149, 155–59,
    163, 164
Modernity
    critical discourses of, 40
    counterdiscourses of, 16, 34,
        35
    unfulfilled promise of, 34
    utopian potential of, 33

Negative dialectics, 78, 80, 87,
    89, 98, 108, 114, 121, 181,
    211, 222
Negativity, consummate, 18
Non-identity thinking,
    feminism and, 108
Nye, Andrea, 16, 64 n.61

Oedipus complex, 67
Oedipal drama, 64
Orthopraxis, 5 n.4

Painted bird, 134–35, 139, 213
Performance principle, 121,
    122, 123, 127, 136
Peukert, Helmut, 158
Pleasure principle, 122, 124
Political economy, 13
Politics, 171, 207
    critical negativity as, 227
    Marcuse and, 173
    refusal of, 172, 223

Postmodernism, 28
    feminism and, 109 nn.68–69,
        216
Praxis, 9
    praxis philosophy and, 14
        n.28
    technique and, 9 n.14

Reason
    ambiguity of, 20
    instrumental, 9, 19, 20, 21,
        29, 30, 99, 219, 224
    justice, freedom and
        happiness and, 12, 20
    purposive-rational, 30
    substantive, 20
Reification, 50, 58
    objectification and, 50 n.28
Reiss, Timothy, 7–8
Ruether, Rosemary Radford,
    agnosticism of, 205
    critical theory of religion
        and, 175, 176, 206
    domination and, 174, 180,
        200, 201, 218, 225
    emancipatory potential of
        Christianity and, 178,
        179
    goddess critique and, 177,
        183–85, 199
    humanist feminism and, 198,
        200, 202, 203, 205, 218,
        225
    identity thinking and, 219,
        220, 222
    programmatic constructivism
        of, 217, 220, 221
    radical feminism and, 175

socialism and, 174, 175, 180,
181–82, 200, 203, 205,
218, 225
women-church and, 177
woman and nature and, 201

Saiving, Valerie, 2
Schüssler Fiorenza, Elisabeth
agency of women and, 162–
63, 166, 196, 214, 219
co-equal discipleship and,
166, 167
dangerous memory and,
150, 164, 167, 169
difference and, 148–49 n.5,
181
feminist critical hermeneutics
and, 162
hermeneutics of
remembrance and, 164,
165
history as incomplete and,
169
Jesus' relations with women
and, 168
kyriocentrism, 167, 217

nonidentity theory and, 214–
15
Syro-Phoenician woman
and, 164, 165, 166, 217
women in early Christian
communities and, 166
Self-management, 181, 204

Thanatos, 121
Theopompus, 194–95
Theory-practice (praxis)
relationship, 5, 6–7, 22,
151, 223

Utopia, 172, 173, 206, 221, 228
Adorno and, 86
feminist critical theory and,
112
hope and, 32, 209
negative as, 32

Warren, Peter, 191–92
Woman
abstract category as, 37 n.1,
38, 57, 60, 107, 165
family and, 94–96, 101–102,
108
nature and, 17, 23, 24, 99
prehistory and, 134